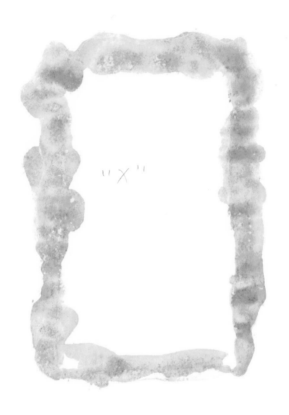

"X"

Social Conflict
and
Television News

Volume 183 Sage Library of Social Research

RECENT VOLUMES IN . . .
SAGE LIBRARY OF SOCIAL RESEARCH

Social Conflict
and
Television News

Akiba A. Cohen
Hanna Adoni
Charles R. Bantz

with
Deanna C. Robinson
Jay G. Blumler
Michael Gurevitch

in association with
Gabriele Bock
Alison Ewbank
Karen Honikman
Friedrich Knilli

Sage Library of Social Research 183

SAGE PUBLICATIONS
The International Professional Publishers
Newbury Park   London   New Delhi

For information address:

SAGE Publications, Inc.
2455 Teller Road
Newbury Park, California 91320

SAGE Publications Ltd.
6 Bonhill Street
London EC2A 4PU
United Kingdom

SAGE Publications India Pvt. Ltd.
M-32 Market
Greater Kailash I
New Delhi 110 048 India

Printed in the United States of America

Library of Congress Cataloging-in-Publication Data

Main entry under title:

Social conflict and television news / by Akiba A. Cohen. . .[et al.].
    p. cm.—Sage library of social research ; v. 183)
  Includes bibliographical references and index.
  ISBN 0-8039-3926-4. — ISBN 0-8039-3927-2 (pbk.)
  1. Television broadcasting of news—Social aspects —Case studies.
2. Television broadcasting of news—Political aspects—Case studies
3. Social conflict—Case studies. 4. World politics—1965- —Case
studies. 5. Journalism—Objectivity—Public opinion. I. Cohen,
Akiba A. II. Series
PN4749.S6. 1990
303.23'45—dc20   90-38951
                                                     CIP

FIRST PRINTING, 1990

Sage Production Editor: Astrid Virding

For

Ettie, Ami, and Sandra

Contents

Preface

The intellectual seeds of the study reported in this volume were sown in Israel in the late 1970s. We were becoming intrigued by two seemingly related phenomena. First, Israel appeared to us then (and still does today) as a highly conflictual society, both in real manifestations and in the way the conflicts seemed (and still seem) to be portrayed on the country's only television station.

Since it gained its independence in 1948, Israel has fought several wars and has suffered continued unrest between itself and its Arab neighbors. Moreover, the country has experienced some highly potent divisions within its social fabric—between Ashkenazi and Sephardic Jews, between the orthodox and the secular, and between the major political parties. Despite Israel's small size (only slightly more than four million people) between 10 and 15 political parties always have been represented in its parliament. There is an old story often told about Israel's first president, Dr. Chaim Weizmann, who visited President Harry Truman soon after the State of Israel was born. Truman, the tale goes, was telling Weizmann about how difficult his task was, being president of a nation of 200 million people. To this Weizmann was said to have replied: "That's nothing, Mr. President, after all I am president of about six hundred thousand presidents" (the size of the population in 1948).

The second phenomenon about which we were curious—and which was not new, of course—was the widely held and often expressed belief among media scholars that television news does not portray things as they really are. Perhaps the fact that such a complaint seemed to be coming from all directions of the Israeli

9

political spectrum could be interpreted as nullifying the protest. But on the other hand, it tended to highlight the fact that the three realms of reality—the *real* world (whatever is happening "out there"), the *symbolic* world (mainly the world of television), and the *subjective* world (the world that people have in their minds, based on a combination of unmediated experiences with the real "things" and "events" as well as with their portrayal on television) — interact in a very complex fashion, particularly in conflict situations.

Thus we soon found ourselves among a growing assortment of academics who share a common interest in what has become known as the study of the social construction of reality. Our first study along these lines dealt with what we called the social construction of *economic* reality. We were interested in the process by which people become familiar with economic issues and their perception of the role television news plays in this process (Adoni & Cohen, 1978). We found that although people did not really know much about the economy (at least as they could express it in a formal way), they believed nonetheless that television was helping them understand the economic conditions of the day.

Some time later we decided to change our focus and to deal with a wide array of social conflicts. We were of the opinion that despite the fact that these phenomena occur in all social systems, and are experienced by most people time and time again, they are nonetheless not understood clearly. Moreover, we were curious as to the role that television news seems to play in the process by which people come to understand social conflicts. Hence we embarked on a study that dealt with how social conflicts are perceived in the "real" world and in the world of television news (Adoni, Cohen, & Mane, 1984; Cohen, Adoni, & Drori, 1983).

Armed with some initial findings, Cohen and Adoni traveled to Acapulco, Mexico, and presented them at the annual meeting of the International Communication Association that was held there in May, 1980. At the end of the presentation we asked our audience if there was any interest in expanding this sort of work into a cross-national study. Several colleagues expressed interest: Charles Bantz, Deanna Robinson, Jay Blumler, Friedrich Knilli, and Gabriele Bock. The seven of us formed a group that later also included Michael Gurevitch, Karen Honikman, and Alison Ewbank.

Work on the study was not an easy task. Each of us had his or her opinions, often quite strong, as to how and why things should be done. The 10 of us worked together on the design of the study and the data collection. Over the years we managed to meet several times—mainly at conferences—but as a result of the passage of time, the geographic distances, and different developing interests among some of us (and perhaps some waning patience), the main thrust of the data analyses and the writing task were placed on Cohen, Adoni, and Bantz. Robinson, Blumler, and Gurevitch also provided input into the preparation of the volume by writing some segments and commenting on others. Honikman and Bock provided the sections on South Africa and West Germany, respectively. When we got down to writing, Ewbank and Knilli were on to other things and did not partake in the process, hence they are spared from any responsibility for errors that may appear in the text. To all our colleagues we are grateful for their friendly and productive collaboration. Without them this study would not be possible. But in the end Cohen, Adoni, and Bantz are ultimately liable for what appears in the volume and also for what is absent from it.

We owe much to many individuals and organizations. Some of the credits are given collectively by the entire group and some are individually awarded. Let us begin with the former. There is an old Jewish saying "If there is no flour, there is no Torah." We wish to acknowledge the Israel National Council for Research and Development, the Konrad Adenauer Foundation of West Germany, and the Israel Foundation Trustees of the Ford Foundation for providing the flour, or the bread. Without the generous support of these three organizations at various stages of the project it would not have been possible.

Several people took interest in our work and provided us with their insights and encouragements. We owe much to Sandra Ball-Rokeach of the University of Southern California and Elihu Katz of the Hebrew University who were helpful with their comments throughout the years of the project. We also wish to remember two departed colleagues and friends: Louis Guttman of the Hebrew University and the Israel Institute for Applied Social Research and Hilde Himmelweit of the London School of Economics, both of whom provided us with very useful feedback at several points along the way.

Akiba Cohen is appreciative of the hospitality afforded him by the Department of Speech–Communication of the University of Minnesota during a sabbatical in the data collection and analysis stages. Niels Krarup, then a student from Denmark, was most helpful. Cohen also wishes to thank the College of Journalism at the University of Maryland where he spent another sabbatical working on the initial draft of the manuscript. Reese Cleghorn and Mark Levy, both at Maryland, were very gracious hosts. Later on, Mark was very instrumental in providing feedback on the manuscript and sound advice on many points.

Hanna Adoni would like to thank William McGuire, who was particularly helpful in the planning stages when she spent her postdoctorate period at Yale University working on some of the theoretical issues involved in the study. She also wishes to thank Elisabeth Noelle-Neumann and Hans M. Kepplinger of the University of Mainz, West Germany, where she spent a sabbatical and did some of the writing. What would we do without sabbaticals?

Cohen and Adoni jointly wish to acknowledge the Hebrew University and especially its Communications Institute: colleagues, staff, and students. It is difficult to cite all those who helped in the distant and recent past, but some deserve special mention: Itzhak Roeh, Shlomit Levy, Shmuel Shye, Sherrill Mane, Gideon Drori, Debbie Steinberg, Rina Matsliah, and Netta Ha'Ilan.

Charles Bantz would like to acknowledge the financial support obtained from the Department of Speech–Communication at the University of Minnesota, the graduate school there, the MacMillan Travel Fund, and the Academic Computing Services. At Arizona State University he would like to thank the Department of Communication, the College of Public Programs, the Auxiliary Resource Center and the Computing Services. Also, several individuals deserve recognition: Kelly Shannon, Helga Kessler, Fred Blume, Lori Beth Fitz, Robert L. Scott, Beatrice Dehler, and Joan Lund.

We all thank Gadi Wolfsfeld of the Hebrew University and Bradley Greenberg of Michigan State University for reading the manuscript and providing us with very useful comments, and Sandra Braman of the University of Illinois for her detailed and profound criticism, and exhaustive editorial comments. We also wish to thank Irit November, the librarian at the Hebrew University, for her professional and friendly assistance in locating the numerous books and articles that we referred to in this project.

Finally, we wish to thank Sage Publications, and especially Ann West, as well as our two anonymous reviewers for their comments, interest, and encouragement. If we have forgotten anyone over these long years, we wish to be excused.

This international collaborative effort was not easy. And yet, the volume we have produced with collective energy and wisdom is finally here. It is surely not perfect, as no book can be, and it probably contains some errors despite our attempt to weed them out. Although we know that much is still left open for further research and discussion on the subject of our inquiry, we believe that our work contributes a fresh approach to at least one aspect of the study of media and society. If we are correct on this latter point alone, that is sufficient.

Prologue

This book attempts to examine how social conflicts *in general* are presented on television news, how people perceive social conflicts, and the extent to which there is a relationship between these two phenomena. Our work was not done in a single country but in a cross-national setting. While the approach to our study was not to examine *specific* conflicts, we thought it wise to begin with a concrete example from the news of the relatively recent past. For this we could have easily selected an example from any one of the countries. We chose what we believe to be an especially potent example that illustrates the kind of conflicts and the main concepts we have been dealing with.

Our illustration comes from Samaria on the West Bank of the Jordan River, part of the territory occupied by Israel since the Six Day War of 1967. It is April 6, 1988, and another tragic incident has taken place during what has become known as the *intifada*, the uprising of the Palestinians. The story has just been reported around the world. Here is a sampling.[1]

NBC Nightly News, New York, United States, 7:00 p.m.

TOM BROKAW: Good evening. The savagery and the hatred of the Israeli-Palestinian fight were never more telling than they were today on the occupied West Bank. For the first time, an Israeli civilian, a teenager, was killed, two Palestinians were shot to death by Jewish settlers, and a resolution of this blood feud seems ever more remote. NBC's Martin Fletcher tonight begins with the story of the dead Israeli teenager who was part of a group of settlers attacked by Palestinians.

MARTIN FLETCHER: Palestinians called the ambulances to treat their wounded. Instead the Arab medics found the Israeli victims. Along the road by the small Arab village they found a dead Jewish girl, a 14-year-old, whose head was smashed in by a rock. And a Jewish man, his head also smashed in, but breathing. Teenage settlers on a holiday hike were surrounded by Arabs and stoned. Two armed Israeli guards killed two Arabs, wounded two more, then ran out of ammunition. The Arabs swarmed over the Israelis, beat them with rocks and fled.

HIKER: Call someone, there is one missing! Please call the *Tzava* [the Israeli army], please!

FLETCHER: The missing child was found later with cuts and bruises. Some Arabs had helped the boy. Most kept out of sight. Why did they attack the hikers?

BYSTANDER: We don't know, we don't know. There is no reason.

FLETCHER: The Israelis are religious settlers living on the West Bank near the Arab town of Nablus. They'd been hiking without army permission. One survivor explained why they'd walked so near an Arab village.

SURVIVOR: So we—we have to show them that we are—the owners of the country. It wasn't good that we had just two guns.

FLETCHER: The settlers have mostly kept out of the uprising, leaving the army to control the Arabs, but the settlers have long warned that if pushed far enough, they'll hit back themselves. They blame the press for helping the Arabs, and called for revenge.

SETTLER: You have to close the village and you have to destroy all the houses in the village, because it was a collective doing, you have to have a collective punishment.

FLETCHER: The settlers' answer to the killing tonight is to establish a new settlement next to the Arab village, if the army lets them. If not, they threaten they'll find another way to take revenge.

ZDF, Mainz, West Germany, 8 p.m.

ANCHOR
[voice over footage]:   A new blood incident took place in Israeli-occupied West Jordan. In a village near Nablus four people lost their lives as a result of the incident; two young Palestinians, one Israeli girl and a Jewish settler were shot. For the first time since the unrest broke out four months ago Israeli citizens, too, have lost their lives. Seventeen other people were badly wounded. The army and the Palestinians gave completely different accounts of the incident. The military spokesman reported an attack by several hundred Palestinians against a group of young Israeli excursionists. Two adults accompanying the group opened fire. The Palestinians for their part speak of an incident provoked by Israelis. Settlers had entered the village, ordering the removal of a PLO flag from the rooftops.

Israel Television, Jerusalem, Israel, 9:00 p.m.
(Text abridged due to its length)

ANCHOR: In the Beita incident, an Elon Moreh girl and two Beita residents were killed. Two Arabs and fourteen Elon Moreh children were wounded. This is the first incident during the past four months between Jewish and Arab residents in which security forces had not been present. At this hour, a massive IDF [Israel Defence Forces] battalion has entered Beita and its environs to secure the area and find the killers of the girl.
                         This evening, the IDF Commander-in-Chief met with settlement leaders to cool down emotions. In the Beita village area, *Ha'tchiya* [a right-wing political party] members put up

a new settlement. The Prime Minister and his
Deputy sharply denounced the murder of the
girl.
Justice Minister, Mr. Avraham Sharir, said tonight that the village of Beita must be destroyed and all of the rioters deported.
The girl who was killed, Tirtza Porat, was hit
by a stone, and one of the escorts was badly
injured.

The Arab-Israeli conflict has been and continues to be one of the
most long-lasting conflicts in this century. Over the years, it probably
has received more media attention than most other regional or
world problems. It is also very likely that a great proportion of
news consumers around the world have some knowledge about it,
including some attitude regarding it. And it is probably also true
that many people have an opinion as to how the media have been
covering this ongoing problem.

What is it about this conflict that has sustained the interest of
politicians, the media, and public opinion for so long? This question can probably be answered by the mere fact that the conflict is
very severe and persistent. More specifically, however, it is a very
complex conflict, involving many nations, peoples, incompatible
goals and aspirations. It is also complex because there are so many
issues and subissues involved in it. The conflict is also very intense.
No fewer than five full-scale wars have erupted and been fought
bitterly since 1948, and an uncountable number of smaller-scale
encounters and acts of terror have taken place inside Israel and
outside its borders, with numerous casualties on all sides. And it is
a conflict that appears—at least at the present time—to be unsolv-
able, if we are to judge by the lack of negotiations among the parties
and their seeming adamant unwillingness to compromise or make
concessions.

The conflict between Israel and its Arab residents and neighbors
is the sort of issue that also seems to make for good media stuff.
The press in general, and television in particular, seem quite adept
in covering such matters. There is much drama and potentially
good footage available for stories of this kind, as the illustrative
example of the incident at Beita village indicates. As a mental

exercise, if our readers would try to imagine what TV viewers around the world were shown on that sad evening in the spring of 1988, they would probably guess correctly because they already have seen so many television reports of similar events in the past.

There is a tragic and ironic twist to the Beita village story, which illustrates even better the complexity, intensity, and difficulty of solving the Arab-Israeli conflict. On the following night, April 7, 1988, it was reported around the world that Tirtza Porat, the young Israeli girl, actually was killed by a bullet fired by one of the Israeli guards, not by a stone thrown by an Arab villager.

As noted at the outset, this book does not deal with the Arab-Israeli conflict nor does it relate to any other specific conflict. Therefore we shall not go into any detailed and comparative analysis of how the Beita story was covered in these different countries. In fact, this event occurred long after the present study was completed. We present this recent story, however, because we believe that it is an excellent example, albeit quite an extreme one.

The data presented in this book are not as contemporary as the Beita affair. The wide-ranging study that we conducted on the presentation of social conflicts in the news and the perception by audiences of social conflicts incorporates data from five countries and two time periods, 1980 and 1984. Although many of the specific stories surely have changed, the general theoretical framework and its mandated methodologies remain valid despite the passage of time.

Our study was conducted simultaneously in the United States, the United Kingdom, the Federal Republic of Germany (West Germany), Israel, and South Africa. In each country we analyzed the contents of newscasts and conducted a survey of young adults. We were trying to determine how television stations present social conflicts and how people make sense of them.

During the time we were busy gathering and analyzing the data the world was not standing still. In December, 1980, when we did the first analysis of the news, the main international story was the Polish crisis with the threat of a Soviet invasion. There were other stories of prominence as well, including: hunger strikes by IRA prisoners in a Belfast jail, severe labor problems throughout the United Kingdom, the beginning of the Iran-Iraq war (which was to go on for eight years), clashes between Israel and Syria, appointments being made to the first Reagan cabinet, nuns killed in San Salvador, riots in Argentina, a major Italian earthquake, and the murder of John Lennon.

In January of 1984, the time of our second news analysis, the central ongoing story was the Lebanese crisis. Additional stories included a major political corruption scandal in West Germany, politicking among Democratic candidates for the forthcoming presidential election in the United States, the West German chancellor's visit to Israel, Egypt's return to the Islamic Conference, more labor troubles in the United Kingdom and Israel, terrorism in South Africa, and negotiations between that country and Mozambique. In both periods there were many more stories of domestic or international interest, as well as stories on sports and (of course) the weather.

In both time periods, some of the stories studied were just beginning, some were in their midst, while others were in the process of ending. Some were short-lived, while others are still going on today. In fact, when we watch the news these days we realize that although the scenes have shifted and some of the actors and issues have changed—the focus now being mainly on Eastern Europe, the Soviet Union, and still on South Africa, albeit in a different vein (just today, as this was written, Nelson Mandela was released from prison)—and while some conflicts seem to be in an advanced state of resolution, others are taking their place. Thus the centrality of social conflicts and their media manifestations are as poignant as ever.

In any event, as we have noted above, the purpose of the study was to look at content of the news that dealt with social conflict and at peoples' perceptions of it, and to see if and how they relate to one another. Also, we wanted to see if things are similar or different in a variety of societies.

In analyzing the findings of our sample of newscasts, we reached several main conclusions. First, we found that social conflicts in the news abound. Although there were variations from country to country, roughly half of the news stories were concerned with social conflict. Moreover, social conflicts in the news were concentrated in a few major categories such as international politics, internal politics, and internal order and labor relations. In addition, conflict items were placed in relatively more prominent positions in the newscast compared with nonconflict items.

Second, social conflicts tended to be presented as relatively complex, difficult to solve, and not particularly intense. Furthermore, foreign conflicts—that is, conflicts not involving the country of broadcast—tended to be portrayed as more severe than domestic conflicts. Foreign conflicts were more complex than domestic conflicts (they generally involved more parties, both opponents and non-opponents), they tended to be presented as more intense than domestic conflicts, and they were displayed as being more difficult to solve than domestic conflicts. All combined, these findings suggest a *severity syndrome* of foreign conflict news.

Third, we found that most of the parties in the conflicts were *opponents*, with few parties serving in the role of arbitrators, mediators, go-betweens, and interested parties (including victims). The major parties to the conflicts were governments, political parties, countries, workers, and dissidents. There were also some differences among the five countries in the prevalence of the various kinds of parties: thus, for example, the U.S., German, and Israeli newscasts presented relatively more countries, governments, and political parties, whereas the U.S. newscasts seldom presented dissidents and workers. On the other hand, South Africa and the United Kingdom presented far more dissidents and workers as opponents in conflicts.

Across all five countries, political parties had the highest average level of representation as opponents in conflicts; thus one would be more likely to hear quotations and see representatives of political parties than of any other kind of conflict entity. Dissidents, on the other hand, were the lowest in terms of representation.

In addition to the content analyses, we also asked young adults in the five countries about how they perceived social conflicts both in the news and in the "real" world. Although our samples of respondents do not purport to represent the entire populations from which they are derived, they do allow us to draw some conclusions—albeit tentative—regarding the perception of social conflict.

The first overall (and nearly uniform) finding was similar to what we found with the news items themselves. In all the countries —when asked about the complexity, the intensity, and the solvability of the conflicts, both on television and in the real world—foreign conflicts nearly always were perceived to be the most severe (that is, more complex, more intense, and more difficult to solve) than domestic conflicts.

The second overall finding was that when controlling for country and for the degree of complexity, intensity, and solvability, conflicts in the "real" world were perceived to be more severe than the same conflicts in television news.

This demonstrates respondents could clearly distinguish between the "real" world and the world of television news. It suggests that the more remote the conflicts are from personal unmediated experience, as in the case of foreign conflicts, the more people are dependent upon the media for their knowledge, understanding, and interpretation of the conflicts.

The respondents in all five countries estimated that there were fairly numerous social conflicts going on in the world: many international conflicts, fewer national conflicts, and even fewer local conflicts. As for the perception of the prominence of conflicts in the news, here, too, many conflicts were perceived to be going on. In the case of international conflicts, however, television news was perceived as presenting more conflicts than there were in the real world. Also, the distinction between foreign and domestic stories proved to be a central factor in understanding the moderate degree of correspondence that we found between the presentation of the news and its perception by audiences.

Ten years have passed from the time the study began until the manuscript was finally ready to go to press. At several points along the way we were tempted to write some papers concerning various aspects of the study. We held off, however, with this desire so that we could present one manuscript that paints the whole picture. Reporting a study as large and complex as this one in a reasonable-length text forced us, however, to omit several lines of analysis. Some of these analyses we plan to present in future articles.

The book consists of four parts. The first part (Chapters 1 through 3) presents the theoretical perspective, the research questions, and the methodologies employed. The second part (Chapters 4 through 6) discusses findings on the presentation of social conflicts in the news of the five countries, focusing on the dimensions of conflict and the parties involved in them. The third part (Chapters 7 and 8) presents findings on the evaluation and perception of social conflicts. And the final part (Chapters 9 and 10) attempts to integrate the findings and looks at the correspondence between presentation and perception.

NOTE

1. The translations of the German and Hebrew news items were done by the authors.

PART I

Theory and Method

ONE

Social Conflicts and Television News: Some Theoretical Issues

The subject of this study is social conflicts in television news. We have chosen to work with Kriesberg's (1973) definition of *social conflict* as a "relationship between two or more parties who (or whose spokesmen) believe they have incompatible goals" (p. 17). Following Gurr (1980) who stipulated that conflict research bears on "collective action" we were concerned in this study only with conflicts that exist in some underlying social context and not with conflicts involving personal goals or motivations.[1] Consequently, our definition is deliberately broad to include various types of conflicts, both social and political.[2]

We have chosen social conflicts because of three basic considerations: first, the ubiquity of social conflicts in society; second, the dominance of social conflict as a subject of television news; and third, the suggestion that the mass media play a central role in the development and regulation of many social conflicts.

It is an accepted postulate that conflicts exist in every type of society, regardless of the degree of social differentiation and specialization (Coser, 1956; Gurr, 1980; Kriesberg, 1973; Simmel, 1955; Wehr, 1979). According to the functional model of society, the regulation of social conflicts operates routinely through a variety of institutional, social, and political mechanisms that provide for the expression and resolution of social disputes and disagreements (e.g., parliaments or political parties). Actions taken outside normal and official channels are understood to be antisocial and deviant from social norms. Both Coser (1956) and Dahrendorf (1959), however, suggest that social conflicts actually serve adaptive functions for society in making social change possible, which usually implies challenges to established institutions and beliefs. For example, conflict within a system can lead to the renewal of old norms or the creation of new ones, and conflicts with an external group may tighten social boundaries and increase cohesiveness.

In the sociological and political science literature dealing with conflict there is an implicit assumption that a relationship exists between external and internal conflicts. One of the most common hypotheses, based on research concerning in-group and out-group relations, maintains that external conflict decreases internal social tensions. Despite the considerable research efforts, this hypothesis has not been supported unequivocally and the interaction between internal and external conflicts is still problematic (Stohl, 1980). At the same time, however, there is consensus among researchers that this is an important issue in conflict research. The theoretical framework of the present study enables an examination of this issue from two perspectives: the presentation of foreign and domestic conflicts in the news, and the differential perception of such conflicts among audience members.

The debate concerning the contribution of social conflict to social stability and change has been a central and ongoing one. Students of conflict suggest that various aspects of social conflicts are influenced by various systemic factors relating to the distribution of power in society, among them the control over the mass media of communication (Pirages, 1980) and the spread of mass media in society (Zimmerman, 1980)

The dominance of social conflict as a subject in television news, and hence its importance in placing various issues on the public agenda, has received considerable attention from scholars holding various points of view (e.g., Arno & Dissanayake, 1984; Davison, 1974; Galtung & Ruge, 1965; Katz, 1977; Park, 1940; Tichenor, Donohue, & Olien, 1980; Tuchman, 1978a; Van Poecke, 1988). Various studies that focused on organizational constraints and journalistic practices and their effects on the content of news have stressed the fact that the nature of news is a product of organizations and their personnel.

These studies all point to two different levels of constraints within the organization: first, journalists themselves, including their professional values, norms, stereotypes, and judgments as well as their fundamental view of the world and their place in society (Altheide, 1976; Galtung & Ruge, 1965; Gans, 1979; Katz, 1989; Tunstall, 1971); second, the organizational structure and routines of news operations as well as the economic and medium-related constraints determining them, such as cost control, format, technology, and programming time (Bantz, McCorkle, & Baade, 1980; Braestrup, 1978; Epstein, 1973; Johnstone, Slawski, & Bowman, 1976; Schudson, 1978; Tuchman, 1973, 1978a). Both sets of constraints, of course, also are reflected in the coverage of social conflicts in the news.

Several researchers have sought to identify additional constraints external to the news organization (Dahlgren, 1981; Gitlin, 1980; Hall, 1977, 1981; Hartley, 1982; Schiller, 1973; Smith, 1973; Turow, 1984). The common interest of all these scholars are the political, economic, and social systems within which the media organizations operate. Included among the external factors are the specific interests of powerful groups who serve as news sources, the audience, the relative autonomy (formal and informal) of the media organization from the state and from business enterprises, and the ideologies of the power-holding groups within society. From this theoretical perspective, the exigencies of the news process itself are seemingly less significant to the news product than are the influences of the environment within which the media organization operates.

Although the first two reasons for choosing social conflicts are relatively straightforward, the third reason needs more elaboration. It relates to the claims of both functional theorists (e.g., Lazarsfeld & Merton, 1948; Lasswell, 1948) and proponents of the critical approach (e.g., Adorno & Horkheimer, 1972; Althusser, 1971; Benjamin, 1970; Gramsci, 1971; Marcuse, 1964) that the mass media play a central role in the development and regulation of social and political conflicts. Although the advocates of these two approaches differ strongly on the nature of media functions regarding social conflicts, they both share the common assumption that the mass media do fulfill a central role in these processes.

The functional theorists stress the integrative role of the media that regulate social conflicts and create the basis for social consensus. Thus Lazarsfeld and Merton (1948) suggest that "the mass media operate toward the maintenance of the ongoing social and cultural structure rather than towards its change" (p. 480). Their argument is similar to Coser's (1956) according to which the exposure of norm violations by the news media causes reaffirmation of public morality and social norms rather than private morality and norms. This "ethiocizing" function of the media (i.e., the enforcement of social norms) serves to strengthen social control and contributes to the media's continuing reaffirmation of the status quo, a notion that is similar to what is advocated by the proponents of the critical approach.

An alternative conceptualization of the mass media acting at times as agents of social change is put forward by Kellner (1981) and by Alexander (1981). Kellner points out the contradictions between state, business, and network television that cause the American networks to be "unreliable defenders of the existing order." Accordingly, the networks transmit contradictory images and messages that reflect the divisions and ideological confusion within the ruling class and society at large. When network news exposes and calls attention to the failures and wrongdoings of government and business, television may serve to jeopardize their interests and status and delegitimize their practices. Ultimately, by promoting awareness of the system's failures, television may contribute to a "legitimization crisis" within society and create a reservoir of discontent available for mobilization in the interests of social change.

Alexander (1981) ascribes to the mass media of democratic societies a social integrative function that creates the possibility for action rather than passive resignation. The mass news media are autonomous, untied to any particular interest or group, and are in constant struggle with the state.

According to the adherents of the critical approach, the mass media support the established social order by acting as the means of social control and thus legitimizing the status quo (e.g., Adorno & Horkheimer, 1972; Marcuse, 1964). Furthermore, media depictions of society tend to minimize the importance of social conflicts, and as such are fundamental to the task of ensuring and maintaining the social and political status quo. Additional scholars further developed these notions and in many instances applied them to television, which was perceived as a powerful agent of the dominant ideological apparatus (e.g., Gitlin, 1978; Hall, 1977; Murdock, 1973).

Another central figure among the critical theorists in the 1930s was Gramsci (1971) who believed that all institutions interact with and mutually depend upon each other within the overall social formation. The interactions of people with each other and with these institutions are interpreted through what Gramsci called "common sense," the shared assumptions of people who live within the social formation. Common sense acts as a "hegemonic ideology" and binds the society together. Gramsci also believed that dissidence is always present within society but is controlled in various ways by the internal workings of the overall formation.

Following Gramsci's notions, Althusser (1971) suggested that states maintain power not just through "repressive state apparatuses" such as armies and police forces but also through "ideological state apparatuses" such as the legal system, educational institutions, religious institutions, and the media. Foucault (1977) extended this notion by viewing every interaction as one involving power that normally served to support the existing power structure. Gramsci's commonsense notion can be seen as the device by which this power is manifested.

THE DIMENSIONS OF CONFLICT

The sociological literature refers to three central dimensions of conflicts: their complexity, intensity and solvability. Moreover, in reviewing the voluminous literature based on a variety of approaches to the mass media, we noticed that notions relating to bias in news coverage also seem to allude to these three dimensions.

Complexity refers to the overall context of the conflict. Specifically it deals with the degree to which a social conflict involves few or many participants and bears upon few or numerous issues. Also included in the complexity notion are the past history of the conflict, its duration, and the magnitude of its possible consequences. Social conflicts low on these characteristics are considered simple, while increments in each of them would contribute to making the conflict more complex (Galtung, 1964; Gamson, 1975; Rex, 1981; Wehr, 1979).

In addition to main opponents, who by definition participate in all conflicts, Schellenberg (1982) offers a typology of "third parties" and distinguished among four basic patterns of third-party involvement: good offices, mediation, arbitration, and adjudication. Because of the dramatic character of the representation of conflict in television news, special attention was paid in the present study to the various parties and roles they played.

Our focus on the complexity dimension also stems from the argument found in numerous sources that television news coverage tends to simplify social conflicts. Although the sociological literature maintains that any conflict in society has several stages, television news focuses only on its manifest stages and minimizes the presentation of its underlying causes, the opponents' motivations, and in general, the analysis of social conflicts as gradually unfolding processes. Television news fails to present the dimension of social power and social processes, and portrays a world that is "unchanging and unchangeable" (Golding, 1981; Golding & Elliott, 1979).

According to Murdock (1973), this type of simplification is the result of *event orientation,* which determines that processes leading to an event do not themselves make news. In the absence of explanations of the underlying causes of social conflicts, television news presents events as being "caused" by the immediately preceding acts of groups or individuals, thereby creating the impression that dissent is confined to small and marginal groups in society. Further simplification typically is depicted by television news whereby social conflicts are presented as struggles between two well-delineated opponents although in many conflict relationships there are actually more than two parties, including various "third parties" who are pursuing incompatible goals.

Intensity is concerned with the behavior and attitudes of participants relative to the conflict itself. Dahrendorf (1959), Stagner (1967), and Kriesberg (1973) all distinguish between the intensity of the participants' feelings and the intensity of their actions or behavior (e.g., violence). Intensity of behavior is a function of the means chosen by the opponents in their struggle to achieve their goal, and may vary independently of the intensity of feeling—that is, the depth of emotional involvement and energy expenditure of the participants (Coleman, 1957; Lewin, 1948). Social conflict situations may be characterized merely by arguments and debates, and the intensity dimension may be manifested in terms of actions other than physical, such as various forms of verbal aggression. Thus, based on the sociological literature, the intensity dimension of social conflicts in this study is conceptualized as being comprised of three components: physical aggression, verbal aggression, and the expression of feelings or emotions by the participants involved in the conflict.

Many media studies point out that television news tends to present only the more intense moments of social conflicts. Tuchman (1978a) illustrates this point with the example of news coverage of riots. Although during riots there usually are periods of lull, "news reporters commonly ignore such phases, collapsing the course of riots into continuous intensive activity" (pp. 190-191). Hall (1977) observed that the characteristic form of coverage of social conflict is "actuality without context" and that this is obtained by the concentration of the news media on "vivid sound and image." The event orientation of television news also is illustrated by Abel (1984) in his study of the role of television in international conflicts.

Furthermore, the presentation of intensive activity usually centers around groups who are not identified with the economic and political power holders in society. Thus the Glasgow University Media Group (1976) found that in television coverage of British industrial disputes management representatives generally are interviewed in their offices—a quiet setting connoting reason, authority, and responsibility—whereas strikers are show "in action" at mass meetings and picket lines—a setting implying that they are the major source of discord.

Solvability, the third and final dimension, deals with the extent to which it is easy or difficult to solve social conflicts. According to sociological analysis of social conflicts, the difficulty of resolution depends on the nature of the incompatible goals pursued by the opponents and on the estimated costs of the possible outcomes to each of the parties involved, as well as to other uninvolved individuals and groups. Thus, for example, social conflicts over basic values and resources such as power, status, civil rights, or religion would tend to be more difficult to solve than conflicts over issues such as economic benefits. In the present study solvability is conceived of as indications that a resolution of the conflict is forthcoming. This would be characterized by a desire to solve the conflict, a willingness to compromise, and actually engaging in some solution-oriented activity (Kriesberg, 1973; Nordlinger, 1972; Oberschall, 1973; Wehr, 1979).

The solvability dimension appears also to be affected by television's portrayal of social conflict. Murdock (1973) contends that as a result of event orientation the social conflicts covered by television news appear to be short-term and easily solved. Connel, Curti, and Hall (1976) also claim that as a result of the ethical and professional importance of objectivity, neutrality, and balance, the presentation of television news gives the solutions to conflicts the appearance of being in the general interest rather than exposing the advantages that the dominant sections of society gain from them.

The underlying message concerning this type of presentation of the three conflict dimensions is that, essentially, society is characterized by consensus, and that as a consequence news serves as a means of regulating social conflicts, thereby either reinforcing the status quo or creating conditions for a nonviolent social change. What we attempted to do in this study was to investigate empirically news presentation of these three dimensions and to test the veracity of these claims.

Following the conflict research literature, this study deals with the differences in the presentation of foreign and domestic conflicts along the three main dimensions elaborated above. We expected to find foreign conflicts to be presented as more severe—that is, more complex, more intense, and more difficult to solve—compared with domestic conflicts. According to various studies on news selection (e.g., Galtung & Ruge, 1965; Gans, 1979) foreign stories would pass the selection threshold when they are sufficiently dramatic. On the other hand, domestic conflicts are included in the news even if their newsworthiness is lower, as long as they are relevant to the country of broadcast. Along the lines of the critical perspective the same outcome would be hypothesized, but for different reasons. The presentation of foreign conflicts as more severe would be an attempt on the part of journalists or media organizations, whether intended or not, to show their audience a more tranquil domestic front in comparison with the outside world and hence to support and maintain the social order.

It should be emphasized that we were not interested in particular conflicts and specific parties in the conflicts. On the contrary, we wanted to develop an abstract, conceptual framework that could be applied to the study of news content and its perception in various societies that differ from one another in their cultural and social systems (Adoni, 1989). Our approach is similar to Oberschall's (1973) evaluation according to which one of the theoretic gains of game theory (Boulding, 1962; Rapoport, 1965) is "uncovering the structure of a great variety of conflict situations without regard to what the substantive issues are or who the opponents are" (Oberschall, 1973, p. 49).

THE SOCIAL CONSTRUCTION OF REALITY

Berger and Luckmann's (1967) far-reaching redefinition of the sociology of knowledge had direct implications for the study of culture and mass communication. They postulate that the sociology of knowledge must concern itself with "everything that passes for 'knowledge' in society" (p. 14). Thus the emphasis should be on various expressions of the social construction of reality and not solely on its intellectual articulations. Recently, Barnes (1988) defined society as "a distribution of knowledge" claiming that "how people act depends upon what they know" (p. 46). In this context, it is also interesting to note that in his analysis of class conflicts, Giddens (1982) uses the term *conflict consciousness* in referring to cognitive recognition of opposition between class differences.

These notions are compatible with Park's (1940) now-classic definition of news as a special type of knowledge and with McQuail's (1972) notion that the mass media play a part in "shaping the individual and collective consciousness by organizing and circulating the knowledge that people have of their own everyday life and of the more remote contexts of their lives" (p. 13).

The process of reality construction is defined as *social* because it can be carried out only through social interaction, either real or symbolic. The social construction of reality is a dialectical process in which human beings act both as the creators and as products of their social world. This is the consequence of a special human faculty of externalization and objectivation of one's own internalized and subjective meanings, experiences, and actions.

For heuristic purposes, a distinction can be made between three types of reality implied in this dialectical process. First is *objective* social reality, which is experienced as the objective world existing outside the individual and confronting him or her as facts. This reality is apprehended by people in a commonsense fashion as reality par excellence, and does not need any further verification over and beyond its simple existence. Although human beings are capable of doubting this reality, they are obliged to suspend such doubt in order to be able to perform the routine actions that ensure both their own existence and their interaction with others.

The second type of reality is *symbolic* social reality, which consists of any form of symbolic expression of objective reality such as art, literature, media contents, or communicative behavior. There are multiple symbolic realities that differ from one another by various symbol systems.

And third, there is *subjective* social reality, where both the objective and symbolic realities serve as an input for the construction of the individual's own reality. In more general terms, it can be said that the objective world and its symbolic representations are fused into individual consciousness. As we are dealing with a dialectical process, however, this individually constructed subjective reality provides the basis for the individual's social actions, and thus ensures the existence of objective reality and the meaningfulness of its symbolic expressions.

When dealing with these three types of reality, one encounters what initially appears to be a paradox. Although symbolic reality and subjective reality can be measured by various acceptable procedures in social research, it is the "real" reality—those "facts" that seem to be self-evident—that cannot be measured in any satisfactory manner. Thus symbolic reality can be measured, for example (albeit imperfectly) by looking at selected attributes of the phenomenon of interest in some content analytical scheme. Also, subjective reality can be measured by using a variety of research methods such as surveys and field observations. It is difficult, however, to tap empirically all the relevant aspects of a complex phenomenon such as social conflict. Even such phenomena (e.g., crime or labor disputes) that can be documented statistically in terms of the number of reported murders or the number of workdays lost because of a strike are surely not precise reflections of the real thing.

In our discussion of the dimensions of social conflicts, we argued that symbolic reality as it appears in television news distorts, at least to some extent, the "real" reality—it tends to present conflicts as less complex, more intense and more solvable than they really are. Any attempt to compare symbolic reality to "real" reality is in most cases impossible. Some exceptions to this have been attempts to relate demographic statistics of symbolically produced contents (e.g., action dramas and soap operas) to their corresponding real-life parameters (see, for example, Gerbner & Gross, 1976; Greenberg, 1980; Tuchman, 1978b). However, when one is concerned (as we are here), with socially intricate phenomena defined by means of abstract concepts even this procedure cannot be applied adequately.

THE PERCEPTION OF CONFLICT: PROXIMITY AND DEPENDENCE

In the present study we focused on various aspects of symbolic and subjective realities and the interactions between them. As mentioned above, these two realities simultaneously interact with objective reality in a dialectic process of the social construction of reality. We believe, therefore, that a study of these interactions also contributes to our understanding of social conflicts in the "real" world.

The individual's subjective reality is organized in terms of *zones of relevance*, which differ on the basis of their proximity from the here and now of the individual's immediate environment. Those social elements and actors with whom the individual interacts frequently in face-to-face situations are part of "close" zones of relevance. The "remote" zones of relevance are composed of general, more abstract social elements that are not accessible to direct experience—for example, social conflicts among various groups in society.

Although Schutz (1967), as well as Berger and Luckmann (1967), refer to mass media only in a tangential manner in their analyses of these psychosocial processes, we believe the media dependency hypothesis advanced by Ball-Rokeach and DeFleur (1976) provides a useful conceptual link between the phenomenological theories and media research. According to this systemic theory, there are relationships of dependency among various parts of society—individuals, groups, and organizations. The media system is a part of a larger system and is in control of information gathering, processing, and dissemination. DeFleur and Ball-Rokeach (1989) suggest that: "An advantage of media system dependency theory is that we can use the same basic concepts that apply to the abstract macro relations between systems to examine the more concrete (and micro) relations between individuals and the mass media" (p. 305). Furthermore, according to the media dependency hypothesis, the degree of media contribution to the individual's construction of subjective reality is a function of one's direct experiences with various phenomena and consequent dependence on the media for information about these phenomena.

The proximity factor of social conflicts can be viewed both in terms of its geographical location and psychosocial context. Proximity has been examined in studies of newsworthiness (e.g., Epstein, 1973; Galtung & Ruge, 1965) where it was found to be important in determining the coverage of events. Accordingly, events that occur in close geographical or psychological proximity would be more likely to be reported.

The proximity factor is also important because it relates to the question of the maintenance of the social status quo. Presenting stories of "distant" conflicts may shift the attention of the population away from its own domestic problems and conflicts toward foreign conflicts. By doing so the dynamics between power holders and the media in society contribute to internal cohesiveness and underplay the significance of social conflicts among various segments in the society.

The final input to the present study comes from a trend of empirical research that focuses on the relationships between mass-media content and public opinion. This trend actually developed early in the history of mass-communication research, beginning with Walter Lippman (1922). The second phase, in the 1930s, produced studies on the effects of types of content on public opinion (e.g., Blumer, 1933). This was followed by the work of Hovland, Lumsdaine, and Sheffield (1949) and Lazarsfeld, Berelson, and Gaudet (1944), who focused on the possibilities of using the media for active persuasion. More recently, McGuire (1981) presented a communication/persuasion matrix that provides a framework for combining media inputs and psychological outputs. In addition, several groups of scholars have been interested in the relationship between media content and public opinion. From this approach to communication research emerged hypotheses and findings on the "spiral of silence" and the dynamics of public opinion (Kepplinger & Hachenberg, 1986; Noelle-Neumann, 1974, 1984), the cultivation effect (Gerbner & Gross, 1976; Gerbner, Gross, Signorielli, & Morgan, 1980; Gerbner, Morgan, & Signorielli, 1980), the agenda-setting function (McCombs & Shaw, 1972), the "knowledge gap" hypothesis (Tichenor, Donohue, & Olien, 1970) and the "media dependency" phenomenon (Ball-Rokeach, 1985; Ball-Rokeach & DeFleur, 1976).

These studies focused on the interaction between the symbolic representations of social reality in different media and genres and the social construction of reality by media consumers (Adoni & Mane, 1984; Hartmann & Husband, 1972; Hawkins & Pingree, 1982). This approach led to the initial research on the perception of social conflicts in "social reality" and "media reality" (Adoni, Cohen, & Mane, 1984; Cohen, Adoni, & Drori, 1983). These studies suggest that individuals are dependent upon the mass media, particularly television, in making sense of various social phenomena, and that the way television presents various social issues influences the way people perceive them (Adoni & Cohen, 1978). Although Gerbner's cultivation theory deals mainly with fictional contents of television, Cohen and Adoni, using news content, suggest that people are able clearly to distinguish between the world of television (the symbolic world) and the reality in which they live. Hence people can determine when television is presenting a distorted picture of the real world. The more familiar people are with the issues and the more knowledgeable they are about the subjects, the more likely people can make those judgments with better acuity.

Using the concepts of complexity, intensity, and solvability, Cohen, Adoni, and their associates were able to demonstrate that people differentially perceived social conflicts (dealing with terrorism, labor troubles and school integration) that varied in terms of the respondents' anticipated familiarity with the issues. The present study expands upon this notion by considering social conflicts that differ in terms of their proximity by examining international, national, and local conflicts.

Our conceptualization of the three dimensions enabled us to generate several hypotheses regarding the modes of perception of social conflicts. Thus, as a consequence of television's emphasis on the relative simplicity of social conflicts, people ought to perceive social conflicts on television news as relatively simple when compared to "real" social reality, particularly when dealing with events that are closer to their everyday experiences.

Furthermore, assuming that television presents social conflicts at their peak of intensity, audiences ought to perceive conflicts on television news as being more intense than in "real" social reality. This would not be the case, of course, if the people were experienced with the specific conflicts and could thereby know on a first-hand basis what the conflicts were like. And lastly, as with the previous two dimensions, we would expect that people perceive social conflicts on television news as relatively easy to solve. With regard to conflicts with which they have direct familiarity, however, they might tend to perceive them as more difficult to solve.

PRESENTATION AND PERCEPTION

The conceptual framework of our research was conceived along the following lines: on the one hand, concern with the basic premises of functional theories and of the critical approach; and on the other hand, the application of theories and findings based on empirical work showing the interaction between media content and the audience's attitudes, opinions, and perceptions of social reality.

This attempt toward an integrative approach is not new in communication research. Communication scholars of different periods and backgrounds have advocated the integration of the American and European main schools of thought. As early as 1949, Merton suggested that both the European sociology of knowledge and the American empirical sociology of mass communication "can be regarded as a species of that genus of research that is concerned with the interplay between social structure and communication" (Merton, 1968, p. 493).

More recently, Carey (1977) suggested that an integrative approach will enrich both traditions. Lang (1979) states that "there is no inherent incompatibility between the 'positivism' of the communication research and the critical approach associated with the Frankfurt School" (p. 83). Blumler (1980) points out that proponents of the two schools of thought should reexamine both their own and each other's basic premises in an effort to refine their theories and analyses. In his paper on the mass media and social change, Rosengren (1981) suggests that recent developments in the area of social and cultural indicators research may be helpful in the integration of the sociologies of knowledge and mass communication. Finally, Lull (1982) advocates the adoption of the communication rules perspective in order to develop a mass communication theory that includes concepts and methodologies associated with both empirical and critical schools of thought.

By conducting the present study we wished to contribute to the current perspective of communication research by focusing on a central social phenomenon—social conflict—and by studying its presentation in an important television genre (the news). We did this simultaneously while studying the perceptual patterns among audiences in several different countries.

This project focuses on three central questions. The first question was concerned with the way television news presents social conflicts. The second question was how people perceive social conflicts on television and in the "real" world. And finally, we wanted to determine the correspondence between the presentation of conflicts in the news and the perception of the conflicts by audiences. In our attempt to answer these three questions we used an eclectic approach by borrowing certain concepts from various sources and adapting them to our needs.

Our work has led us also to search for abstract concepts that will enable us to analyze patterns of presentation and perception of various social conflicts without relating to the specific and exact nature of the particular conflict situation and its participating parties. In other words, these concepts can serve as an abstract common denominator ensuring a nonculture-bound analysis and enabling us to study content and people from different societies within the same conceptual and operational framework. This brings us to the cross-national component of the study that is explicated in the following chapter.

NOTES

1. Thus, for example, if a man robs a bank because the man has no money to buy food, this case would be considered as an individual problem that might have led to the robbery, and hence would not be the object of our present interest. If an individual robs a bank, however, because the bank symbolizes for him or her (or for a group to which he or she belongs) the oppressing forces of society, we would then consider this as a social conflict (recall, for instance, the case of Patty Hearst and the Symbionese Liberation Army in 1974). Indeed, we can assume that some people would regard the poor person robbing the bank as indicative of a social problem—perhaps even a class conflict—but within the legal framework of our culture this would be considered as an individual problem. In studying social conflicts as presented on television we are, of course, limited to analyzing the report of events. Thus social conflict is defined as it is presented or reported and not by some a priori judgment.

2. There is a distinction in the political science literature between social and political conflicts, according to the types of parties and their goals. Even this body of literature, however, points out the difficulty of distinguishing between these two types in any given instance (Dahrendorf, 1959; Rex, 1981).

The Cross-National Perspective

Much of the literature we have discussed in the previous chapter is steeped in predominantly unquestioned presumptions of cross-national universality. In this literature, culturally unconditioned statements are made both about the content of television news and about the social functions it serves, as if they applied everywhere.

Stories featuring conflict appear often and prominently in television news. As indicated earlier, television (it is said) tends to simplify social conflicts, presenting only surface events, ignoring underlying causes, and focusing mostly on just two clearly opposed sides to contested issues. Television news also intensifies conflict (it is alleged) by highlighting the more dramatic, antagonistic, and violent facets of disputes, while filtering out the 'dull bits.' In addition, television news suggests (so the critique continues) that conflicts are or ought to be solvable, shying away from the presentation of structurally incompatible interests that cannot be bridged, and implying the existence of an overarching public interest to which opposed groups and leaders then are expected to respond by compromising their differences in a pragmatic spirit of "live and let live." Finally, by encouraging viewers to follow the ups and downs of conflicts in the role of spectators, by failing to cultivate a more mature understanding, and by projecting the message that all is fundamentally well in society (or would be if sectional interests would only behave sufficiently rationally), television news stands for social order and thereby sells the status quo.

Such generalizations, however, have been rarely subjected to systematic comparative scrutiny. They have emerged mainly from case studies, either of television news organizations or of television news representations of selected social and political issues (e.g., industrial relations; race relations; crime, law, and order; social welfare; Northern Ireland; terrorism), carried out in two Anglo-Saxon societies: the United Kingdom and the United States. Thus, to date, the overtly comparative literature on the subject is thin and inconclusive.

One attempt to answer the above question has been supplied by Golding and Elliott (1979) in their cross-cultural study of broadcast organizations in Sweden, Ireland, and Nigeria. They concluded that in

> all three countries, government intervention and control either seem less important, as determinants of broadcast journalism, than the values by which the job is conducted, and exert their effect through distortion or amplification of news values . . . even in highly varied cultural and organizational settings broadcast news emerges with surprisingly similar forms and contents. (pp. 137, 207)

Golding and Elliott further contend that although there are differences between countries in news output, the important determinants of output are those that belong to the organization—that is, constraints on material available to newsrooms and shared perceptions of audience interests and demands. Notwithstanding the differences in the relationship between broadcast organizations and government, the "same institutional areas, illustrated by the same events and the same people, dominate the news" (p. 48).

Golding and Elliott found many similarities of organization, work routine, and responsiveness to external influences in television newsrooms in Ireland, Nigeria, and Sweden, but their examination of the resulting output was not detailed and lacked a close focus on the reporting of conflict.

In a nine-country study of television portrayals of the first European Community elections of 1979, Siune (1983) found certain transnationally common elements in journalists' contributions to the campaign (as distinct from those of politicians), including emphases on events, conflicts, personalities, topicality, and the election strategies of the main contenders. Nevertheless, the issues of the elections as depicted on television varied greatly from country to country, depending largely on how the major national parties had resolved to fight the elections.

Three limitations are underscored by this cursory review. First, the literature carries a (largely unstated) implication of the existence of a transnational news-value culture to which reporters tend to adhere regardless of the countries in which individual journalists happen to be working, although the extent of its dominance is unevenly charted. Second, the reporting of conflicts by the television news systems of different countries has not been examined systematically on like topics and aligned dimensions of coverage. Third, comparative theorizing about this subject is virtually nonexistent. Little sustained thought has been given to the respects in which news portrayals of social conflicts should be expected to be similar across different countries and to the identification of influences that might be expected to differentiate them. This leaves something of an intellectual vacuum: It is difficult to know where to turn for theoretical inspiration when approaching conflict news reporting comparatively.

THE COMPARATIVE FRAMEWORK

News reports of social conflict were analyzed cross-nationally in order to identify patterns of variation in the participating countries. Five countries were included in the study: the United States, the United Kingdom, West Germany, Israel, and South Africa. These five countries share several relevant common features. In all of them, television news is viewed by relatively large audiences and can be assumed to be an important source of information about political, social, and economic affairs occurring at home and abroad (Robinson & Levy, 1986; Roper Organization, 1985). Also, the national broadcasting organizations in each of these countries nominally subscribe to—and usually practice—the norms and routines of "objective" journalism, which may influence broadcast organizations to produce similar news output, particularly because the sources of news are similar and common (Epstein, 1973; Gans, 1979; Schlesinger, 1978; Tuchman, 1978a).

At the same time, however, the broadcast organizations in the different countries operate in political, social, and economic settings that vary with regard to two systemic factors. The first factor is the relationship between the broadcasting organizations and government, which as Smith (1973) notes, is the "most crucial of all the relationships which bind a broadcasting organization to its society" (p. 142). The second factor is the form and degree of competition that each of the news organizations faces from other media organizations.

In order to compare and contrast among the five countries, we examined the television broadcasting system in each country focusing on the information necessary to consider the similarities and differences among them on four major points: (1) degree of government influence, (2) source of revenue, (3) extent of competition, and (4) journalistic norms and traditions. (This information is presented in Appendix A for the benefit of readers unfamiliar with these five national systems.)

Based on an analysis of the five broadcasting systems we reached the conclusion that two continua exist, one for the degree of government influence and regulation and one for the degree of competition among the media. What is even more remarkable about these continua is that the five countries are located along both of them in the identical order: the United States, the United Kingdom, West Germany, Israel, and South Africa. As far as government influence is concerned, there is the least in the United States and the most in South Africa, and regarding competition there is the least in South Africa and the most in the United States.

POSTULATED SIMILARITIES AND
DIFFERENCES IN PRESENTATION

As we have noted above, the basic journalistic norms are shared by news professionals in all the countries examined in the present study. Accordingly we assumed that similarities that may exist among the countries will be the result mainly of the common journalistic ethos and practice. On the other hand, two sets of factors will push simultaneously toward differences among the countries: the systemic variables of government influence and media competition, as well as the special idiosyncracies of each of the societies. Several of the articles appearing in Martin and Chaudhary (1983) analyze some of these variables in concrete societies.

Blumler and Gurevitch (1981) have stressed the advantage of analyzing the behavior of journalists (as well as politicians) in terms of role relationships. This provides us with a dual perspective. First, journalists are anchored in a framework of tasks assigned to them by their occupations and organizations. Thus their reactions both to other social institutions and to the types of news they must regularly report will stem in large part from their occupancy of defined positions in the organizational hierarchy. Second, however, through their professional culture journalists are exposed to a national value system, which implicitly ranks social institutions and groups for respectability and defines norms, the violation of which would be regarded as societally significant and therefore meriting attention in news organs (Blumler & Gurevitch, 1986; Lazarsfeld & Merton, 1948). Thus an emphasis on role relations alerts us to the dualistic field of forces within which journalists operate, comprising influence from their professional culture on the one hand, and from extra-professional influences inherent in their roles as citizens of the larger society on the other.

Specifically, we hypothesized that the differences in the presentation based on the three dimensions will be modified by the two central systemic variables of government influence and media competition. The complexity and intensity of conflict stories may vary according to the degree of governmental control—often considered as the distinction between public service and commercial—among broadcasting systems. In public service systems, norms of "social responsibility" and obligations to educate and inform may mitigate the more "purely" journalistic impulses to simplify and to shock. In addition, conflict stories are most likely to be intense and simple where the competition between news organizations is keen (e.g., the United States, perhaps), less so where it is contained with some framework of mutually shared public goals (e.g., the United Kingdom, West Germany), and least marked where competition is virtually nonexistent (as in the monopolistic broadcasting systems of Israel and South Africa).

The projection of conflicts as solvable could also depend on two sources of differentiation. First, for broadcasting systems a subordination-autonomy axis, or dimension of degree of political institutional control over television organization, may be relevant (Blumler & Gurevitch, 1975; Roshco, 1975). Given a disposition among political leaders to perceive and present themselves as architects of national unity, television news is likely to be more constrained toward "solvable conflict reporting" in those broadcasting systems that are subordinated more closely to the state (as, say, in South Africa) than in those where "arm's-length" conventions insulate broadcasting from political pressure to some degree (the United Kingdom) and especially in those where news autonomy enjoys a highly authoritative constitutional protection (the United States).[1]

Finally, this preliminary framework of expectations should take account of the distinction built into the empirical research design between the reporting of domestic and foreign conflicts. Following some of the notions offered by Galtung and Ruge (1965) concerning the nature of "foreign" news, we discern here two alternative prospects. The first would maintain that the extraprofessional constraints tending to differentiate conflict news cross-nationally should apply chiefly to coverage of domestic controversies and disputes. This perspective suggests that reporters everywhere will be more free to deal with foreign events according to their journalistic lights than they can with situations closer to home. If so, a greater similarity would be predicted for portrayals of foreign conflicts across the five countries than for equivalent domestic stories.

This line of thought ignores the fact, however, that for all countries in the study, certain situations and events abroad will be highly relevant to the perceived national interest and ultimately to elite and mass evaluations of government performance. For the United States, relations with the Soviet Union and the Communist bloc and developments elsewhere that may tip the East-West power balance are highly preoccupying. South Africa is especially sensitive to foreign reactions to its apartheid regime and concerned with relations to bordering black states. For Israel, relations with its Arab neighbors and the Middle East policies of the United States are virtually matters of national survival. West Germany is close to the political firing line of East-West relations. Questions of nuclear disarmament and relations with the United States have played a central part in the recent politics of the United Kingdom. Thus certain international conflicts reported in the news may have domestic implications and therefore tend to come under the mixed influences governing the presentation of both domestic and foreign news. Accordingly, we hypothesized that the magnitude of the variables for these "domestic-foreign" conflicts will fall in between the magnitudes of the distinctly domestic or foreign conflicts.

POSTULATED SIMILARITIES
AND DIFFERENCES IN PERCEPTION

As we have argued above, our study of the perception of social conflicts closely follows our investigation of the related presentation of television news. Just as in the case of comparative news research, the absence of previous and cumulative findings makes it difficult to formulate precise hypotheses concerning the domain of perception. In the case of the perception of conflicts, our main proposition is that there is a relationship between the way the conflicts are presented and the way they are perceived.

This type of relationship, if it were all that simple, would suggest that if, say, conflicts are presented in the news as being of low complexity, high in intensity, and easy to solve, then the viewing public would perceive conflicts as being of low complexity, high intensity, and high solvability.

As we have argued in the first chapter, however, the relationship between media content and perceptions of social reality is not simple, and it is the subject of a prolonged and ongoing debate among communication scholars. In the research that has led to this study (based on theories of social construction of reality and media dependency), Adoni, Cohen, and their colleagues arrived at two main conclusions. First, they found that people are able to differentiate between conflicts in social reality and their presentation in television news according to their complexity, intensity, and solvability. And second, the degree of personal experience, relevance to the individual, and the extent to which he or she is dependent on the media for information tend to mediate the modes of perception. In the present study the degree of personal experience and relevance was operationalized as the proximity (or location) variable that differentiated among local, national and international conflicts.

To assess the relationship between content and perception we employed a cross-national design, because such a comparison permits us to identify what aspects of that relationship are consistent across countries and what aspects vary by country. Without a between-country comparison, the influence of a country's idiosyncratic broadcasting structure cannot be identified.

What we are looking for in our study of social conflicts, then, are possible overall universal patterns of perception of conflicts, which are a function of media dependency as well as unmediated experiences. And yet, we clearly do not wish to ignore the possible impact of the specific portrayal of the conflicts in the various countries on how people perceive the conflicts.

As an illustration of this point, let us return to the Beita village story that we presented in the prologue. The presentation of that item by the various countries had some common threads, although they were clearly different in emphasis and detail.[2] Also, we know from public opinion studies conducted in different countries that the overall image of the situation in the occupied areas is not favorable to Israel (e.g., Graber, 1988). To what extent, then, would the perception of people in the different countries regarding the complexity, intensity, and solvability of the conflict in the Middle East (for all of whom—except the Israelis—it is a "foreign" story) be a function of what they have seen on their television screens (in this and similar stories over time), and a function of other factors that shape their opinions? The way a story is told would be at least in part a function of the "local" attitudes concerning it, and hence the perception of the story by the audiences in different countries might vary. This should be particularly evident if one examines stories that are domestic in one country and foreign in others. Also, the perception might vary as a function of the extent to which television news (and perhaps other media as well) cover certain kinds of stories in the first place. Thus if television does not cover certain kinds of stories because of political pressures, for example, then people would be more dependent upon other sources to know about them, or they would remain ignorant about them.

This single example of Beita village—and there are many more—clearly illustrates that the problem we have undertaken is quite complex. And, as we shall explain in the next chapter we have not been interested in this or any other specific conflict per se, but rather in the overall presentation and perception of social conflicts, which makes the situation even more difficult.

TOWARD THE INTEGRATION
OF THEORY AND RESEARCH

In this chapter we have asked how comparative analysis can contribute to the study of conflict news in a field where much of the literature has appeared to adopt an implicitly universalistic stance. First, we contend that comparative theorizing helps to specify a set of national system conditions which may differentiate the activities of news organizations and the kinds of stories they produce. And second, in this study we looked at these stories as the output of a dialogue between a (presumed) universal professional culture and a culture-specific set of extra professional influences. The former were expected mainly to result in similarities across countries, while the latter is more likely to differentiate among countries.

Cross-national research of content among the various news organizations in the variety of countries could indicate whether and to what extent media competition and the ties between the broadcast organizations and their respective governments are factors that influence the presentation of news, to the extent that they override the organizational factors that cause a tendency toward uniformity in the news content of the different countries. Such a plan of research should, on the one hand, identify some features of news content that may be examined simultaneously in all the countries, and on the other hand develop conceptual continua concerning competition and government influence along which the various countries can be compared. After careful analysis, this plan might lead to conclusions about the relative influence of the various factors.

And finally, examining the perception of social conflicts in a cross-national context and how it relates to the content of television news will tell us (it is hoped) something about the role of television in the process by which individuals make sense of the world around them, namely in their social construction of reality.

Believing that theory and method are inseparable, Louis Guttman (cited in Gratch, 1973) provided a definition of *theory* that relates concepts and observations in an attempt to formulate hypotheses. Accordingly, a theory is "an hypothesis of a correspondence between a definitional system for a universe of observations and an aspect of the empirical structure of those observations, together with a rationale for such an hypothesis" (1973, p. 35). To assist in theory formulation, Guttman developed the *mapping sentence*, which is "a verbal statement of the domain and of the range of a mapping including connectives between facets as in ordinary language" (Shye, 1978, p. 413).

The conceptual background we have presented so far in a somewhat eclectic fashion is rich and the methods we propose (see Chapter 3) are intricate. This background provides the rationales for the various hypotheses that we have proposed. We believe that the integration between the two can be explicated best in Figure 2.1.

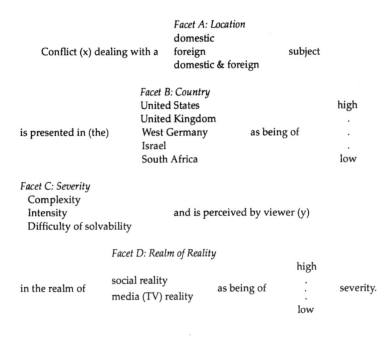

Figure 2.1. A Mapping Sentence of the Presentation and Perception of Social Conflicts

The mapping sentence has four facets that form the domain of the study. The first facet, *location,* deals with the location of the conflict (domestic to the country of broadcast, foreign, or a combined foreign and domestic conflict) and represents the various levels of media dependency as a function of the proximity factor.

The second facet, *country,* orders the five countries of the study according to the two continua explained above, based on the relative degree of political influence and media competition in their respective media systems.

The third facet, *severity,* is composed of the three dimensions of conflict: complexity, intensity, and solvability (the latter being defined as *difficulty of solving* so that its magnitude would be ordered in the same direction as complexity and intensity with regard to severity).

The fourth facet, *realm of reality*, pertains to the distinction between social reality and media reality (in our case, that of television news), both based on the theoretical notions of the social construction of reality.

The range of the mapping sentence, going from high to low severity, relates both to the presentation and perception of conflicts. This mapping sentence represents the main core of the study, and its direct implications are tested in Chapter 5 (for presentation) and Chapter 7 (for perception). Clearly, however, the study includes an additional array of variables that are not explicit in the current mapping sentence. Although these variables could be added to the mapping sentence, we chose not to include them and thus to avoid an extremely elaborate mapping sentence.

In reading through the mapping sentence, taking one element at a time from each facet, one can generate an hypothesis as to the way the four facets are related. Thus, for example, one hypothesis could state that a foreign conflict presented in the news of the United States as relatively low in complexity would also be perceived in the realm of media reality (TV news) as relatively low in complexity. It should be noted that we did not "duplicate" the country and the location facets for the perception, because in the present study the perception of the conflicts obviously were measured and reported by respondents in each of the five countries only with respect to the conflicts that were presented in their own country.

NOTES

1. An additional possible source of variegating influence could be the legitimating creed of political journalism that exists in the societies concerned (Blumler & Gurevitch, 1975). The presentation of conflict as solvable may be favored in professional cultures where norms of journalistic independence are weak (South Africa) or journalists are politicized heavily (West Germany) and may be less common where the culture of national political journalism is strongly adversarial (as is often maintained for the United States).

2. The notion that the identical subject in the news will be presented differently was pointed out in a classic newspaper study by Schramm (1959).

THREE

Two Methods: Content Analysis and Survey Research

This chapter details the two methods and respective instruments utilized in the study: First, it describes the content analytic scheme designed to assess the presentation of social conflicts in television news; and second, it presents an overview of the survey conducted to measure audience perception of social conflicts.

Before describing the two instruments, it is important to emphasize the relationship between the content analysis and the survey. A central aspect of the study's theoretical framework is the conceptualization of the three dimensions of conflict—complexity, intensity, and solvability. In order to bridge the gap between the world of television presentation and the domain of perception, an attempt was made to construct measurable attributes of these three dimensions in both realms. Accordingly, the dimensions were operationalized in the content-analysis codebook as well as in the survey questionnaire in order to allow for comparisons between them. Moreover, as far as the perception of conflict is concerned, this methodological approach was based on the assumption mentioned earlier that individuals are able to draw a distinction between the "real" world and the world of television.

THE CONTENT ANALYSIS

The content analysis was the first of the two methods employed and was clearly the most difficult to plan, organize, and execute.

Selection of Newscast Populations

We selected the newscasts according to three main considerations: (1) our focus on national newscasts, rather than local newscasts; (2) our interest in the overall patterns in the presentation of social conflict—not in the presentation of any specific story; and (3) our desire to be able to compare the presentation of social conflicts in the different countries at the same points in time.

National newscasts were selected because the study was designed to explore the presentation of social conflict and its perception by people in the five countries at a level that would be meaningful in all the countries, and hence comparable. In Israel and South Africa, all television news is broadcast at the national level. In West Germany and the United Kingdom brief segments of the newscast are devoted to "regional" news. In the United States, however, there are distinctly separate "local" news programs as contrasted with the national news programs. Hence to establish commonality only national newscasts were selected. Furthermore, given our knowledge about the prevalence of social conflict in international news and the paucity of international news in U.S. local news, the focus on national news was essential.

Consequently, the main evening national newscasts in all five countries were selected: ABC's *World News Tonight*, NBC's *Nightly News*, and CBS's *Evening News* in the United States, the BBC's *Nine O'Clock News* in the United Kingdom,[1] *Tagesschau* on the ARD network and *Heute* on the ZDF network in West Germany, *Mabat* in Israel, and SABC's *Eight O'Clock News* in South Africa.

In order to provide comparability and to examine the programs with the largest possible audiences, only the Monday through Thursday newscasts were analyzed. This was done because the formats of the weekend newscasts differ in the various countries (Friday newscasts also were omitted from the analyses because the

Israeli newscasts on Friday nights have a different format—a brief news bulletin followed by a magazine-type weekly review). Also, choosing Mondays through Thursdays enabled us to span a wider period of time with the same number of newscasts.

The study focuses on the *overall* patterns in the presentation and perception of social conflict. It was not a case study of specific news stories as they were presented in the five countries, nor was it a study of a series of stories or any particular conflict. Hence the focus of the content analysis was on the overall manner in which social conflicts were portrayed. As a consequence, the dates for gathering newscasts were not selected to record any particular event.

In fact, given our concern for overall patterns in the portrayal of social conflict, our a priori selection of dates took into account one major substantive consideration. The dates were selected after checking the anticipated schedule of events in each of the five countries to exclude national elections and any other foreseeable major conflicts that might, if they occurred, heavily bias the coverage of other events. Contingency plans called for halting the recordings of the news if such an event was to occur. Fortunately, no such specific events of major importance occurred during the sample time periods.

Finally, in order to provide a temporal basis of comparison, we decided to record and analyze two sets of newscasts at two points in time. Two sets of newscasts were needed in order to attempt to isolate those factors in the nature and format of presentation of conflicts that might change over time and those factors that seem to be stable over time.

The Sample of Newscasts

The first set of newscasts (Wave I) was gathered in December of 1980. The second set (Wave II) was assembled in January and early February of 1984. The Wave I data included December 1–4, 8–10, and 15–18 for a total of 11 evenings (December 11, 1980 was deleted because of a technical mishap in one country, which precluded comparable data in all five countries). The Wave II data consisted of January 16–19, 23–26, 30–31, and February 1–2, thus providing 12 evening newscasts. Thus the entire sample consisted of 23 newscasts in each of the networks.

Although all the newscasts were recorded on the predetermined nights in all the countries, some adjustments were necessary because in the United States, the United Kingdom, and West Germany more than one network newscast is presented each evening. Thus special consideration was given to balancing the sample of newscasts. In the United Kingdom, as noted, we were unable to record the ITN news. Based on prior research demonstrating little difference between the news on the BBC and on ITN (e.g., Glasgow University Media Group, 1976), however, we felt that this did not create a significant bias, particularly since the BBC news was the most heavily viewed. In the United States and West Germany news from all networks was gathered; however, in order to weight the newscasts properly, their number was reduced in each of these two countries by a random sampling procedure to 11 newscasts from Wave I and 12 from Wave II. The random-sampling procedure was stratified to assure that at least one newscast from each network was analyzed for each week. [2]

Once videotaped copies of the newscasts were available, the researchers in each country either obtained or prepared transcriptions of the text of the newscasts.

The Unitizing Process and Coding Scheme

The codebook (see Appendix B) for the content analysis was developed by the research team in a series of meetings spanning more than two years, including a trial analysis done on newscasts of the first wave. The final version of the codebook contained three major parts: variables dealing with conflict and nonconflict items, variables pertaining to social conflict items in their totality, and variables related to the parties to the conflicts.

The precoding stage of the content analysis required the division of the newscast into news items. This unitizing or itemization process can be especially problematic, for example, when a newscast reported on a series of related events (e.g., strikes). Should three strikes be considered as part of one news item, or should they be treated as three separate items? In the present study, because we were interested in social conflict with special interest in disputes between parties, the conceptual framework implied that the operationalization should break the series of three strike reports into three separate items. Accordingly, our itemization procedure stated that whenever an issue or a party changed, a new item had begun. As another example, when fighting in Lebanon was described followed by a report on congressional debate on U.S. involvement in the fighting, two items were coded even though the newscast provided no obvious separation of the items. Thus the definition of a news item was not necessarily the same as journalistic practice, which might link the three strike reports together to form a single news item or combine the reports on the fighting and the debate as a single item.

The unitizing and itemization task was done by the senior researchers in each country following and based upon an agreed set of criteria. This task was performed by the researchers themselves, and not by the student coders, in order to maximize the likelihood that the process was being done in an identical manner in each country. The enumeration of items was clearly marked on the transcripts and on the rundown sheets that listed each story in the newscast. Following the initial itemization, the researchers identified and marked clearly the social conflict items using the agreed-upon definition: "a dispute between two or more social groups or their representatives concerning at least one issue, goal, topic, or idea." With the social conflict items identified, the researchers then proceeded to identify and list all the parties to the conflict, explicitly noting whether they were opponents, mediators, arbitrators, go-betweens, or interested parties.

Opponents were defined as parties directly involved in the conflict. *Mediators* and *arbitrators* were defined as parties trying to assist the opponents in reaching a resolution to the conflict. The two differ, however, in that mediators typically only bring the sides together and help facilitate the interaction between them, whereas arbitrators usually offer their own proposals for resolving the conflict. The role of *go-between* is merely a technical one and is defined as a party that relays messages from one opponent to another, but does not partake in the actual negotiations. Finally, the *interested party* is defined as a party that has some stake in the conflict but is not involved in it. This category includes potential or actual victims.

It is important to emphasize that the classification of the parties was done only on the basis of information that was included in the news items, and not on the basis of additional information that might have been available or known to the researchers. This minimized the possibility of a party being coded as one kind of party or another on the basis of a totally subjective interpretation of the researcher and his or her attitude towards that party and the conflict. Incidentally, this general coding rule of relying upon information contained in the item was used almost without exception (the few departures from this rule are indicated at the appropriate places in the codebook and the coders' guide—see below and Appendix B).

In most items there were no more than six parties; hence the party variables were included in the codebook six times, once for each party in the order of their mention in the news item (in the rare cases with more than six parties, the seventh and above were not coded).

The variables in the first part of the codebook—which applied to all items (conflict and non-conflict)—also were coded by the senior researchers. These variables included item–country identification information: date, network, length of the item, and length of the newscast with and without commercials (the latter only applies to the United States).

The senior researchers also indicated (a) the number of related social conflict items, and (b) the number of related non-conflict items presented in a newscast. An item would be coded as being related to another item if both items either were connected verbally by a news anchor or reporter or if the items were placed immediately following each other with no separate introduction given to the latter item. Thus in most cases related items would follow one another immediately, but in certain cases an item could be considered as being related to another even if they were separated by one or more other items (or by commercials in the case of the U.S. networks). This could only be indicated after the entire newscast was coded.

The researchers also coded each item for its general topic. This categorization included the country of location, the generic topic area (e.g., economics), and a subtopic (e.g., rise in cost of living). The topic of each item also was categorized as foreign, domestic, or both foreign and domestic from the point of view of the country of broadcast.

Finally, for each item the researchers indicated whether the journalists provided historical context in the item by connecting the story to prior events. This connection could be made by direct reference to other events, either with or without a precise statement as to when the other event occurred, or it could be limited to some general reference to another event. The "connections" were identified by examining the verbal text.

The second and third parts of the coding scheme was done by trained coders (see below). The second part of the codebook consisted of all the variables pertaining to the social conflict items in their totality, as complete items including indicators of the complexity, intensity, and solvability of the conflict as well as numerous other verbal and visual variables.

For complexity, the variables included the number of opponents in the item and the breadth of the conflict's potential consequences; for intensity we measured the presence of verbal and visual presentation of physical aggression, verbal aggression, and emotional display; and for solvability we included whether anyone was calling for resolution of the conflict, the state of negotiations presented in the item, indicators of willingness to compromise, and the outcome of the conflict (e.g., withdrawal or compromise). Also included were measures of the use of slides and photos, graphics, printed words, moving film, clips of correspondents in the field, anchorperson screen time, number and time of correspondents reporting from the field, time devoted to the presentation of physical aggression, number and time of non-anchors in the studio, and the number of voice-overs and cuts in the item.

The third and final part of the codebook dealt with the parties to the conflict. As noted above, the parties were classified by whether they were an opponent, a mediator, an arbitrator, a go-between, or an interested party.

The codebook recorded how the newscast presented each party. This included recording the number of official and nonofficial persons speaking, quoted, seen, and interviewed on behalf of the party. In addition, each representative was coded to indicate its relative position (i.e., highest, middle, or lowest level in the hierarchy or structure of its group). Finally, the length of interviews and visual presentations were noted.

The manner in which the newscasts presented the party's point of view was assayed by coding whether the party described another's position or accused another of initiating the conflict, whether the journalist described or advocated the party's position, whether journalists accused the party of initiating the conflict, and whether the journalist presented the party as connecting the conflict to prior events.

Coders and Reliability

As noted, following the itemization process and the coding of the first part of the codebook done by the senior researchers themselves, pairs of trained coders in each of the countries completed the coding of the other variables. The coders were students in communication. In some countries all the coding was done by the same two coders while in other countries several pairs of coders worked on the material.

In each of the countries several training sessions were held. The coders were given an overall introduction to the project as well as a detailed explanation of all the variables in the codebook. The codebook was accompanied by a coder's guide (see latter part of Appendix B) that contained explanations of key variables and some examples.

The coders were provided with the videotapes of the newscasts, transcripts, codebooks, coding forms, and a stopwatch. Coders were encouraged to view the newscast and read the transcript as often as necessary to code effectively.

The coders were urged to work for no more than several hours in one session to avoid fatigue. The average time it took a pair of coders to code the social conflict items in a single newscast was about seven hours—with much variability depending on the number of social conflicts and the amount of visual material.

Coders were instructed to decide individually on the proper code for each variable and then to indicate to each other what the code for each of the variables should be. If there was agreement, the code was recorded. If there was disagreement, the coders were instructed to discuss the diverging point of view with each other and reach a common judgment, while indicating that there was initial disagreement. If they were absolutely unable to reach consensus, they were told to refer the dilemma to the senior investigator. This consensual model was adopted as many of the variables were nominal and differences could not be averaged.

The reliability of the coding needs to be discussed at two levels. First, with regard to the itemization process and coding done by the researchers themselves, we believe that there was very strong agreement among them. We base this argument upon the fact that the definitions and procedures for the entire coding process were created by all the investigators in unison, with complete understanding among them. Moreover, at one of the weeklong meetings, conducted in Jerusalem, a large batch of first-wave items from the five countries were coded together and agreement was reached. This constituted a modified form of cross-national reliability checking.

The consensus model of coding appeared to be successful in achieving a high level of agreement among the student coders. The notes taken by the student coders during the coding process provide evidence of high agreement. The notes indicate that by and large there were fewer than 15% disagreements prior to the forced-negotiations stage of the coding designed for such occurrences, and in fewer than 5% of the cases did the coders need to approach the senior investigators in order to referee and determine a verdict. This success is likely the consequence of (1) the high cross-national agreement obtained by the senior investigators who then thoroughly trained the student coders, (2) the complete coding of the 1980 data set as a practice, then recoding it after the senior researchers met in Jerusalem, and (3) the availability of the senior researchers to assist throughout the coding process.

TREATING THE CONTENT DATA

Once the data for all countries were coded and entered on a computer file, they were examined for out-of-range codes. All problems were resolved by the researchers checking the data and corrections being made.

Although two content waves were gathered and coded, we decided to combine both waves for the analysis. The main rationale for combining the two waves was to obtain a much larger and hence more stable sample, which would not be dependent upon any particular set of events that might have taken place in any particular time period. What this means is that throughout this book we shall be treating the content data as one sample.

Two separate data files were then prepared. The *items* file contained the data that pertain to the complete news item and the overall description of the conflicts. It also contained the basic information on the nonconflict items. This file consisted of 1957 cases for both waves combined. The second file contained the information on the *parties* to the conflicts. The parties file contained a total of 2611 cases, which were derived from the 895 conflict items.

THE SURVEY

In order to assess the perception of social conflict in television news and social reality a survey questionnaire was developed based on the work reported by Cohen, Adoni and Drori (1983) and Adoni, Cohen, and Mane (1984). The questionnaire was modified significantly and expanded, however, in order to adapt it to the present study. The questionnaire was administered to respondents in the five countries in exactly the same form.

The Samples

Because it was impossible as a result of budgetary constraints to use randomly selected samples of the entire adult populations in each of the countries, we decided to use more homogeneous groups. In each of the five countries the respondents to the questionnaire represent, therefore, purposive nonprobability quota samples of young adults 17- to 22-years-old.[3] The choice of this age group was to be able to examine how young adults, just before or after their first opportunity to vote in their respective country's elections, perceive social conflicts.

The sample was balanced for gender and educational tracks. The latter variable was operationalized as respondents from *academic* or *vocational* educational institutions. In West Germany, the United Kingdom, and Israel high school students from college-preparatory schools constituted the academic students, whereas students in vocational high schools constituted the vocational students. In the United States, the academic sample consisted of university students attending first-year courses at a major university, whereas the vocational students were attending postsecondary vocational-technical schools. In South Africa, the entire sample consisted of first-year university students because it was impossible to obtain a sample of vocational students. The target of the questionnaire administration was 240 respondents per country, with 60 males and 60 females in each of the two educational tracks.

The samples in each country were gathered in one metropolitan area, as follows: Minneapolis-St. Paul, United States; Leeds, England; West Berlin, West Germany; Jerusalem, Israel; and Cape Town, South Africa.[4] The complete sample consisted of 1229 respondents and is presented in Table 3.1. Thus the samples should be considered at best as representative of the specified age groups in the indicated parts of the five countries.

The Questionnaire

The questionnaire (see Appendix C) had several sections. The basic structure of many of the questions utilizes one or more of three major variates: (1) dimension of social conflict: complexity, intensity, and solvability; (2) location of conflict: local, national, international; and (3) realm of reality—television news and the "real" or social reality.

Table 3.1 The Survey Sample by Country, Educational Track, and Gender

| | Academic | | Vocational | | |
	Male	Female	Male	Female	Total
United States	55	75	50	58	238
United Kingdom	56	68	70	35	229
West Germany	50	91	99	23	263
Israel	82	89	60	22	253
South Africa	102	144	—	—	246

The instructions described the questionnaire in general terms; assured the respondents that the questionnaire was not a test with correct or incorrect answers; asked for their voluntary participation; defined what was meant by social conflict; illustrated local, national, and international conflicts; and explained the requirement that they respond to conflicts "in general" or what they considered as "typical" conflicts.

Three questions assessed the individual's judgment of the importance of knowing about international, national, and local social conflicts. The respondents were asked nine questions on the value of television news, radio news, and newspapers in providing information about international, national, and local conflicts. Three questions asked for the respondent's judgment of the number of international, national, and local conflicts going on simultaneously.

These questions were followed by 18 critical questions assaying the respondent's perception of the complexity, intensity, and solvability of international, national, and local social conflicts as presented on television news or as they occured in the "real" world. Thus 18 questions probed for all combinations of dimensions, location, and realm of reality. The questions pertaining to real-life occurrence of social conflict and television news occurrence were balanced in their order of presentation, with half the questionnaire booklets presenting real-world questions first, and television news questions appearing first in the other half.

In the initial work on the perception of social conflict by Adoni and Cohen cited earlier in which the measurement of the three dimensions was developed, we used specific measures for each dimension. In preparing the instrument for that study, we asked the respondents (Israeli high school students) to evaluate *in general* how complex, intense, and difficult to solve social conflicts were in the three life areas we were studying—political terror, labor disputes, and school integration. We also asked three *specific* questions about each of the dimensions (e.g., how many parties generally are involved in conflicts about labor disputes). In validating the questionnaire items, we then correlated the specific items with general questions about the perceived complexity, intensity, and solvability. We found high correlations between the specific and the general questions. In the report of that study we reported only on the responses to the specific questions. In the present study, however, given the fact that we were working in five countries where specific social conflicts are somewhat different, we opted to use the more general questions.

But in order to be absolutely sure that the respondents in the five countries would be referring to the same concepts when we asked them about complexity, intensity, and solvability, we conducted still another pretest. Accordingly, we asked about 50 high school seniors in each of the five countries to write a brief but detailed essay describing any ongoing social conflicts in their respective countries. These essays for analyzed in an attempt to discover to what extent their authors related to elements of the conflict dimensions. Most of the writers made reference to attributes of the complexity, intensity, and solvability of the conflicts. This strengthened our belief even further that people indeed think in terms of these dimensions when relating to social conflicts. Thus we were satisfied that by asking the respondents about the three dimensions, *in general*, they would be thinking about the same attributes of conflicts.

Several questions surveyed the respondents' judgment of the frequency with which in real-life conflicts impact on each other and are caused by past events. There were also questions used to ascertain the respondents' judgment of the proportion of the newscast taken up with conflict; whether the conflicts are primarily local, national, international, or some combination thereof; and how frequently local, national, and international conflicts are presented on television news

We also asked for the respondents' perception of the way newscasts present conflicts: how often journalists link conflicts together, present background material, advocate the position of one of the parties to the conflict, actually show the parties to conflicts, and/or use technical devices in presenting conflicts.

A series of questions recorded the respondents' general beliefs about and experience with social conflict and measured their perception of the similarity of their beliefs to those of their peers. These questions related to the degree of "reality" in television's presentations of conflict; the value of conflict for society, both on television news and in real life; whether the respondent had any personal experience with social conflicts; whether the respondent felt that reporting on conflicts is desirable; and whether his or her view of life is similar to or different from the views of their parents, friends, or peers.

Finally, the respondents were asked demographic-related questions and for information on media-usage, including weekday television viewing, viewing of television news, reading of the news section of newspaper, and listening to radio news.

Translation

The earliest version of the questionnaire was written in Hebrew, then translated to English for the working group. In order to guarantee comparable translations in the three languages (English, Hebrew, and German) the final version was translated from English into German and back into English (for Germany) and also translated back from English to Hebrew (for Israel). This latter version was compared with the earlier Hebrew version and no significant variation was identified.

Administration

The questionnaires were administered in classroom settings in all five countries during the months of March, April, and May of 1984, two to four months after the second wave of content data were obtained.[5]

The administration was approved by the appropriate review body in each case. Respondents were read the cover sheet instructions by the supervisor and they also were asked to follow along. They were given an opportunity to ask questions at any time during the completion of the questionnaire. The respondents were given as much time as necessary to complete the questionnaire; most respondents completed the entire questionnaire within 45 minutes.

DATA ANALYSIS

The data for the content analysis as well as the surveys were analyzed using the Statistical Package for the Social Sciences (SPSS) and the later SPSS[x] version. Smallest-space analysis (SSA) was conducted utilizing the Hebrew University Data Analysis Package (HUDAP). In addition to general and overall descriptive analyses, indices were developed to measure the three dimensions of social conflict, the level of visual and verbal representation afforded the parties, and the extent to which an item was connected to other items and historical context. Each of these indices is described in subsequent chapters where the results are reported.

Correlating Presentation and Perception

Although the portrayal of social conflicts in television news and their perception by individuals are related conceptually, the two respective data sets used in this study were generated from two totally different sources. In other words, the presentation data did not come from respondents and the perception data were not derived from the newscasts. Thus in order to correlate between the two data sets it was necessary to create variability along some other common parameter.

This was done utilizing the cross-national design. Accordingly, it was possible to rank order the various countries on both the presentation data and the perception data and thereby correlate between the rankings. For example, it was possible to rank the countries in terms of the degree of intensity of international social conflicts as presented on television news and also to rank the countries on how the respondents perceived the intensity of the portrayal. Hence the correlation between the two data sets could provide some indication as to the relationship between the presentation and the perception variables.

Significance Testing

For the most part in both the content analysis and the survey research, as well as in examining the relationships between these two sets of data, we have chosen to join the growing trend away from doctrinal use of statistical hypothesis testing. Thus we present the data without resorting to conventional tests of statistical significance. We regard the statistics as descriptive in nature and look upon our treatment of the information gathered in the study as exploratory.

We have taken this approach for two main reasons. First, because we were dealing with large samples many of the analyses would yield significant results anyway, a fact that might tend to pressure the reader (as well as ourselves) to place too much emphasis on what turned out to be highly significant findings. And second, because we were interested primarily in trends in the data and considered the design of the study to be one of a series of replications in the various countries, it would not be crucial if a particular difference or relationship were statistically significant in the orthodox sense of the term (Guttman, 1977). This does not mean, however, that we have refrained totally from statistical testing when we felt that it absolutely was warranted by the data.

By no means have we avoided statistics, however, as the numerous tables will make clear. But in this regard we need to make one final caveat. The amount of data generated by this study, both for the content and the perception, was enormous. Even in book form we could not possibly deal with all the variables that were measured. Hence, although the content-analytic codebook and the questionnaire as presented in the appendix section are unabridged, not all the variables are treated in the data chapters that follow.

NOTES

1. Although we wanted to do so, we were unable to analyze ITN's *News at Ten* because of financial limitations

2. Thus, of the 33 newscasts recorded in 1980 (Wave I) in the United States, the following 11 were used: ABC (December 4, 9, and 16), CBS (December 3, 10, 11, and 17) and NBC (December 1, 2, 8, and 18). In 1984 (Wave II), of the 36 U.S. newscasts recorded, the 12 used in the analysis were: ABC (January 17, 18, and 23, and February 1 and 2), CBS (January 16, 24, and 26), and NBC (January 19, 25, 30, and 31). In Germany, of the 22 newscasts in 1980 the following 11 were analyzed: ARD (December 2, 4, 8, 9, and 16) and ZDF (December 1, 3, 10, 11, 17, and 18). In 1984, of the 24 German newscasts the following 12 were used: ARD (January 17, 19, 23, 25, and 31, and February 2) and ZDF (January 16, 18, 24, 26, and 30, and February 1).

3. We use the term survey throughout the text, although technically speaking the research design might be viewed as a quasi-experimental field study. But as we stressed earlier, we had no intention of generalizing the findings from the samples to the general populations of the five countries. In fact, this relates once again to the notion of replication, a point that we raise later in the text.

4. Given the particularly large variability expected in the United States, attributable to its size, the questionnaire was administered to an additional 120 academic respondents from several high schools, a college, and a university in Oregon. No significant differences were found between the Minnesota and Oregon samples. Therefore, in order to retain comparable sample sizes in each country we shall only report on the Minnesota sample.

5. There seems to be one additional important justification for combining the two waves of content data, even if it was conceived *ex post factum*. Because the objective of the study was to compare the contents of the news as presented on television with the perception of the news by young adults, the time period of the survey must have been coordinated with the content analysis. Moreover, because only *one* survey was conducted, following Wave II, the combining of Wave I and Wave II presentation data made it possible to relate the questions in the survey to the general period prior to the administration of the survey, but not limiting it to the immediate past.

PART II

Presentation

FOUR

Parameters of Conflict Presentation in Television News

In this chapter we begin our exploration of the similarities and differences among the newscasts of the five countries. We do so by comparing several parameters of conflict and non-conflict items: their degree of salience in the newscast, whether they are domestic or foreign, their main topics, the extent to which they are inter-related within the newscasts, and the extent to which historical context is provided.

THE SALIENCE OF CONFLICT ITEMS

The first issue we looked at was the salience of conflict items in the newscasts. We did so by: (a) determining the relative frequency of social conflicts in the complete newscast; (b) comparing the frequency of conflicts in domestic and foreign news items; and (c) looking at the relative position of the conflict and non-conflict items in the lineup of the newscasts.

Based on the initial itemization of the newscasts, it was possible to determine the number and percentage of news items containing any reference to social conflict. In addition to the clearly visible social conflict items there were three types of pseudo conflicts:

- First, items in which a conflict is reported, but where the conflict is not central to the news story. For example, in an item based on an interview with a former Nazi war criminal there was a background story on the Nazi era in Europe. The conflict in the background story was not the topic of the main story and was, therefore, coded as inconsequential.
- Second, the parties are not mentioned but are taken for granted. The report of a Supreme Court decision that does not present the actual details of the case or specify the parties illustrates this type. Thus a report saying that the Court decided to declare a certain law unconstitutional, without telling who the plaintiff was (a form of reporting not uncommon), would be a case of a conflict without the parties being mentioned.
- Third, conflicts "created" by journalists, which parallel Boorstin's (1961) notion of "pseudo events." Often in such items journalists speculate that something *might* take place and *may* become a conflict, yet there is no actual conflict at the time the story is being reported.

Across all five countries 46% of all the 1,957 news items were coded as dealing with social conflict (see Table 4.1). Moreover, while relatively few in number, the additional 7% of the items classified as pseudo conflicts increased the overall figures past the 50% level. Thus, 53% of all the items presented some form of social conflict, a finding not entirely unexpected given the theoretical literature.

The country with the highest relative percentage of social conflicts was Israel, with 60% of all its news items; the lowest was South Africa with 32% of all its items; and the three other countries were in a middle position—the United States with 42%, and West Germany and the United Kingdom, both with 48% of all their respective news items.

There were relatively few conflicts with unspecified parties, ranging from 1% to 4%; no such conflicts appeared on West German television. Also, there were hardly any "journalistically created" social conflict items. Such conflict items ranged from 1% to 2%, and did not occur at all in West Germany and South Africa.

Another measure of the salience of conflict items is their relative positioning in the newscast compared with the non-conflict items. In general, the conflict items were placed higher up, that is, closer to the beginning of the newscast (see Table 4.2). Across all the countries, the mean ordinal position for conflict items was 8.0,

Table 4.1 Percentage of Conflict and Pseudo Conflict Items by Country

	Total	U.S.	UK	FRG	Isr.	SA
Conflict	46	42	48	48	60	32
Inconsequential	3	—	9	6	2	1
Created by journalist	1	2	1	—	1	—
Unspecified parties	3	3	3	2	1	4
Non-conflict	47	53	39	44	36	63
Total	100	100	100	100	100	100
(n)	1957	389	367	323	431	447

Table 4.2 Mean Order of Item in the Newscast by Country and Location

	Total	U.S.	UK	FRG	Isr.	SA
Conflict items						
Domestic	8.1	7.5	6.5	6.6	9.9	8.8
Foreign	8.4	8.1	8.3	8.1	9.6	8.3
Domestic & Foreign	6.7	5.9	7.4	5.8	8.2	6.0
Total	8.0	7.3	7.2	6.9	9.5	8.1
(n)	895	163	176	155	259	142
Non-conflict items						
Domestic	11.6	10.5	11.0	9.7	12.1	12.7
Foreign	10.6	9.8	10.2	9.5	11.8	11.5
Domestic & Foreign	12.4	11.0	10.0	8.8	9.0	13.3
Total	11.2	10.4	10.7	9.4	11.7	12.6
(n)	928	206	143	142	155	282

whereas for non-conflict items the mean ordinal position was 11.2. This pattern appears in all the countries and is probably the result of the common and shared practice by journalists of highlighting social conflicts because they believe conflict is one of the criteria for newsworthiness.[1] The story location (i.e., whether the story is domestic or foreign) also influences the ordinal position of the items. This relationship seems to exhibit two patterns in two different sets of countries. In the United States, the United Kingdom, and West Germany domestic items appeared higher in the newscasts, while in Israel and South Africa the position of foreign items was higher.

In sum, conflict items are salient in the news: they comprise over half the items in the newscasts and they are given more prominent positions than non-conflict items.

CONFLICT LOCATION:
DOMESTIC OR FOREIGN

Indeed, a critical element in the presentation of social conflicts in the news is the location of the conflict. As suggested by Galtung and Ruge (1965), this factor is an important consideration at the selection level when the newscast is prepared. In some countries, location might even be a determining factor as to whether or not an item will be included in the lineup, particularly if there are other news formats that place special emphasis on domestic issues rather than on foreign issues.

Our sample indicated that there was a distinct and not unexpected bias toward presenting news items as dealing with domestic matters. Of the 1823 news items, 1061 (58%) were concerned with purely domestic issues; 435 (24%) of the items dealt with purely foreign issues; and the remaining 327 (18%) were related to issues that included both domestic and foreign elements from the point of view of the country of broadcast.

The relationship between location and presentation of social conflict was examined from two points of view. First, the proportion of domestic conflict items, foreign conflict items, and combined foreign and domestic conflict items were examined (see Table 4.3).

Among the foreign items the percentage of conflicts was much higher than among the domestic items: 41% of the domestic items contained social conflict, whereas 66% of the foreign items contained social conflict. Also, 54% of the items that combine domestic and foreign issues contained social conflict. This phenomenon was

Table 4.3 Percentage of Domestic and Foreign Conflict Items by Country

	Total	U.S.	UK	FRG	Isr.	SA	(n)[1]
Domestic	41	28	48	55	59	21	1061
Foreign	66	70	78	54	69	62	431
Domestic & Foreign	54	75	53	43	68	34	327
Total	46	42	48	48	60	32	1823

1. Not including pseudoconflict items

strongly evident in all the countries except West Germany, which has essentially the same level of conflict among the items with domestic and foreign issues.

Although this may be quite obvious, given the fact that news editors will be more likely to select items dealing with foreign issues only if they contain something of special interest, such as social conflict—a staple ingredient of a good news story—it seems that there could also be a latent interpretation of this finding. Accordingly, in selecting and portraying relatively heavy doses of social conflict in stories having to do with other countries, the viewer can be given the impression that the level of conflict in society is quite high abroad and relatively lower at home. In other words, the news may suggest to viewers that "the grass is actually greener on our side of the fence."

In the present study, moreover, the difference in the level of conflict between domestic and foreign items is particularly great in South Africa and the United States. In the case of American television, this may simply be a function of the fact that local newscasts inherently emphasize local and regional news while national network news programs are mainly devoted to national and international news. In the case of South Africa, we suggest that this is attributable, at least in part, to the South African government's response to socio-political controversy and its particularly close relationship to the South African Broadcasting Corporation (SABC).

Table 4.4 Percentage of Domestic and Foreign Conflict and
Non-Conflict Items by Country

	Total	U.S.	UK	FRG	Isr.	SA
Conflict items[1]						
Domestic	49	40	54	49	57	37
Foreign	32	32	28	32	27	44
Domestic & Foreign	19	28	19	18	19	16
Total	100	100	100	100	100	100
(n)	895	163	176	155	259	142
Non-conflict items						
Domestic	67	81	71	43	67	68
Foreign	16	16	10	29	20	14
Domestic & Foreign	17	8	19	28	13	18
Total	100	100	100	100	100	100
(n)	928	206	143	142	155	282

1. Not including pseudoconflict items

The second perspective examined the conflict and non-conflict items separately, in order to determine what proportion of conflict items were located at home, abroad, or both. This comparison indicated the distribution of location *within* conflict or non-conflict items, thus suggesting, for example, the likelihood that a conflict story is located domestically.

Table 4.4 shows that although a small percentage of the countries' non-conflict items presented foreign topics (ranging from 10% to 29%), a more substantial percentage of the countries' conflict items presented foreign topics (ranging from 27% to 44%). In contrast, a large percentage of the countries' non-conflict items presented domestic topics (ranging from 43% to 81%), while a smaller but substantial percentage of the countries' conflict items presented domestic topics (ranging from 37% to 57%).

Considering these data by country indicated an interaction between country, conflict, and location. Hence, the most striking finding was that while in the United States, West Germany, the

Table 4.5 Percentage of Each Topic Category Containing Conflict by Country[1] (in overall descending order) (N = 1821)

	Total	U.S.	UK	FRG	Isr.	SA	(n total)
Labor relations	87	—	89	79	96	82	111
Social relations	79	79	—	—	9	—	39
International politics	78	88	80	62	76	87	344
Internal politics	62	44	91	66	61	71	278
Internal order	53	44	53	57	65	44	265
Defense	52	—	—	27	74	40	53
Communication	46	—	—.	—	60	—	28
Health and welfare	40	—	—	—	67	0	48
Business	37	20	64	—	46	—	70
Economics	35	13	38	50	61	8	105
Other[2]	23	29	42	13	28	12	176
Disasters	9	5	26	10	30	0	112
Sports	8	—	17	—	—	5	101
Human Interest	3	7	5	—	0	0	91

1. Countries that had fewer than 10 items in any given topic category were excluded from this analysis and are indicated by a dash (—). Zero (0) represents no conflict items in any given topic category.
2. Includes items of the following topic categories: transportation, agriculture, population/immigration, education, housing, environment, energy, science, culture, and ceremonial.

United Kingdom, and Israel a greater percentage of conflicts were domestic rather than foreign, in South Africa that relationship was reversed. The SABC presented a greater percentage of conflict items as foreign rather than as domestic. When examining the non-conflict items, in all five countries the relative frequency of domestic items greatly exceeded the foreign items.

TOPICS OF THE NEWS ITEMS

This section presents two analyses of the topics of the news items, condensed from the original 24 topic categories (see Appendix B). The collapsing of categories was done taking into account the frequencies for each category.[2]

Table 4.5 suggests differences among the countries in the extent to which certain topics are conflictual or not. In the United Kingdom, for example, 91% of all items dealing with internal politics presented social conflict, whereas in the United States only 44% of the internal politics items were conflictual. On the other hand, the percentages of items dealing with internal order that presented conflicts were less varied, ranging from 44% in the United States and South Africa to 65% in Israel.

Across all the countries, the topic that had the highest percentage of social conflicts was labor relations. The next three topics in descending percentages were social relations, international politics, and internal politics. When considering only the high-frequency topics (i.e., more than 100 items), the top four ranked topics in terms of social conflict were labor relations, international politics, internal politics, and internal order (social relations, such as among ethnic groups, was an infrequent topic on American and Israeli newscasts).

When examining each country separately using the criterion of at least 10 cases per country, the topic categories with the most conflicts were as follows: internal politics in the United Kingdom (91%), international politics in the United States (88%) and in South Africa (87%), and labor relations in Israel (96%) and in West Germany (79%).

One of the questions of the study was to determine if conflict items dealt with similar or different social issues compared with non-conflict items. Reviewing the conflict items across the five countries (see Table 4.6), four categories encompassed over 75% of the items: international politics (30%), internal politics (19%), internal order (16%), and labor relations (11%). There was more variation for the non-conflict items. The highest category (15%) was the "other" category, which included a variety of topics such as transportation, agriculture, education, housing, energy, environment, science, and culture. The second highest topic category was internal order (13%), followed by internal politics (12%), disasters (11%), and sports (10%). Thus the conflict items were concentrated in a few high-frequency topic categories, while the non-conflict items included a wider variety of topics with lower frequencies in each category.

Table 4.6 Topics of Conflict and Non-Conflict Items by Country (in descending overall percentage order)

	Total	U.S.	UK	FRG	Isr.	SA
Conflict items[1]						
International politics	30.1	43.6	21.1	29.0	26.3	33.9
Internal politics	19.1	20.9	11.9	25.8	16.3	23.9
Internal order	15.8	11.0	19.3	12.9	16.6	18.3
Labor relations	10.9	1.8	19.3	12.3	10.5	9.9
Other[2]	4.6	3.7	9.1	2.6	3.1	4.9
Economics	4.1	2.5	2.8	6.5	6.6	0.7
Social relations	3.5	6.7	2.3	2.6	4.3	0.7
Defense	3.1	2.5	1.7	1.9	5.4	2.8
Business	2.9	3.7	5.1	2.6	2.3	0.7
Health and welfare	2.1	1.8	0.6	1.9	4.7	0.0
Communication	1.5	0.0	1.1	1.3	2.3	2.1
Disasters	1.1	0.6	2.8	0.6	1.2	0.0
Sports	0.9	0.0	2.3	0.0	0.4	2.1
Human Interest	0.3	1.2	0.6	0.0	0.0	0.0
Total	100.0	100.0	100.0	100.0	100.0	100.0
(n)	894	163	176	155	258	142
Non-conflict items						
Other[2]	14.7	7.3	15.4	19.1	13.4	17.7
Internal order	13.4	11.2	19.9	10.6	14.8	11.7
Internal politics	11.5	20.8	1.4	14.9	17.5	5.0
Disasters	11.0	10.2	9.8	6.4	4.5	18.0
Sports	10.0	1.0	13.3	5.0	3.2	21.2
Human Interest	9.5	12.6	12.6	2.8	10.3	8.5
International politics	8.1	4.9	6.3	20.0	13.4	2.5
Economics	7.3	13.5	5.6	7.1	7.1	3.9
Business	4.7	11.7	3.5	1.4	4.5	2.1
Health and welfare	3.1	1.9	4.9	1.4	3.9	3.5
Defense	2.7	1.9	1.4	5.7	3.2	2.1
Communication	1.6	1.0	1.4	0.7	2.6	2.1
Labor relations	1.5	0.5	2.8	3.5	0.6	1.1
Social relations	0.9	1.5	0.7	1.4	0.6	0.6
Total	100.0	100.0	100.0	100.0	100.0	100.0
(n)	927	206	143	141	155	282

1. Not including pseudoconflicts
2. Includes items of the following topic categories: transportation, agriculture, population / immigration, education, housing, environment, energy, science, culture, and ceremonial

When considering each country's presentation of conflict, the United States stood out for its particularly strong emphasis on international politics (44% of all conflict items, which was 10% to 22% higher than in the other countries). This enhanced emphasis may reflect the network newscasts' emphasis on national and international affairs, as well as the U.S. newscasts' judgment that international affairs are more newsworthy when they are conflictual. Also quite striking were the country differences in labor-relations coverage (see Tables 4.5 and 4.6): 19% of British conflict items were labor relations items, whereas the percentages decreased to 12% in West Germany, 11% in Israel, and 10% for South Africa, to only 2% for the United States. Another noteworthy difference was the presentation of conflicts concerning social relations, which ranged from 7% in the United States to only 1% in South Africa.

As for the non-conflict items, there were relatively many items on internal politics (15% to 21%) in West Germany, Israel, and the United States, while in the United Kingdom and South Africa this topic was an infrequent non-conflict item. Both West Germany and Israel presented non-conflict items on international politics, while the other three countries did so infrequently. Economic and business news was more salient in the United States (more than 25% of the non-conflict items) compared with the other countries. South Africa, which stood out for its high percentage of non-conflict items, focused on disasters (18%) and sports (21%). Finally, although general non-conflict human interest stories were given some prominence in the United States, the United Kingdom, Israel, and South Africa (ranging from 13% to 9%), this topic was rare in West Germany (3%).

What these findings seem to indicate is that the picture for the conflict items seemed to be fairly similar in the five countries, with the four major categories cited above (international politics, internal politics, internal order, and labor relations) constituting between 70% and 86% of all the items, whereas among the non-conflict items there was far less consistency among the countries. This suggests a journalistic cross-national agenda for conflict, whereas the news agenda for non-conflicts was more country and culture specific.

INTERRELATEDNESS OF ITEMS
WITHIN THE NEWSCAST AND
THEIR HISTORICAL CONTEXT

Television newscasts can be viewed not only as an amalgam of individual items, but also as a set of inter-related items, topics, and forms. Our earlier discussion of the salience of conflict items used such an approach by considering the ordinal position of the items in the line-up.

As suggested in Chapter 1, one of the main critiques of television news is its fragmentation, which might be one of the direct causes of over-simplification of the portrayal of conflicts. This point was examined by exploring additional aspects of newscast composition, namely, the relationship among items within a newscast and historical context or background provided by a journalist.

Based on the mean number of related *conflict* items (i.e., the average number of social conflict stories presented as being related to a particular item), the findings show a tendency in all the countries to present conflict items as being related to other conflict items (see Table 4.7). This was particularly pronounced in the United Kingdom, where each conflict item was related to a mean of 1.15 additional conflict items, and least evident in South Africa with a mean of only 0.44 related conflict items. Non-conflict items were related only slightly to conflict items.

Examining the differences between the domestic and foreign items reveals that among the conflict items in all the countries but the United States there were more conflicts related to the domestic items. Among the non-conflict items, however, there were more conflict items related to the foreign items than to the domestic ones (once again in all countries except for the United States).

Whereas the presentation of related conflict items was prevalent, very few news items were related to non-conflict items (see Table 4.8). Nonetheless, there were substantial differences among the countries (with the United Kingdom and West Germany tending to be above average) and between the conflict and non-conflict items (with more non-conflict items related to other non-conflict items).

Table 4.7 Mean Number of Related Conflict Items in Newscast by Country and Location

	Total	U.S.	UK	FRG	Isr.	SA
Conflict items						
Domestic	0.74	0.42	1.46	0.68	0.57	0.38
Foreign	0.43	0.58	0.54	0.45	0.30	0.35
Domestic & Foreign	0.71	0.84	1.16	0.57	0.31	0.78
Total	0.64	0.59	1.15	0.59	0.46	0.44
(n)	895	163	176	155	259	142
Non-conflict items						
Domestic	0.16	0.14	0.35	0.43	0.07	0.05
Foreign	0.25	0.04	0.57	0.50	0.13	0.10
Domestic & Foreign	0.32	0.53	0.39	0.51	0.30	0.10
Total	0.20	0.16	0.38	0.47	0.11	0.06
(n)	928	206	143	142	155	282

The substantially higher prevalence of conflict items being related to conflict items (total mean = .64) than the other combinations (total means = .32, .36, .33) suggests the "packaging" of conflict items. Thus when the newscast is produced, it seems that there is a tendency to make a point of relating conflict items that have something in common with other conflict items of the day's news. In fact, it may be possible that an item previously prepared but not broadcast will be scheduled back-to-back with another item that was on that day's news agenda.

Our final comparison between conflict and non-conflict items was the extent to which journalists connect a given item to previous events, either general or historical in nature (see Table 4.9). The most clear conclusion was that conflict items were connected by journalists to other events more frequently than non-conflict items. Across all five countries, 56% of the conflicts were connected in some way, whereas only 45% of the non-conflict items were connected. Moreover, this

Table 4.8 Mean Number of Related Non-Conflict Items in Newscast by Country and Location

	Total	U.S.	UK	FRG	Isr.	SA
Conflict items						
Domestic	0.23	0.25	0.43	0.41	0.04	0.08
Foreign	0.26	0.09	0.38	0.57	0.23	0.08
Domestic & Foreign	0.33	0.27	0.32	0.67	0.29	0.15
Total	0.26	0.20	0.40	0.51	0.13	0.09
(n)	895	163	176	155	259	142
Non-conflict items						
Domestic	0.31	0.35	0.41	0.49	0.12	0.27
Foreign	0.35	0.22	0.50	0.57	0.19	0.26
Domestic & Foreign	0.38	0.53	0.49	0.25	0.27	0.50
Total	0.33	0.35	0.38	0.51	0.18	0.27
(n)	928	206	143	142	155	282

phenomenon was found to be the case in all five countries. West German news provided context with the greatest percentage of conflict items (70%) and non-conflict items (61%), while Israeli news provided context in the smallest percentage of conflict items (39%) and non-conflict items (31%).

Interestingly, among conflict items, the most frequent kind of connection was to other events with no specified date (nearly 22%), followed by events that were said to have occurred at least one year earlier. Few specific references were made to events that had occurred in the days or weeks immediately prior to the event being broadcast. Among the non-conflict items, however, there was about an equal percentage of connections made to events that occurred more than one year previous to the event being studied and to events that occurred at an unspecified date. Thus conflicts were more likely than non-conflicts to be contextualized, but the frequency of precise references to prior events was minimal—especially in Israel.

Table 4.9 Connections Made by Journalist to Previous Events for
Conflict and Non-Conflict News Items by Country

	Total	U.S.	UK	FRG	Isr.	SA
Conflict items						
No connection made	44.0	49.1	33.0	29.7	60.7	37.3
To previous day	3.8	2.5	3.4	5.2	4.6	2.8
To previous week	5.1	2.5	8.5	3.9	5.4	4.9
To previous month	3.8	2.5	6.8	4.5	1.9	4.2
To previous year	7.5	8.0	10.2	3.9	5.0	12.0
To more than year	14.2	17.7	17.6	21.9	7.7	9.2
To unspecified date	21.6	17.7	20.5	30.9	14.7	29.6
Total	100.0	100.0	100.0	100.0	100.0	100.0
(n)	895	163	176	155	259	142
Non-conflict items						
No connection made	54.8	52.0	55.9	38.8	68.5	57.1
To previous day	3.1	1.9	1.4	4.2	1.3	5.3
To previous week	3.6	3.9	5.6	2.8	1.9	3.5
To previous month	2.2	1.9	2.1	3.5	0.6	2.5
To previous year	7.7	6.8	9.8	5.6	4.5	9.9
To more than year	14.5	26.2	13.3	17.6	7.1	9.2
To unspecified date	14.1	7.3	11.9	27.5	16.1	12.4
Total	100.0	100.0	100.0	100.0	100.0	100.0
(n)	928	206	143	142	155	282

CONCLUSIONS

There were five points of similarity across the countries in
their presentations of conflict that warrant consideration.
First, in all five countries almost all the conflict items dealt
with "genuine" conflicts, and only a few (1% to 4%) items
presented conflicts in which the parties were unspecified,
with an additional 1% to 2% of the items coded as conflicts
created by journalists. The only exception to this cross-country
similarity was the conflicts coded as inconsequential to the news
item. The West German and British newscasts included far
more inconsequential conflict items than did newscasts from the

other countries (6% and 9% respectively). These two countries were also the countries with the highest level of connection made by journalists to other events. This may suggest that the introduction of incidental conflict to an item reflects the editors' efforts to provide continuity and background information.

The second similarity is that in four of the five countries the items categorized as having to do with foreign issues were more likely to contain conflict than the items categorized as domestic. West Germany, the exception, had virtually identical percentages of conflicts in domestic and foreign stories.

The third point of similarity was that conflict items appeared higher up in the newscast line-up compared with the non-conflict news items. This placement of conflict items is interpreted as evidence of higher salience or priority as judged by journalists in all five countries.

The fourth point was that in all the countries, without exception, the conflict items were presented as being related to other conflict items substantially more often than were the non-conflict items. Finally, the fifth cross-national similarity—which might be somewhat related to the previous one—was that the conflict items were presented along with more background information than were the non-conflict items.

These similarities, in combination, clearly suggest that television news highlights social conflict by conveying an overall impression of the importance of social conflict in society. This was reinforced by the generally clear distinction between conflict and non-conflict items. This uniform presentation of social conflict was disturbing particularly because four of the five countries presented foreign news as more conflictive—a pattern that might contribute to a xenophobic view of the world.

There were two major differences among the five countries. First, there were clear differences in the prevalence of conflicts in the countries' newscasts, with South Africa having the lowest presented level (32% of all the news items) and Israel having the highest level (60% of all the items). Second, there were differences in the frequency of presenting a particular topic as a conflict.

Taken together, we have attempted to create what may be termed country "profiles" in terms of how the news on television presented social conflict.

The United States. Commercial television in the United States contained a moderate percentage of social conflicts, with the vast majority of them foreign conflicts and a small minority of domestic conflicts. At the same time, however, domestic conflicts were placed higher in the line-up than the foreign conflicts. The most prevalent conflict items dealt with international politics, with the United States having the highest percentage of such stories. In contrast, it was tied with South Africa for the lowest percentage of internal-order conflict stories, and there were very few labor-relations conflict stories. There was a moderate amount of background information and connection of conflicts with previous events.

The United Kingdom. The BBC also presented a moderate percentage of social conflicts. BBC foreign items were far more likely to be conflict items than were domestic items, which were placed higher in the line-up than the foreign conflict items. The conflict topics that received the most coverage were international politics, labor relations, and internal order, and there was a moderate amount of connecting the stories by means of background information.

The Federal Republic of Germany. West German television also presented a moderate percentage of social conflicts, with an equal proportion of foreign and domestic items presented as conflicts. Here, too, the conflict items dealing with domestic issues were higher in the line-up compared with the items dealing with foreign conflicts. The topics most often reported on in conflict stories were international politics, internal politics, and labor relations. There was a relatively high degree of connecting the stories by means of background information.

Israel. Israel presented the highest percentage of conflict items among the five countries studied. Similar to the other countries, foreign items on Israel Television contained a higher percentage of conflicts than the domestic items. In contrast to the United States, the United Kingdom, and West Germany, conflicts dealing with foreign issues were placed higher in the Israeli line-ups than conflicts dealing with domestic issues. The most prevalent conflict topics were international politics and internal order, and there was a low level of background information about the items given by the journalists.

South Africa. South Africa, in contrast with the other countries, presented relatively few social conflicts in its television news. The SABC was also more likely to present foreign items as conflicts than domestic items. As was the case in Israel, however, foreign conflict items appeared higher in the line-up compared with domestic conflict items. International and internal politics were the most frequently reported conflict topics, and there was a medium amount of background information given.

This comparison of the five countries, contrasting the presentation of stories that report social conflicts with those that do not, indicates that there are both similarities across the five countries as well as country-specific patterns. We suggest that the similarities are the result of journalistic norms reflecting a high news value placed on conflict. On the other hand, we believe the differences among the countries, are attributable to the systemic variables of government influence and media competition as well as to particular sociopolitical conditions existing in the countries at the time of the study. We shall return to these points at the conclusion of the volume.

NOTES

1. Caution must be exercised to avoid an over-interpretation of the absolute mean order scores among the different countries, because they are a function of the total number of news items in the newscast. For example, German newscasts are the shortest in duration and have the fewest items, while Israeli newscasts are the longest in duration and have the most items. Hence the mean rank orderings of the conflict and non-conflict items reflect these differences.

2. In general, the overall figure for the five countries was used as the criterion, with a 1.5% threshold in either the conflict or non-conflict categories; however, when a topic was especially prevalent in one country, it was retained as a separate category even though its overall frequency was low and did not attain the threshold.

The Dimensions of Social Conflict in Television News

In this chapter we explore how the social conflict items were presented in the newscasts of the five countries by focusing on the three dimensions of social conflict: complexity, intensity, and solvability. The majority of the chapter presents each of the three dimensions separately, both in terms of their respective component variables and as overall indices. Then we consider the interrelationships among the dimensions before concluding with an assessment of how our expected structural factors—such as competition and government influence—relate to the dimensions of conflict as presented on television news.

THE PRESENTATION OF COMPLEXITY, INTENSITY, AND SOLVABILITY

Complexity

Of the three dimensions, complexity is actually the most difficult to operationalize satisfactorily.[1] The most conceptually sound and reliable measure of complexity is the nature and number of parties involved in the conflict, as presented in the news. Conceptually, the parties to a conflict are critical to its trajectory and its pattern. By distinguishing between opponents and non-opponents (including arbitrators, mediators, and go-betweens) the coding permits examination of the pattern of conflict. Furthermore, the involvement of *non*-opponents in the conflict is a subtle indicator of the complexity of the conflict, for such a conflict involves not only two or more parties in opposition, but also one or more entities that might be affected by the conflict or might seek to influence it.

The most striking finding in Table 5.1 is that across all the conflict items, when based on the total number of parties, the most complex portrayal of conflict was in South Africa (3.3 parties per conflict), followed by Israel (2.9), and with virtually no differences for the other three countries (averaging 2.8 parties per conflict). Moreover, when examining the mean number of opponents per conflict there were only minute differences between the five countries, with Israel slightly higher (2.6, versus a mean of 2.5 or 2.4 for all the other countries). This pattern was reinforced further with the measure of the mean number of non-opponents: South Africa with its mean of 0.80 stands dramatically higher than any of the other countries, with their respective means ranging from 0.35 to 0.40.

In many of the news items there were only two opponents—ranging from 56% of all items in the United Kingdom to 70% in West Germany. On the other hand, between 17% (in West Germany) and 25% (in the United Kingdom) had three opponents, and between 8% (in West Germany) and 16% of all the conflicts (in South Africa) had four to six opponents specified in the items. This seems to suggest relatively high complexity.

In the breakdown by domestic and foreign news items, we found additional evidence of the differential presentation of foreign and domestic items. On all three measures of complexity and in four of the countries (the exception being West Germany), foreign conflicts were presented as involving more parties (opponents as well as non-opponents) than were domestic conflicts. Foreign conflicts were presented, therefore, as being more complex than domestic conflicts. Items that were coded as being both domestic and foreign fall, in most cases, in between the foreign and domestic scores—which is what would be expected.

Table 5.1 Mean Complexity Measures by Country and Location[1]

	Total (895)	U.S. (163)	UK (176)	FRG (155)	Isr. (259)	SA (142)
Mean number of parties[2]						
Domestic	2.8	2.5	2.7	3.0	2.7	3.0
Foreign	3.2	3.1	3.1	2.6	3.4	3.6
Domestic & Foreign	2.9	2.8	2.7	2.6	2.8	3.5
Total	2.9	2.8	2.8	2.8	2.9	3.3
Mean number of opponents						
Domestic	2.5	2.2	2.4	2.5	2.6	2.4
Foreign	2.7	2.7	2.7	2.3	2.9	2.6
Domestic & Foreign	2.4	2.5	2.5	2.3	2.3	2.6
Total	2.5	2.4	2.5	2.4	2.6	2.5
Mean number of non-opponents						
Domestic	0.32	0.25	0.29	0.46	0.22	0.58
Foreign	0.56	0.49	0.46	0.29	0.54	0.92
Domestic & Foreign	0.51	0.53	0.22	0.43	0.50	0.93
Total	0.44	0.40	0.33	0.40	0.35	0.80

1. The subsample sizes are presented in chapter note 10.
2. The sum of the mean number of opponents and mean number of non-opponents is not always equal to the mean number of parties because of rounding of last digits.

As an example of a relatively complex foreign and domestic conflict, we present a story on the fighting in Beirut, Lebanon, aired on CBS on January 16, 1984 (eighth item in newscast). We quote Dan Rather and the text of correspondent Larry Pintak reporting from Beirut (for emphasis we have italicized the six parties):[2]

RATHER: In Beirut, at least 18 people were killed today in escalating artillery duels between *Christian militia* and *Druze Moslem forces*. Larry Pintak has more about this.

LARRY PINTAK: The day-long violence came as *U.S. envoy Donald Rumsfeld* met *Lebanese President Amin Gemayel*, trying to patch things back together. The importance of his mission was underlined by last night's assault on the *Marines*

This is one of the areas the Marines say the attack came from. The Americans hit back here with tanks and mortars. This was a

	doctor's office; next door, a dental clinic. This plastics factory burned for hours. All have a clear line of fire on the Marines' airport compound. But it's the Marines, not the militiamen, who the people blame.
MAN:	We call them to make peace here, not to renew war.
MAJOR DENNIS BROOKS:	We're sorry about that. We can't control where we take fire from.
PINTAK:	Marine officers say last night was a good example of what's to come if the attacks continue. The policy is now: if you hit us, we'll hit you back a lot harder.

Another example, this time of a foreign conflict, comes from the 10th of December, 1980, broadcast on Israel Television (first item in newscast). The story dealt with the preliminary measures being taken by the NATO countries in view of the Soviet threat to Poland. It is unusually high in complexity, with nine parties mentioned, some opponents and some interested parties. The parties in the order of their appearance in the item were as follows: The United States, the USSR, Poland, Czechoslovakia, East Germany, NATO, West Germany, the Polish people, and the Solidarity union.

In sum, many conflict items presented more than two opponents, and there is evidence that foreign conflicts were presented as more complex. South Africa's portrayal of conflict tended to be more complex than the other countries by virtue of its presentation of the highest number of non-opponents in combination with an average number of opponents.

Intensity

Overall, the most salient point was the relatively low levels of aggression in all the countries, particularly of the emotional-display and the verbal-aggression varieties (see Table 5.2). Furthermore, only one-third of the items *verbally* reported physical aggression and only one-sixth *visually* presented physical aggression.

Table 5.2 Percentage of Conflict Items Presenting Six Types
of Aggression and Emotion by Country[1]

	Total (895)	U.S. (163)	UK (176)	FRG (155)	Isr. (259)	SA (142)
Verbally reported physical aggression						
None	68.5	71.6	59.1	74.3	73.1	62.7
Aggression without damage	10.8	6.8	12.1	11.6	10.4	13.4
Imprisonment	3.7	3.1	6.9	1.9	1.9	5.6
Property damage	3.4	1.9	5.2	1.3	4.2	3.5
Wounding	0.8	0.6	1.7	0.0	1.2	0.0
Damage and wounding	0.9	0.6	0.6	0.0	1.5	1.4
Killing	4.7	4.9	4.6	4.5	2.7	8.5
Damage and killing	0.8	0.0	0.6	0.0	1.2	2.1
Wounding and killing	1.7	1.9	2.3	1.9	1.9	0.0
Damage, wounding, & killing	4.7	8.6	6.9	4.5	1.9	2.8
Total	100.0	100.0	100.0	100.0	100.0	100.0
Visually shown physical aggression						
None	84.7	80.3	78.1	93.0	85.3	87.4
Aggression without damage	7.3	9.9	9.8	3.9	7.3	4.2
Imprisonment	0.6	0.6	0.6	0.0	0.8	0.7
Property damage	4.8	5.6	6.9	0.6	5.0	5.6
Wounding	0.3	0.0	0.6	0.0	0.4	0.7
Damage and wounding	1.0	1.2	1.7	0.6	0.4	1.4
Killing	0.4	0.6	0.0	1.3	0.4	0.0
Damage and killing	0.4	0.0	1.1	0.6	0.4	0.0
Wounding and killing	0.2	0.6	0.6	0.0	0.0	0.0
Damage, wounding & killing	0.3	1.2	0.6	0.0	0.0	0.0
Total	100.0	100.0	100.0	100.0	100.0	100.0
Verbally reported verbal aggression						
None	85.2	87.7	71.9	96.8	82.7	90.8
Profanity	6.7	8.0	13.8	2.6	6.9	0.7
Heated debate	3.6	1.2	2.3	0.0	8.1	3.5
Threat to property	0.6	1.9	1.1	0.6	0.8	0.0
Threat to well-being	3.9	1.2	10.9	0.0	1.5	4.9

(continued)

Table 5.2 Continued

	Total (895)	U.S. (163)	UK (176)	FRG (155)	Isr. (259)	SA (142)
Visually shown verbal aggression						
None	94.0	91.4	87.4	98.1	96.2	96.5
Profanity	3.1	6.2	6.3	1.3	1.9	0.0
Heated debate	1.9	0.6	5.2	0.6	1.5	1.4
Threat to property	0.1	0.6	0.0	0.0	0.4	0.0
Threat to well-being	0.9	1.2	1.1	0.0	0.0	2.1
Total	100.0	100.0	100.0	100.0	100.0	100.0
Verbally reported emotional display						
None	93.8	93.8	90.3	93.6	95.4	95.8
Nonverbal	5.2	5.6	8.0	5.2	4.6	2.1
Vocal	0.8	0.6	1.7	0.6	0.0	1.4
Hysteria	0.2	0.0	0.0	0.6	0.0	0.7
Total	100.0	100.0	100.0	100.0	100.0	100.0
Visually shown emotional display						
None	87.0	85.7	78.2	93.5	90.0	87.3
Nonverbal	8.2	10.5	12.1	5.2	8.5	3.5
Vocal	3.3	1.9	5.7	1.3	1.5	7.0
Hysteria	1.5	1.9	4.0	0.0	0.0	2.1
Total	100.0	100.0	100.0	100.0	100.0	100.0

1. The subsample sizes are presented in chapter note 10.

There were some specific differences, however, regarding the various components of the intensity dimension.

The United Kingdom and South Africa reported more physical aggression than did the other three countries, with South Africa highest in reports of killing without other forms of aggression (8.5%) and the United Kingdom highest with reports of imprisonment (6.9%) and second highest with reports of damage, wounding, and killing (6.9%). In contrast, Israel presented only 1.9% of items with imprisonment and 1.9% with damage, wounding, and killing. The United States and the United Kingdom more frequently presented visual physical aggression, showing more aggression without damage as well as more damage, wounding, and killing. West German news seldom presented visual physical aggression (7%), particularly in presenting virtually no property damage (0.6%) compared to the other countries that showed property damage in 5% to 6% of the social conflict items.

Nearly 14% of the British items reported the use of profane language compared with only 7% to 8% in Israel and the United States and very little in West Germany (2.6%) and South Africa (0.7%). In Britain 10.9% of the items contained threats to the well-being of an opponent, 4.9% in South Africa, and hardly any or none in the other three countries. British newscasts also showed far more heated debates (5.2% of conflict items) than did news in the other countries. Israel reported more verbal aggression than did the United States, West Germany, and South Africa as a consequence of its reports of heated debate (8.1% of conflict items).

Finally, British newscasts once again reported and presented the most examples of emotion. They were the highest in reporting nonverbal display of emotion (8% of all items), compared with 4% to 5% in the United States, West Germany, and Israel and only 2% in South Africa. In the visual display of emotion, the British news was the most frequent in showing nonverbal emotional display (12%) compared with the four other countries (3.5% to 10.5%), with the lowest frequency being once again in South Africa. The BBC news was the second most frequent in showing vocal emotional display (5.7%), following South Africa (7%), with the other three countries showing very little (1.3% to 1.7%).

Thus for all six measures of intensity, the British newscasts presented and reported the most aggression and emotion. The BBC portrayal of conflicts was consistently more intense than that of the other countries, while West German news was the least intense in physical aggression, verbal aggression, and visual reports of emotion.

To illustrate the high intensity of the BBC news, we present two examples. First is a domestic conflict: a violent demonstration by Welsh unemployed during a visit to Cardiff by Prime Minister

Margaret Thatcher. The item was first in the newscast on January 11, 1980. Following are excerpts of the voice-over by correspondent Michael Sullivan:

SULLIVAN: Welsh trade union organizers had promised a huge and angry reception for the Prime Minister . . . and the police had acted accordingly. More than a thousand of them closed the streets around the big city hall, ringed it with crush barriers, and filled the road in front of the main entrance. . . . And a few minutes later Mrs. Thatcher's convoy of government and police cars appeared between the demonstrators and the building. . . . There followed a long struggle between the police and the demonstrators, who despite their modest numbers, well under a thousand, kept up a fierce pressure on the barriers. Eggs, beer cans and some flares were lobbed towards the city hall and twenty or so people were dragged from the crowd and bundled into police vans.

The second example, a foreign conflict, showed protestors in a bloody riot in the streets of Buenos Aires, Argentina. It was shown on January 18, 1984, as the ninth item in the newscast:

ANCHOR: In Argentina protestors have stoned a retired army general who said people who complained about human rights under military rule were subversives. . . . General Menendez . . . was besieged in Buenos Aires by a hostile crowd after his remarks incensed friends and relatives of some of the thousands who've disappeared during the military rule. Our diplomatic editor, John Simpson, was there.

SIMPSON: The mood turned angry when they shouted that Menendez is a killer. By this time the crowd has heard that he'd refused to take back his accusations that critics of the military were subversive. And they were getting so violent that the police called in their shock troops to clear a way for Menendez's escape. But after his two-hour siege inside the building he emerged ignoring the stones and insults, much as he'd ignored the new government's orders. The police and military haven't been used to this kind of opposition in Argentina, and at first they withdrew, perhaps under orders to avoid more trouble. Demonstrators, for their part, took out their frustrations on the congressional offices, regardless of the fact that the Congress is mostly on their side. But the police didn't stay away long, and when they came back they made straight for the human rights enforcers a short way down the street. And they singled out known civil rights activists. There's considerable tension here, outside the civil rights office. The police have made an abortive effort once already to smash it up, and there are about a hundred people gathered inside there and the fear is that the police may come back. . . . It had been a brief but savage episode—another sign of how hard it will be to bring reconciliation to Argentina.

Foreign news items consistently included more components of intensity than domestic news items, although the absolute levels differed from country to country (see Table 5.3). This was the case for all five countries regarding physical and verbal aggression. As for the display of emotion, the same pattern held for all the countries except for Israel. There the same low 3% level appears for both foreign and domestic verbally reported emotional display and a reverse in the trend for visually shown emotional displays (12% in domestic items and only 7% in foreign items). Finally, as with the complexity dimension, items coded as being both foreign and domestic were often in the expected middle position between the purely domestic and purely foreign items.[3]

In sum, foreign conflicts are presented as more intense than domestic conflicts, across all countries and for nearly all six measures of aggression and emotion. The British newscasts presented the most intense conflicts, while the conflicts on West German television presented the lowest intensity level.

Table 5.3 Percentage of Items Containing Intensity of Components by County

	Total	U.S.	UK	FRG	Isr.	SA
Verbally reported physical aggression						
Domestic	19	16	30	14	19	11
Foreign	51	41	64	49	40	63
Domestic & Foreign	29	31	35	17	33	26
Visually shown physical aggression						
Domestic	19	16	16	7	5	0
Foreign	26	23	38	10	29	27
Domestic & Foreign	15	21	13	3	24	4
Verbally reported verbal aggression						
Domestic	13	9	25	1	15	6
Foreign	20	17	42	4	24	14
Domestic & Foreign	11	11	16	4	14	11
Visually shown verbal aggression						
Domestic	6	8	13	1	5	2
Foreign	7	9	16	2	3	6
Domestic & Foreign	5	9	6	3	2	0
Verbally reported emotional display						
Domestic	5	6	7	4	3	4
Foreign	7	7	14	11	3	6
Domestic & Foreign	7	4	10	7	12	0
Visually shown emotional display						
Domestic	12	20	17	7	12	6
Foreign	17	13	36	10	7	24
Domestic & Foreign	6	7	13	0	9	0

1. The subsample sizes are presented in chapter note 10.

Table 5.4 Percentage of Conflict Items Containing
Solvability Components by Country[1]

	Total (895)	U.S. (163)	UK (176)	FRG (155)	Isr. (259)	SA (142)
Call for resolution						
No opponent	58.7	63.6	35.6	47.8	77.2	60.0
All opponents	5.7	3.7	6.3	7.1	5.4	6.3
At least one opponent	27.6	28.4	44.9	37.5	11.2	24.6
At least one opponent denies	2.1	0.6	8.0	0.6	1.2	0.0
All opponents deny	0.6	0.0	0.0	1.3	0.4	1.4
Non-opponents	3.8	1.9	2.9	3.2	4.6	6.3
Opponents and non-opponents	0.9	1.8	1.2	0.6	0.0	0.0
News media	0.6	0.0	1.1	1.9	0.0	1.4
Total	100.0	100.0	100.0	100.0	100.0	100.0
State of negotiations						
None taking place	59.4	71.0	53.4	51.0	66.8	49.4
Attempts to start	8.5	8.0	11.5	14.2	4.2	7.0
Taking place	20.2	14.8	23.6	20.0	15.1	31.7
Intensive taking place	4.5	3.1	0.6	1.9	10.0	3.5
Opponent(s) oppose	1.8	0.6	6.9	0.6	0.4	0.7
Took place in past	5.6	2.5	4.0	12.3	3.5	7.7
Total	100.0	100.0	100.0	100.0	100.0	100.0
Willingness to compromise						
None	83.0	88.3	79.3	85.8	84.5	75.4
All opponents	2.7	0.6	2.9	2.6	2.7	4.9
At least one opponent	11.0	8.6	13.2	5.8	0.7	19.0
One opponent not willing	0.8	0.0	1.7	1.9	0.4	0.0
One willing and one not	2.6	2.5	2.9	3.9	2.7	0.7
Total	100.0	100.0	100.0	100.0	100.0	100.0
Outcome of conflict						
None	81.7	78.4	81.6	79.4	87.3	77.5
Imposition	9.1	13.6	7.5	11.0	6.2	9.2
Compromise	4.8	6.2	4.0	3.9	3.1	8.5
Conversion	2.2	1.2	4.0	2.6	0.4	4.2
Withdrawal	2.2	0.6	2.9	3.2	3.1	0.7
Total	100.0	100.0	100.0	100.0	100.0	100.0

1. The subsample sizes are presented in chapter note 10.

Solvability

The call for resolution is an indication that something is being done toward reaching an end to the conflict, albeit often times quite distant from an actual resolution (see Table 5.4). Across the five countries, in one-third of the cases there was a call for resolution by all or at least one of the opponents involved in the conflict. In addition, in 4% of the cases non-opponents—such as mediators and arbitrators—called for resolution.

There were also some clear differences among the countries. Thus, for example, the relative frequency of opponents calling for resolution was highest in the United Kingdom (52%) and the lowest in Israel (17%). In South Africa and the United States, respectively, there was a call for resolution by opponents in 31% and 34% of the cases, and in South Africa an additional 6% contained similar calls by non-opponents. In West Germany, there was a call for resolution in approximately half of the conflicts, including 3% of such calls by non-opponents.

In one-fourth of the conflicts analyzed, some form of negotiations was taking place (including 4.5% characterized as "intensive" negotiations, in which the parties declared they would continue negotiating until a solution was forthcoming). In South Africa, negotiations were reported in 35% of the items, while in the United States only 18% of the items reported negotiations. In the remaining three countries negotiations were taking place in roughly 23% to 25% of the conflict items.[4]

A stated willingness to compromise occurred overall in only about 14% of the conflicts, with an additional 2.6% of the conflicts in which at least one opponent was willing to compromise while another explicitly was not. Here, too, however, there were differences among the countries. In South Africa, once again, in 24% of the conflicts one or more of the opponents was reported to have been willing to compromise, whereas in Israel the comparable figure was less than 3%. In the other three countries, there was a moderate willingness to compromise: 8% in West Germany, 9% in the United States, and 16% in the United Kingdom.

Table 5.5 Percentage of Conflict Items Containing Solvability Components by Country and Location

	Total (895)	U.S. (163)	UK (176)	FRG (155)	Isr. (259)	SA (142)
Percent reporting a call for resolution						
Domestic	40	31	62	54	24	36
Foreign	39	32	68	43	21	40
Domestic & Foreign	47	49	64	63	19	48
Percent reporting negotiations taking place						
Domestic	42	20	52	62	31	58
Foreign	32	28	36	26	30	38
Domestic & Foreign	50	42	48	53	48	67
Percent reporting willingness to compromise						
Domestic	19	8	26	16	16	33
Foreign	15	15	12	12	14	19
Domestic & Foreign	17	13	19	13	17	22
Percent reporting an outcome of some kind						
Domestic	24	31	25	24	15	38
Foreign	14	13	8	26	10	13
Domestic & Foreign	13	18	3	16	9	15

1. The subsample sizes are presented in chapter note 10.

Finally, in 18.4% of the conflicts across the board, some outcome of the conflict was noted in the newscasts, with imposing a solution being the most prevalent (9.1%), followed by compromise (4.8%). South Africa (23%), the United States (22%), and West Germany (21%) reported the most outcomes, while Israel (13%) reported the least. The United States reported the most imposed outcomes (13.6%)—such as Supreme Court decisions—while Israel reported the least (6.2%). As for compromise, the highest number reported was in South Africa (8.5%) and the lowest in Israel (3.1%). These country comparisons suggest that Israeli news presented social conflicts as least solvable while South Africa presented conflicts, relatively speaking, as the most solvable.

Across the five countries there was a consistent trend in all components of solvability for domestic stories to be more solvable than foreign stories (see Table 5.5). This was most pronounced for reporting negotiations and some form of outcome. Only in the case of reporting "willingness to compromise," however, did the combined foreign and domestic stories fit their "logical" position in between the foreign and domestic stories.[5]

An illustration of the high level of solvability in South African domestic news comes from an item dealing with the status of teachers in that country, which was a subject of an inquiry by a national commission. The report, on December 2, 1980 (second item in newscast), tells of the solution in a studio interview with the minister of national education. Note that the solution is described as more than temporary, and that the issue itself was said to be complex and difficult:

ANCHOR: The Minister of National Education has undertaken to submit the report of the two investigations directly to the cabinet. Announcing this in Pretoria today he assured the Federal Council of Teachers' Associations that the reports and the interim report to the two investigations would go straight to the cabinet and not first to the Commission for Administration. The Minister's statement today followed a meeting between him and the Federal Council yesterday at which a measure of agreement was reached. We asked Dr. Viljoen if this agreement was of a temporary nature.

Dr. VILJOEN: No, I think this is really much more than a temporary solution. For the first time in many years, I'd almost say in decades, as the result of this research project on the status of the educator, the teaching profession and the government departments concerned will have really reliable scientifically based data about the

> relative complexity and difficulty of different
> teaching posts compared to some of the posts
> in the public section and some of the posts in
> the private sector.

A second example of solvability comes from CBS on its January 26th, 1984 newscast (fifth item). The report dealt with Israel's agreement to a United States arms deal with Jordan. It is interesting to note that although the item from the American point of view is a combined foreign and domestic item (involving the United States and Israel) it was not reported on Israeli television, which—as indicated above—was low on solvability.

DAN RATHER: U.S. Mideast policy striving for an evenhand-
              edness between Arab and Israeli fears has
              overcome a crucial obstacle that threatened
              to block U.S. military influence in the re-
              gion. State Department correspondent Bill
              McLaughlin reports how.

McLAUGHLIN: CBS News has learned that Israel agreed this
              week not to oppose the Reagan Administra-
              tion's plans to fund, equip and train a Jordanian
              Rapid Deployment Force. The Israeli decision is
              unprecedented. It's the first time that country
              has agreed not to fight U.S. plans to back a
              Muslim strike force in the Middle East. With-
              out that agreement, sources say, the $200 mil-
              lion Jordanian force would never make it
              through Congress. The agreement was
              reached in Washington this week but stems
              from a personal appeal that President Reagan
              made to Israeli Prime Minister Itzhak Shamir
              when the two met last November.

Index Measures

To present a more concise picture, three simple indices were also used. Given the problems with complexity, we simply used the total number of opponents appearing in the conflicts as it was used above. For intensity and solvability, we counted and summed the occurrence of all component variables (e.g., verbal report of physical

Table 5.6 Mean Index Scores for Complexity, Intensity and Solvability by Country and Location[1]

	Total (895)	U.S. (163)	UK (176)	FRG (155)	Isr. (259)	SA (142)
Complexity[2]						
Domestic	2.5	2.2	2.4	2.5	2.6	2.4
Foreign	2.7	2.7	2.7	2.3	2.9	2.6
Domestic & Foreign	2.4	2.5	2.5	2.3	2.3	2.6
Total	2.5	2.4	2.5	2.4	2.6	2.5
Intensity[3]						
Domestic	0.64	0.75	1.09	0.34	0.59	0.29
Foreign	1.29	1.11	2.10	0.86	1.06	1.41
Domestic & Foreign	0.73	0.84	0.94	0.37	0.95	0.33
Total	0.87	0.90	1.35	0.51	0.78	0.80
Solvability[4]						
Domestic	0.71	0.56	0.82	0.72	0.55	1.15
Foreign	0.55	0.51	0.48	0.59	0.51	0.63
Domestic & Foreign	0.67	0.64	0.71	0.57	0.57	0.96
Total	0.65	0.57	0.70	0.65	0.54	0.89

1. The subsample sizes are presented in chapter note 10.
2. This index is the mean number of opponents (see Table 5.1).
3. The scores for this index can range from 0 to 6.
4. The scores for this index can range from 0 to 4.

aggression, description of outcome). Thus the intensity index could range from zero to six, and the solvability index could range from zero to four. All components were assigned equal weights in their respective indices.

The overall country ranking on complexity of the conflicts was as follows: Israel was most complex, South Africa and the United Kingdom were tied in second place, and the United States and West Germany were tied in third place as least complex (see Table 5.6). Also, as seen in both Tables 5.1 and 5.6, in all countries but West Germany domestic conflicts were presented as less complex than were foreign conflicts.

Ranking the five countries in terms of intensity showed British news as most intense, followed by U.S. news, South African news, and Israeli news, with West German news as least intense. In all five countries, foreign conflicts were more intense than were domestic conflicts. With the exception of the United Kingdom, the combined domestic and foreign stories are somewhere in between the complexity level of the separate domestic and foreign stories. South Africa's presentation is noteworthy because foreign stories were more than four times more intense than were domestic stories, whereas the comparable ratio was approximately 2.5 to 1 in West Germany, and less than 2 to 1 in the remaining three countries.

Lastly, the overall level of solvability ranked South Africa as having the most solvable presentation of social conflict news items, followed by the United Kingdom, West Germany, the United States, and Israel with the lowest level of solvability. Also, the solvability pattern was highly consistent in terms of domestic conflicts being presented as more solvable than foreign conflicts.[6]

Overall, the most salient and important findings for the dimensions—taken separately—highlight differences between foreign and domestic conflicts. In particular, foreign conflicts were presented as more complex, more intense, and less solvable than were domestic conflicts (except in West Germany). Furthermore, South Africa was a particularly interesting case as it scored highest on complexity, intensity, *and* solvability, thus seeming to present difficult conflicts as being solved. However, South Africa's high scores on complexity and intensity were a consequence of its high scores on foreign conflicts, while its high scores on solvability were a consequence of its high score on domestic conflicts. Hence South African news portrayed foreign conflicts as complex and intense (i.e., more severe) and domestic conflicts as more solvable (i.e., less severe).

The Structural Interrelationships Among the Variables

As an overall assessment of the portrayal of conflict on television news we wished to determine the structure of interrelationships between the elements of the three dimensions for the domestic and foreign conflict items. This was done using smallest space analysis

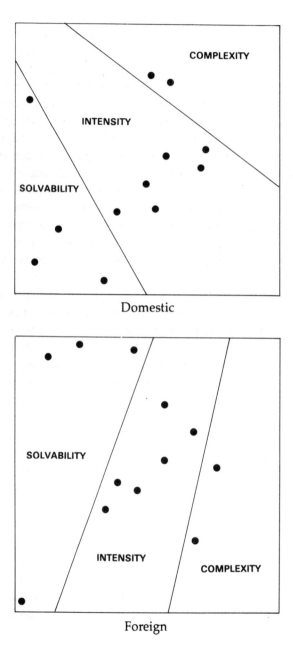

Figure 5.1 SSA Maps for Domestic and Foreign Conflicts

(SSA).[7] The conceptual framework of the SSA was based on the "mapping sentence" presented in Chapter 2.

The data for the SSA maps consisted of two elements of complexity, six of intensity and four of solvability. Two separate runs were made—one for domestic items and the other for foreign items—for all five countries combined (the items that were coded as both domestic and foreign were excluded from this analysis).[8]

In both maps there was a clear division of the space according to the three conflict dimensions (see Figure 5.1). Also, there seemed to be slightly better differentiation among the dimensions in the map of the foreign conflicts (despite the minutely lower coefficient of alienation for the domestic conflicts). In both maps, the center region is occupied by the intensity components while the regions on either side comprise the components of complexity and solvability. In other words, the intensity dimension lies in between and connects with complexity and solvability. Because the three dimensions were not expected to be ordered in any particular way, the output may be interpreted as indicating that intensity is the more central among the three dimensions in determining the severity of the conflicts.[9]

CONCLUSIONS

This chapter has shown that complexity, intensity, and solvability can indeed characterize the way social conflicts are presented in the news in a variety of countries. We also have shown that there is a differential magnitude of the dimensions among the domestic and foreign conflicts.

We hypothesized at the outset that the more competition there is among media, the greater the tendency to simplify content in order to attract a larger audience. This was only partially supported by our data. In South Africa, with the least amount of competition, there was indeed the most complex portrayal (in large portion because of the greater complexity of foreign items compared with domestic items). On the other hand, in Israel—also with virtually no competition for the television news audience—we found low complexity of portrayal.

Our findings clearly show that domestic conflicts were presented generally as being less complex compared with foreign conflicts. This would fit squarely with the notions of the critical theorists to the effect that one of the main functions of the media is to preserve the status quo in society. Although all news events would tend to be portrayed as less complex than they really are (these scholars would say), it seems highly plausible that the events concerning the country of broadcast would be presented even more simplistically. This is not by any means because domestic conflicts are really less complex, but because this mode of presentation might blind media consumers (in our case, the television viewers) to the complexity of domestic conflict. It may also be, as these theorists would argue, that there is at least some unconscious motivation on the part of the media—particularly those governed more closely by the political establishment of the country—to present the domestic scene as less complex (i.e., as less severe), and thus as more manageable.

The intensity dimension of social conflict dramatically supports this view of television news coverage. First, when intensity is examined across countries it is clear that foreign conflicts were always presented as more intense than were local ones. As we suggested earlier, once again it seems that "the grass is greener at home." Second, the countries did range on continua that differed for foreign and domestic items. The highest intensity levels were for the domestic items in the United Kingdom and the United States and the lowest were in South Africa. For foreign conflicts, although British news was still the most intense, South African news was next in line.

The first foreign-domestic difference meshes with the argument that social control and the status quo can be better preserved if the media lead people to believe that things are not really that bad, and in any event they are much worse elsewhere. The second finding extends this to specific countries that are interested in emphasizing the good or the positive in society by focusing on the troubles and social problems of others while presenting a relatively more idyllic picture of the home front. This is more likely to operate in societies with greater governmental control over the media. Our findings that the ratio of intensity abroad and at home was nearly 5 to 1 in South Africa and only 1.5 to 1 in the United States—with the other countries in between—suggest that in comparison with the United States, South Africa was far more interested in obscuring domestic conflict by dramatizing foreign conflict. South Africa's differential treatment of domestic and foreign conflict stood in contrast with British television, which presented conflict as highly intense regardless of its location.

On the dimension of solvability we found that there were differences among the countries and also between domestic and foreign stories. South Africa presented both foreign and domestic conflicts as more solvable than did other countries. Other countries, however, did not lie on the continuum as we would have expected. In fact, Israel which was closest to South Africa in terms of both government control and media competition, presented its conflicts as the least solvable among the five countries. Our data supported the general pattern by portraying domestic conflicts as more solvable than foreign conflicts, suggesting that the media tended to minimize internal conflict while maximizing external conflict. On the other hand, it seems that government control and media competition cannot explain the entire realm of cross-national variation in portraying the solvability of conflicts.

This brings us to our final thoughts on the relationships among the three dimensions. As we have shown, there was a similar structure of interrelationships among dimensions for both domestic and foreign conflicts. This structure relates to what we call the *severity* of the conflicts. Conflicts that are presented as being of high complexity, high intensity, and low solvability are probably the most severe. Moreover, they are probably most difficult to live with and deal with in the media.

But this does not mean that there is a perfect relationship among these dimensions. Thus when each individual conflict is analyzed, it can be shown that sometimes all three dimensions seem to operate in the same direction of severity, thereby manifesting a conflict that is high in complexity and intensity while low in solvability, or vice versa; but on other occasions, a conflict can be low in complexity and high in intensity and solvability, or it can take various other permutations.

An example of this possibility is a BBC item from February 2nd, 1984 (fifth item in the newscast), describing the difficult situation in Beirut, Lebanon. Although the lead-in by the news anchor talks about the southern suburbs that have "come under some of the heaviest shelling for several months," the reporter (Keith Graves) interviewed several residents about their difficulties living in the city. Visually there is little intensity, for all one could see were some scenes of partially destroyed buildings. Graves described the difficult situation, however, and by mentioning the various parties to the conflict (italicized in the text), he makes it appear quite complex. The low solvability of the item appears in the final sentence:

> For nearly a decade Lebanon has suffered an orgy of destruction and bloodshed. Beirut carries the scars of violence that has cost maybe a hundred thousand lives. No one knows for sure. Throughout, the one constant has been the ability of the *Lebanese* to adapt to life in a country at war. But now they've had enough. The legendary resilience of the people is crumbling. It's being replaced by a mood of despair. . . . The *Israelis* control the south . . . the *Syrians* have crippled the Bekaa valley. . . . The capital is constantly threatened and frequently attacked by Lebanese *Druze militiamen* from their strongholds in the mountains. . . . *The Multi-National Force* upon which so many hopes were pinned has proved totally ineffective. . . . With no end in sight to the agony of Lebanon, Arab aid is being withheld; tens of thousands of Lebanese are emigrating; socially and economically the country has started on a downward spiral which may prove more destructive than the bombs and the bullets.

In Chapter 6 we discuss how we analyzed what we found concerning the way the parties to the conflicts were presented.

NOTES

1. This difficulty is a consequence of some conceptual vicissitudes as well as pragmatic issues. The critical problem concerns the important distinction between the inherent complexity of the conflict itself and the complexity of its presentation. For example, attributes of television news such as the use of fast editing, brief audio "sound bites," and intricate visual effects may appear to indicate complexity. These characteristics actually indicate complexity of the presentation, however, not of the conflict itself. On the other hand, there are attributes of complexity that are inherent to the conflict story. For example, we suspected the more issues involved in a specific conflict, the more complex the conflict. And yet, the number of issues per se does not take into account the complexity of the individual issues. Thus a conflict involving two highly complex issues (e.g., the possibility of establishing a Palestinian state on the West Bank and the nature of its leadership) may be a far more complex conflict than a conflict with as many as four or five simpler issues. As a result of this problem, we were unable to develop a measure of issue complexity that would be both valid and reliable. Counting the number of issues is difficult and unlikely to be valid, while coding the complexity of issues may be valid but is very difficult to code reliably.

2. This item also illustrates the difficulty that often existed in determining and identifying the parties to the conflict. The six parties and their respective representatives specified here were all spelled out in the item *as presented* (Donald Rumsfeld was considered as a representative of the U.S. government, Lebanese President Gemayel was regarded as representative of the Lebanese government). The Lebanese Christian militia, the Druze militia, and the Marines were directly mentioned as opponents. The Lebanese people appear as interested parties as represented by the man interviewed and the people presented in the video.

3. Variations from that expectation typically occurred in categories with such small frequencies that stability is unlikely (e.g., emotional display); in contrast, the highest-frequency category (verbally reported physical aggression) met our theoretical expectation.

4. It should be pointed out that given the nature of the study—with its emphasis on the overall level of the severity of social conflict and without going into specific case studies—it could be very likely that the negotiations that were taking place concerning a given conflict on a given day (and reported on the news) could have been continuing on subsequent days and been reported again. This, however, did not detract from the significance of these findings.

5. A closer look reveals that in 14 of the 20 within-country contrasts between domestic and foreign items, the domestic conflicts were presented as more solvable than were the foreign stories. A comparison of the five countries showed that South Africa presented conflicts as most solvable, with domestic conflicts more solvable than foreign. Israel presented conflicts as least solvable, with domestic conflicts also more solvable than foreign. West Germany and the United Kingdom fell in between for overall solvability, but also presented domestic conflicts as more solvable. The United States, although in between overall, did not follow the pattern of presenting domestic conflicts as more solvable.

6. There was variability in the magnitude of the difference between foreign and domestic solvability. Domestic conflicts were only slightly more solvable on Israel and American newscasts. The difference was greater in West Germany, and was greatest in the United Kingdom and in South Africa where domestic conflicts were far more solvable than foreign conflicts.

7. Smallest space analysis produces geometric representations (maps) of the input correlation matrix whereby the distance between any two variables, represented by points in the space, is inverse to the magnitude of the correlation between them (Guttman, 1968). In the SSA procedure the expected partitioning of the space of the map is predetermined by the researcher according to a priori theoretical expectations. SSA does not require any conventional test of significance. Instead, the only criterion of goodness of fit used is a *coefficient of alienation*, which indicates the magnitude of the correlation between the input correlations among the variables and the distances between the data points on the SSA map (the actual measure used is unity minus that correlation; hence the smaller the coefficient of alienation, the better the fit, and the rule of thumb is that a coefficient of alienation of less than .15 is considered satisfactory).

8. The input matrix of intercorrelations for the SSAs consisted of weak monotonicity coefficients (Raveh, 1978) between all the components of the three dimensions. The resultant SSA maps had coefficients of alienation of .11 (for the domestic conflicts) and .13 (for the foreign conflicts), which are considered to be highly satisfactory.

9. To assess whether or not grouping the five countries together for the SSA maps was justified, five pairs of SSA maps were created, one for each country, run separately for the domestic and foreign conflict items. The 10 individual country maps were nearly identical to the two maps obtained for the five countries combined. In these maps we also obtained somewhat better differentiation for the foreign conflicts compared with the domestic conflicts. Hence we only present the two maps for the five countries combined.

10. The sub-sample sizes for Tables 5.1 to 5.6 were as follows:

	Total	U.S.	UK	FRG	Isr.	SA
Sub-sample sizes						
Domestic	435	65	95	76	147	52
Foreign	285	53	50	49	70	63
Domestic & Foreign	175	45	31	30	42	27
Total	895	163	176	155	259	142

Parties to Conflict:
Actors and Roles

This chapter is devoted to a description of the parties in the conflicts. It focuses on three aspects of actors and roles—first, the overall distribution of parties (who they are and how frequently they appear); second, the differential roles the parties take as actors in the conflicts (which parties are presented as opponents, mediators, arbitrators, go-betweens, and interested parties); and third, the relationships among the parties—in an attempt to determine the nature and degree of bias in their presentation of the various parties in the conflicts.

The definition of social conflict as a dispute between two or more parties over an issue, goal, topic, idea, or the means to obtain them, makes understanding parties to conflict an integral element in the total puzzle. Above and beyond this a priori justification, which inherently makes the analysis of parties vital to our work, there are other substantive grounds for the centrality of parties.

The dramatic form of social conflict rests on the juxtaposition of forces that are dramaturgically portrayed in opposition. Such conflictual presentation of forces has long been used in characterizing television news. The nature of the actors—their appeal, their appearance, their time "on stage," and their position in societal structures—affects their viability as characters in the drama of conflict.

Thus drama has long utilized the high and mighty, who have the farthest to fall, as the most effective tragic figures. Further, the interrelationship of actors involved in a conflict influences the characters' import and effect. For example, it takes little familarity with Shakespeare to understand that the effect of Macbeth's character was produced, in part, by the interplay among Macbeth himself, Banquo, and Lady Macbeth.

In our view it is critical to locate actors in the social structure and assay their location relative to the other parties in a conflict, not only for considerations of dramatic form. Much of the claim that the media sustain societal consensus through their failure to expose the flaws of the social structure is based on the notion that news replicates existing social hierarchies. From this perspective, the actors in social conflicts would be presented as occupying the central roles in society that are consistent with the dominant ideology's view of the social hierarchy. Thus the finding of the Glasgow University Media Group (1976) that labor unions were presented as the aggressors in industrial disputes was not surprising because, they argued, that is the role that the dominant ideology assigns to labor unions.

If one assumes that the media preserve consensus through replication, we would expect privileged groups to be gifted with news presence. That is, the status and privilege hierarchy would be replicated by appearance opportunities on television news. We are, therefore, interested in ascertaining which parties in disputes are privileged by appearing on the news, being allowed to speak on the news, or having their side presented by journalists. Our expectation is that those with high status and power will have this privilege reinforced and their status reconfirmed by their appearance on the news—whereas those of low status, the weak "outcasts," will be denied such appearances (Lazarsfeld & Merton, 1948). Such differential presentation of parties and their viewpoints will be an indicator of *establishment bias*, as the news organization replicates the dominant ideology's definition of parties' positions in a hierarchical society.

Table 6.1 Entities in Social Conflict Items by Decreasing Frequency

Entity	Frequency	Adjusted Percentage
Country	307	11.9
Government: Ruling Body	270	10.5
Government: Ministry, Department	184	7.1
Government Head: Prime Minister, President	178	6.9
Opposition Party	151	5.9
People	149	5.8
Organized Dissident Group	140	5.4
Public Authorities	124	4.8
Organized Workers	122	4.7
Armed Forces	120	4.7
Private Industry	89	3.5
Ruling Party: Unspecified	87	3.4
Group of Countries	76	2.9
Parliament: Member, Committee	69	2.7
Faction of a Political Party	61	2.4
All Religious: Groups & Leaders	55	2.1
Unorganized Dissidents	41	1.6
Courts	34	1.3
National Roof Labor Organization	30	1.2
Media	27	1.0
Government: Cabinet	25	1.0
National Industries	25	1.0
All Clubs	24	0.9
All Nongovernmental Experts	24	0.9
Nonrepresentative Political Party	21	0.8
Unorganized Workers	19	0.7
Group of Countries: Armed Forces	18	0.7
Educational Institutions	15	0.6
Workers: Mixed	15	0.6
National Police	14	0.5
Public Inquiry Commission	14	0.5
Group of Countries: Observers	9	0.3
Junta	9	0.3
European Parliament	6	0.2
Hostages	4	0.2
Other	21	0.8
Total	2577	100.0

ACTORS AND ROLES IN
SOCIAL CONFLICT

The 895 conflict items presented 2611 parties. Only 34 parties (less than 2%) could not be coded for their identity within our coding scheme. Thus 2577 parties are the focus of the following analyses.

A *country* was the most frequent entity, accounting for nearly 12% of all parties (see Table 6.1). Next in frequency were three *governmental* entities: *ruling bodies* (10.5%); *ministries* (7.1%); or *heads of government* (6.9%). The distinction between *country* and *government* is important because a country entity is amorphous and lacks a specific "address" (e.g., "Israel announced today . . .") while references to governments or their agencies are more concrete and "personalized" (e.g., "The government announced today . . ." or "The Prime Minister today . . .").

By combining entities, the types of dominant parties become even more clear. Thus the overall picture indicates that groups of authority and power, whether legitimate or illegitimate in society, are the most prevalent parties: *government and other authorities, political parties, countries, workers, dissident groups, armed forces/police,* and *people.* On the other hand, the facilitators of society (i.e., *courts, media,* and *educational institutions*) are almost invisible on the newscasts—at least as far as being portrayed as parties to social conflicts.

Examining Table 6.2 for differences among the five countries reveals substantial variability. For example: in South Africa, fewer than 24% of the parties to conflicts were governments and authorities, while in West Germany and Israel more than 40% were of this category. Israel, which always has had at least a dozen political parties represented in the Knesseth, portrayed many more political parties in the news, while South Africa portrayed political parties considerably less than the mean of all the countries (although several parties are represented in its Parliament). American news displayed a marked tendency to refer to parties as *countries* rather than to *governments* of countries (e.g., "Iran today refused . . ." without making a clear attribution of

Table 6.2 Percentage of Entities in Selected Collapsed Categories
by Country (N = 2577)

Entity	Total	U.S.	UK	FRG	Isr.	SA
Government, Authorities	33.3	29.0	31.1	38.1	40.5	23.8
Political Parties	12.4	13.3	11.0	12.3	15.3	8.6
Country	11.9	23.2	4.1	12.3	7.0	17.1
Workers: Organized and Not	7.2	3.0	13.6	6.5	5.8	7.3
Dissident Groups & Dissidents	7.0	4.8	8.5	5.3	6.4	10.1
Armed Forces, Police	5.9	3.4	2.4	8.6	7.7	6.4
People (including hostages)	5.9	7.1	8.3	2.8	4.1	8.1
Industry	4.4	3.7	8.1	6.0	2.7	2.6
Formal Groups of Countries	3.5	3.0	3.9	2.8	2.1	6.6
Religious Groups and Leaders	2.1	2.3	2.8	0.2	2.7	2.1
Courts	1.3	1.8	0.8	2.1	0.7	1.7
Media	1.0	0.5	0.8	0.5	1.3	1.9
Educational Institutions	0.6	1.1	0.4	0.5	0.5	0.4
Other	3.5	3.8	4.2	2.0	3.2	3.3
Total	100.0	100.0	100.0	100.0	100.0	100.0
(n)	2577	435	492	430	753	467

which element of the country "refused"). In the presentation of *workers* as parties there was great variation: the United States presented them as only 3% of its parties, whereas in the United Kingdom 14% of the parties were workers. Nearly as large a variation was found in the presentation of *dissidents*, with the United States lowest (less than 5%), and South Africa highest with over 10%.

Roles of the Parties

The dominant role played by a party was that of *opponent* (85.4%). The only other role that appears in a substantial number of conflict items was that of *interested parties* with 9.2% of all the roles (see Table 6.3).

Table 6.3 Percentage of Parties in Various Roles by Country (N = 2577)

Role	Total	U.S.	UK	FRG	Isr.	SA
Opponents	85.4	86.7	88.7	85.5	88.1	76.7
Interested Parties	9.2	8.5	8.3	7.7	9.0	12.2
Mediators	2.7	2.1	2.2	2.8	2.0	4.9
Arbitrators	2.0	1.6	0.4	3.3	0.8	4.9
Go-Betweens	0.7	1.1	0.4	0.7	0.1	1.3
Total	100.0	100.0	100.0	100.0	100.0	100.0
(n)	2577	435	492	430	753	467

Four of the five countries were quite consistent in their presentation of parties as opponents, with South Africa being the exception. As discussed in the previous chapter, the analysis of complexity in South African newscasts presented more variety in the parties to social conflicts, with the fewest percentage of opponents (77%), the highest percentage of interested parties (12%), mediators (5%), arbitrators (5%), and go-betweens (1%).

Most of the parties were classified as opponents, yet Table 6.4 suggests several entities were over- or underrepresented as opponents. Using plus or minus 10 percentage points as a rough indicator of divergence, *industry* and *workers* were over-represented in their roles as opponents, while *courts, people, groups of countries,* and *religious groups and leaders* were underrepresented as opponents in social conflicts.

The overrepresentation in opponents' roles was quite predictable. Industry and workers were presented almost exclusively as opponents in social conflicts. Such a presentation is consistent with Epstein's (1973) discussion of dramaturgical news practice as well as the Glasgow University Media Group's (1976) characterization of the presentation of industrial disputes.

Given the very high frequency of opponents as parties to conflicts, it was interesting to examine which entities appeared with greater-than-average frequency in *non*-opponent roles. The entities

Table 6.4 Percentage of Role Types for Selected Entities in all Countries

Entity	Opponent	Interested Party	Mediator	Arbitrator	Go Between	Total	(n)[1]
Industry	97.4	2.6	—	—	—	100.0	114
Workers, Labor	96.2	2.7	0.5	0.5	—	100.0	186
Political Parties	94.7	3.4	1.6	—	0.3	100.0	320
Dissidents	93.4	6.1	—	—	—	100.0	181
Armed Forces/ Police	88.8	9.2	1.3	—	0.7	100.0	152
All Government	88.4	7.2	2.6	1.5	0.3	100.0	859
Media	85.2	14.8	—	—	—	100.0	127
Country	79.5	9.1	8.1	0.7	2.6	100.0	307
Religious Groups	72.7	10.9	16.4	—	—	100.0	55
Groups of Countries	63.7	22.0	6.6	6.6	1.1	100.0	91
People, Hostages	58.8	40.5	—	—	0.7	100.0	153
Courts	26.5	—	—	73.5	—	100.0	34
All entities	85.4	9.2	2.7	2.0	0.7	100.0	2479

1. Entity categories containing few cases were omitted; hence this table is based on 2479 cases and not on all 2577 entities.

appearing as relatively high in *non*-opponent roles were: religious groups and leaders as mediators (16%), courts as arbitrators, and groups of countries and people as interested parties.

The finding that more than 40% of those categorized as *people* were cast in the role of interested parties, is provocative. Interested parties were seldom active participants in the conflicts. Instead, they were concerned with what was going on, they were often affected as innocent bystanders, and often they were even victims of conflicts in which other parties were pitched against each other. Thus *people* often were portrayed as objects of social conflict rather than actors—a characterization consistent with an ideology that makes them something acted upon, rather than initiators of action.

Co-Occurring Opponents in Television News

The next phase of the analysis sketches the patterns of combinations in which parties consistently are presented together as

Table 6.5 Percentage of Opponent Co-Occurrences
by Country (N = 876)

Co-Occurrence	Total	U.S.	UK	FRG	Isr.	SA
Government-Government	21.1	19.4	14.1	25.3	30.2	10.1
Government-Political Party	13.4	12.5	18.0	17.3	14.0	5.8
Political Party-Political Party	10.0	11.3	8.0	8.7	14.3	5.8
Country-Country	9.5	20.6	2.9	9.3	3.9	15.2
Government-Workers	9.5	3.1	17.1	8.0	10.1	8.0
Government-Dissidents	8.8	3.8	12.9	8.0	6.2	15.2
Government-People	5.9	5.0	8.2	4.0	6.2	5.8
Industry-Workers	5.6	1.3	14.2	6.7	1.9	5.8
Armed Forces-Dissidents	5.3	3.1	2.4	1.3	8.5	9.4

NOTE: Parties are assigned a rank score reflecting the highest level of representation they were afforded.

opponents in the same conflict item.[1] The examination of the pattern of co-occurring opponents utilized the combined-entity classification scheme and presents the percentage of the most frequently appearing co-occurrences of opponents (Table 6.5).

The most prevalent co-occurrence was a government with another government (21% had two or more governments presented as opponents). Quite obviously, governments and other public authorities were highly visible as opponents, appearing six times in five different combinations in which one entity was a government. This pattern is consistent with the work of Galtung and Ruge (1965) in which they stressed the salience of elite groups and personalities in journalists' perceptions of newsworthiness.

The relatively frequent pairing of governments and countries as parties to the conflicts highlights a stereotypical view of social conflict as beyond the scope of an individual's control. This might express a somewhat xenophobic view of international relations in which countries are frequently in conflict with one another and, therefore, other countries are "my country's" enemies. It also coincides with the perspective suggested earlier that television news content constructs a view of international relations founded in conflict between and among countries and their governments.

Further evidence of the construction of a conflictual symbolic reality was apparent in the prevalence of the co-occurring opponents of several combinations (industry versus workers, government versus dissidents, government versus workers, government versus political party, and political party versus political party). Television news frequently presented the relationships between these parties as one of opposition, thus defining a pattern of adversarial relationships in society.

Although the pattern described above was quite prevalent, an examination of the data indicated some variation among the five countries. The United States, for example, quite frequently presented country versus country co-occurrences, indicating a marked tendency to present social conflicts with countries as parties— rather than a specific government ministry or people of those countries. Such generalized presentations of parties to conflicts might have meant that U.S. audiences did not hear what South Africa's prime minister, P. W. Botha, recommended or what West Germany's *Bundestag* decided; rather, the audience could only hear that South Africa did this and West Germany did that. Such lack of precision characterizes international conflicts as occurring between generalized opponents, thus reinforcing stereotypes of foreign countries and doing little to inform the audience about the other country's government.

The U.S. coverage also differed in its less frequent presentation of government versus workers, government versus dissidents, and industry versus workers as co-occurring opponents. Some of this difference may reflect the fact that governing bodies in the United States (local, state, and federal) operate fewer businesses than do governments of other countries and hence there are fewer labor-management disputes where government is involved. The infrequency of industry versus workers and government versus dissidents, however, suggests that U.S. national newscasts may be nonetheless minimizing these important societal conflicts.

The BBC newscasts varied widely from the overall data, with government versus political party, government versus workers, government versus dissidents, and industry versus workers appearing substantially more than the overall percentages. Concomitantly, government versus government, country versus country, and armed forces versus dissidents appeared less frequently than in the other countries. The British newscasts thus emphasized conflictual opponents *within* the United Kingdom and de-emphasized opponents outside the country. Further, as suggested in *Bad News* (Glasgow University Media Group, 1976), there was a high frequency of industrial conflicts presented on the BBC news. It seems that this phenomenon remained stable from the 1970s into the 1980s.

West Germany's presentation of opponents was quite average, with only government versus political parties somewhat above the overall percentage and armed forces versus dissidents somewhat below the overall percentage.

Israeli newscasts presented a higher frequency of government versus government, political party versus political party, and armed forces versus dissidents conflicts than the five-country average. On the other hand, the IBA newscasts presented country versus country and industry versus workers less frequently than the other countries.

The South African newscasts more frequently presented opponents as country versus country, government versus dissidents, and armed forces versus dissidents than did newscasts in the other countries. At the same time the SABC presented relatively less frequent government versus government, government versus political party, and political party versus political party opponent co-occurrences. For the latter three co-occurrences, South African presentations occurred approximately half as often as the five-country average. The SABC newscasts seemed to present conflicts as revolving around international country versus country disputes or government/armed forces/police versus dissidents. This pattern suggested an emphasis on internal political harmony with fewer political party disputes than the norm, and with dissension being treated as a law-and-order issue.[2]

Table 6.6 Distribution of Level of Representation Measure[1]
(in Percent, N = 2577)

Presentation	Rank Score	Percentage
No representation	0	22.2
Description of position	1	30.7
Quotation	2	24.3
Speaking	3	6.4
Interview	4	13.9
Journalist advocates party's position	5	2.5
Total		100.0

1. Parties are assigned a rank score reflecting the highest level of representation they were afforded.

ACTORS, ROLES, AND BIAS

The final section of this chapter considers the roles that the actors play as well as the interrelationships among the actors in the conflicts. To do this we constructed two indices of bias in the presentation of the actors: *level of representation* (LR) and *reinforcement of representation (RR)*.

For any given party, the LR measure was based on five generally available opportunities a journalist might use in presenting a party to a conflict. A score of 0 was assigned if the journalist utilized *none* of the five opportunities to present the party. When the journalist did utilize any of the five opportunities, however, then the measure was scored for the highest opportunity utilized using the following scale of opportunities (from low to high): (a) presenting a description of the party's position, (b) quoting the party, (c) presenting the party as a speaker, (d) interviewing the party, and (e) actually advocating the party's position. The theoretical rationale was that the five opportunities could be ranked by their importance in representing the party—with a journalist advocating a party's position (something that seldom actually occurred) as the most

Table 6.7 Selected Entities Ranked by Mean Score on Level of Representation Measure (N = 2577)

Entity	Total[1]	U.S.	UK	FRG	Isr.	SA
Political Parties	2.0	2.2	2.4*	1.8	2.0	1.9
People	2.0	2.0	2.4*	0.8	1.9	1.9
Industry	1.8	2.4*	1.7	1.4	2.2	1.9
Workers, Labor	1.8	2.1	2.3*	1.4	1.5	1.4
All Government Entities	1.7	1.7	2.1*	1.6	1.5	1.8
Group of Countries	1.5	1.5	1.8*	1.7	1.1	1.5
Armed Forces, Police	1.3	1.2	1.0	1.1	1.5*	1.4
Country	1.3	1.4	1.4	0.9	1.2	1.6*
Dissidents	1.1	1.3*	1.1	0.7	1.0	1.2
All Entities	1.7	1.7	2.0	1.4	1.6	1.6

1. The entities are ordered from high to low based on their overall LR scores.
* Indicates the country with the highest score for that entity.

forceful representation of a party, while no presentation of the party was clearly the lowest level of representation. The overall mean LR was 1.7 and the standard deviation was 1.4 (see Table 6.6).

The RR measure was based upon the LR measure, and emphasized three of its elements. Thus, in the RR measure, reinforcement was indicated not merely by signaling the presence or absence of the modes of representation, but by weighting three specific modes: (a) the reporter quoting the party, (b) presenting the party actually speaking, and (c) the party being interviewed. Accordingly, the number of quotations was given a weight of 2, the number of on-camera speaking opportunities was given a weight of 3, and the number of interviews was given a weight of 4. The sum of the three products yielded the RR score for each party.[3] The distribution of the RR measure was highly skewed, ranging from 0 to 57, with a mean of 2.6, and standard deviation of 4.7.

Across all five countries (Table 6.7) political parties had the highest average level of representation, thus suggesting that people are more likely to see interviews, hear quotations, and so on, of political parties than of any other party entity. Dissidents were at

Table 6.8 Selected Entities Ranked by Mean Score on Representation Reinforcement Measure (N = 2577)

Entity	Total	U.S.	UK	FRG	Isr.	SA
Political Parties	4.1	6.6*	4.3	3.1	3.6	2.6
People	4.0	6.3*	4.0	1.8	4.8	2.0
Workers, Labor	3.2	7.3*	4.5	1.6	2.2	1.4
Industry	2.8	6.1*	2.0	0.9	4.8	2.3
All Government Entities	2.5	2.7	3.2*	2.3	2.2	2.3
Group of Countries	2.5	2.4	3.2	3.7*	1.3	2.3
Country	1.5	1.9*	1.1	0.8	1.3	1.7
Armed Forces, Police	1.5	1.1	0.3	1.6	2.1*	0.7
Dissidents	1.0	2.3*	0.7	0.2	1.5	0.7
All Entities	2.6	3.7	3.3	2.0	2.6	1.8

* Indicates the country with the highest score for that entity.

the very bottom in level of representation, with country and armed forces/police scoring just slightly above dissidents.

When comparing the five countries, the most distinctive finding was the consistent and relatively high levels of representation of the party entities on the British newscasts and the consistently lower levels on the other countries' newscasts.

When one examines the presentation of each entity across the five countries, for five of the nine entities (political parties, people, workers/labor, government entities, and groups of countries) the United Kingdom ranked highest on LR. Two of the other countries had but a single entity for whom the presentation scores were highest (South Africa for country and Israel for armed forces). The United States had two entities that appear infrequently on the news but were ranked highest on LR (industry and dissidents). German television news consistently afforded a lower LR to parties in conflicts than did the newscasts of the other countries. Despite the differences in absolute values of the LR scores among the five countries, the relative ordering of those entities by level of representation was reasonably consistent.[4]

As for the representation-reinforcement measure, Table 6.8 demonstrated that there was substantial variance among the countries, with the overall mean scores ranging from 1.04 to 4.05. As in the case of the LR measure, the lowest frequencies were for dissidents, armed forces/police, and countries while the highest frequencies were for political parties and people.

The cross-national comparisons put the United States at the highest level of RR for six of the nine party entities. Israeli, German, and British newscasts each had the highest score on only a single entity. The South African news programs did not score highest on any entity.

As with the LR measure, the rank-order correlations among countries were moderate to high, despite the differences in the absolute score levels among the countries. This suggests once again that the United States, the United Kingdom, Israel, and South Africa presented parties in a consistent order—and that West Germany substantially deviated from this pattern.[5]

When simultaneously considering patterns obtained from the two measures, one can delineate three groups of parties. The most visibility was given to political parties, followed closely by people. The second group, which had the widest variation in visibility, included industry, workers, government, and groups of countries. The least visibility was given to countries, armed forces/police, and to dissidents.

There was some seeming inconsistency when looking at the five countries on the two measures. Although British newscasts were particularly high on the LR measure, American newscasts received notably high scores on the RR measure. This differentiation was probably the result of the extensive use of brief and rapidly changing shots and interviews in the American news—more than in the United Kingdom or in any of the other countries, a fact that strongly affected the American RR scores. And yet, Spearman rank-order correlations between the rankings based on the two scores for each of the five countries produced very high coefficients ranging from a low of .87 in the United States to a high of .96 in the

Table 6.9 Mean Scores on Level of Representation Measure and
Representation Reinforcement Measure for Opponents, Interested
Parties, Mediators, Arbitrators, and Go-Betweens (N = 2577)

	Role				
Measure	Opponent	Interested Party	Mediator	Arbitrator	Go-Between
	(2202)	(236)	(70)	(52)	(17)
LR	1.71	1.30	1.39	1.65	1.77
RR	2.78	1.80	1.43	2.12	1.53

United Kingdom. Thus there were differences in the countries'
levels of LR and RR, but at the same time there was at least a
four-nation consistency in the *pattern* of presentation. That is, the
same parties received high representation in four countries, the
same parties received moderate representation, and the same
received low representation.

Finally, we briefly surveyed how the various party entities
scored on the two measures of representation. It was apparent
from Table 6.9 that *opponents* were the primary beneficiaries of
news prominence. In the case of the RR measure the range of
difference was very large (i.e., opponents versus go-betweens).
Go-betweens scored high on LR during their infrequent appearances (only 17 of 2577 parties), but go-betweens and mediators
did not have that representation reinforced by the use of news
production techniques. Clearly, as might be expected, these findings indicated that opponents are the central figures in conflicts.
Somewhat surprisingly, however, those parties seeking to intervene in the conflict—sometimes by attempting to solve it—were
substantially less important in the newscasts' presentations. Moreover, interested parties (who were often victims in the conflict)
were not granted substantial representation.

CONCLUSIONS

Television news in all five countries presented governmental and political forces as the most dominant and frequently appearing parties to social conflicts. The drama of social conflicts did indeed present the viewer with several classic pairs of dramatic opponents: industry versus workers, political parties versus political parties, government/countries versus government/countries, government versus dissidents, and government versus workers. Some of these opponents were matched fairly well in representation (e.g., industry and workers); others, however, differed greatly, as when government ranked higher on both measures of representation than did dissidents.

The newscasts did present stereotypical and generalized pictures of conflicts by highlighting opponents both as the primary parties to conflicts and by providing them with the most representation. Furthermore, the newscasts presented many conflicts as government versus government and country versus country, while characterizing people as interested parties. Finally, the consistency among the four countries (excepting West Germany) suggests a uniformity in the relative presentation of parties across countries.

These patterns lend additional support to our finding that newscasts tend to dramatize social conflict as beyond the control of the people, basing this on the pattern of emphasizing governments and countries as principal opponents in social conflict.

Although the evidence in this chapter tended to support a critical-theory perspective, we also must consider inconsistencies with the argument that television news replicates the dominant ideology's vision of societal structure. In particular, the cross-national pattern of variations require additional consideration before such a conclusion can be established. For example, although dissidents were given low representation in the newscasts (something that obviously would be predicted if the dominant ideology dictates television coverage), armed forces/police consistently scored as low as dissidents in their representation. Although it is possible to argue that the invisibility of armed forces/police reflects the dominant ideology's attempt to understate the presentation of its control forces, thereby masking its exercise of physical force, that argument becomes problematic when taking into account the cross-national data.

The cross-national juxtaposition of the presentation of armed forces and police with that of dissidents is quite intriguing. Whereas in the United States and the United Kingdom dissidents receive higher representation reinforcement scores than armed forces and police, in Israel and West Germany the situation is reversed, namely, higher representation reinforcement scores for the police and armed forces than for dissidents. In South Africa, the level of representation reinforcement was the same for both entities.

Are the dominant ideologies of United States and the United Kingdom more open to portraying dissidents than control forces? Is that pattern reversed in Israel and West Germany? At this point, we are reluctant to base our explanations on such broad societal claims. In our opinion only future research, focusing on a country-by-country analysis of its dominant ideology and its expression in television news can answer these poignant questions.

A central impetus to this study was understanding the relationship between media content and audience perception. Having covered many aspects of content in detail, the next two chapters present our data on audience perception of social conflicts and television news.

NOTES

1. This analysis was based on 876 of the 895 conflict items that presented two or more opponents and that could be identified and coded. In these 876 items there were a total of 2203 opponents appearing in 571 pairs, 194 triples, 83 quadruples, 21 quintets, and 7 sextets. For example, each time an industry opponent appeared in the same item with a workers opponent, a co-occurrence of industry versus workers was noted. Given that the codebook allowed for up to six entities to be coded in any item, it was possible to have multiple opponent co-occurrences in the same item. For example, in one item, six opponents could appear: government A, government B, political party A, political party B, political party C, and armed forces/police. Such an item could produce different combinations of co-occurrences: government versus government; government versus political party; government versus armed forces; political party versus political party; political party versus armed forces.

2. These intercountry differences can be demonstrated in still another manner. Using the data of Table 6.5, Spearman rank-order correlations were computed between each of the 10 pairs of countries. Except for two relatively high correlations (.79 between the rankings of West Germany and the United States and .75 between West Germany and the United Kingdom) all the other eight correlations range from -.29 to +.46, indicating substantial differences between the countries.

3. We consider all the elements in the RR measure as hierarchical. There surely can be no disagreement regarding the mere description of the position and its advocation as being clearly different on the ordinal scale. We wish to argue, however, that the quoting, presenting, and interviewing of parties also exhibit ordinality. Although the latter three elements are all formats in which information on the party's position is provided, making them perhaps laterally equivalent, nevertheless we believe that they do differ in the qualitative way in which the parties are given airtime, hence there is an implied increment in strength. Thus,

RR = (2 × number of quotations) +
     (3 × number of on-camera speaking opportunities) +
     (4 × number of interview clips)

For example, a party who was quoted three times, was not given any on-camera speaking opportunity, but was shown being interviewed by a reporter in two different clips would receive a score of 14 [(2 × 3) + (3 × 0) + (4 × 2) = 14].

4. The 10 Spearman rank-order correlation coefficients (i.e., all permutations of the pairs among the five countries) ranged from .30 to .85. The four lowest correlations, ranging between .30 and .47, were between each of the four countries and West Germany.

5. Of the 10 Spearman rank-order coefficients, nine ranged from .39 to .93, and the one between Israel and West Germany was essentially zero (-.03). Again the correlations between West Germany and the other countries were, on average, the lowest.

PART III

Perception

SEVEN

The Evaluation of News and Social Conflicts

This chapter examines news consumption patterns of young adults and their evaluation of several aspects of social conflicts as they are portrayed in television news. The findings reported here are based on the surveys conducted in the five countries (see Appendix C). The Chapter 8 examines the patterns of perception of the dimensions of social conflict.

NEWS CONSUMPTION AND SOURCES OF INFORMATION ABOUT CONFLICTS

There were substantial differences in the extent to which the young adults in the five countries consumed news on television, radio, and in newspapers (see Table 7.1). As for television, the British and Israeli respondents were relatively heavy viewers of news, whereas the respondents from the United States were relatively light viewers. The data indicated that 40% of the British respondents, 28% of the Israelis, and only 9% of the Americans claimed they watch the news nightly, while 16% of those in West Germany and 17% in South Africa watched the news nightly.[1] As for listening to the news on radio, the Israeli respondents were

Table 7.1 Mean Consumption of News from Television,
Radio, and Newspapers

	Total (1229)	U.S. (238)	UK (229)	FRG (263)	Isr. (253)	SA (246)
Watches national TV news[1]	2.89	2.54	3.24	2.74	3.13	2.81
Listens to radio newscasts[2]	3.23	2.87	3.08	3.29	4.15	2.71
Reads news section of newspapers[3]	2.71	2.61	2.84	2.32	2.91	2.91

1. 1 = never; 2 = rarely; 3 = several times per week; 4 = every evening.
2. 1 = never; 2 = on some days; 3 = once each day; 4 = twice each day; 5 = several times each day.
3. 1 = never; 2 = rarely; 3 = almost every day; 4 = every day.

clearly the heaviest listeners (47% listened to several radio news bulletins each day). In West Germany, 25% listened to several bulletins, and in the remaining three countries listening to radio news was even less frequent.[2] With regard to reading the news section of the daily newspaper, both in Israel and in South Africa 24% read every day, in the United Kingdom 20% read every day, in the United States 15% read every day, and in West Germany only 10% read the news section of a newspaper every day.[3]

We asked the respondents how much each of the three media helped them get information concerning international, national, and local social conflicts. Overall, across all five countries and the three proximity levels (Table 7.2), newspapers were perceived to be most helpful in providing information about social conflicts, followed by television, with radio being least helpful.

As for the levels of proximity, generally speaking across all the countries the three media were most helpful in providing information on international and national conflicts (with very little or no difference among them), whereas they were considerably less helpful in providing information on local conflicts. There were some exceptions, however: in the United States, radio was perceived to be more helpful in providing information on local conflicts than on

Table 7.2 Mean Perceived Utility of Mass Media and
Importance of Information on Social Conflicts

	Total (1229)	U.S. (238)	UK (229)	FRG (263)	Isr. (253)	SA (246)
How helpful is television news in getting information on . . .?[1]						
International conflicts	2.98	2.97	3.27	2.79	3.20	2.69
National conflicts	2.94	3.05	3.24	2.71	3.17	2.55
Local conflicts	2.42	2.90	2.33	2.26	2.65	1.98
How helpful is radio news in getting information on . . .?[1]						
International conflicts	2.44	2.16	2.23	2.38	2.91	2.49
National conflicts	2.50	2.28	2.38	2.41	3.01	2.38
Local conflicts	2.35	2.50	2.11	2.43	2.65	2.05
How helpful are newspapers in getting information on . . .?[1]						
International conflicts	2.96	2.90	2.94	2.74	3.22	3.02
National conflicts	2.99	2.94	3.06	2.76	3.28	2.94
Local conflicts	2.79	2.89	2.51	2.76	3.07	2.72
How important is it for you to know about . . .?[2]						
International conflicts	3.07	2.90	3.25	3.06	2.98	3.20
National conflicts	3.24	2.97	3.36	3.30	3.18	3.39
Local conflicts	3.10	3.00	3.17	3.09	3.03	3.22

1. 1 = doesn't help at all; 2 = helps a little; 3 = helps quite a lot; 4 = helps very much.
2. 1 = not important at all; 2 = not so important; 3 = quite important; 4 = very important.

national or international conflicts, while no differences for radio were
found in West Germany among the three proximity levels. Also, in both
the United States and West Germany there were no differences among
the three proximity levels in terms of the extent to which newspapers
helped in providing information on social conflicts.

As for the differences among the five countries, it seems clear
that in the Israeli case the three media—but mainly radio and
newspapers—were considered as relatively most useful in providing information on social conflicts at the three proximity levels. In
the United Kingdom, television was considered as most useful only
for national and international conflicts. In South Africa television

was considered to be least useful in providing information on conflicts, particularly regarding local conflicts.[4]

Concerning the importance of knowing about conflicts, in all the countries but the United States national conflicts were considered to be most important to know about (in the United States local conflicts were considered most important to know about, but only slightly more than national conflicts). On the other hand, conflicts least important to know about were international conflicts, with the exception of the United Kingdom where the least important conflict category reported was local conflicts.

Across the countries, the greatest perceived importance of knowing about social conflicts was in South Africa, followed by the United Kingdom, West Germany, Israel, and the United States. Looking at each level of proximity, this overall pattern was consistent except for one switch between the United Kingdom and South Africa for first and second place regarding international conflicts. Particularly noticeable differences occurred at the national level between South Africa and the United States, where 51% versus 22% respectively claimed that it was very important to know about social conflicts.

The importance attached by the respondents to knowledge about social conflicts and their evaluation of media usefulness in providing relevant information definitely were correlated with the amount of news consumption, especially with regard to television and newspapers. These findings suggest that the more people want to know about social conflicts, the more they go to the mass media to find out about them. Also, the more they believe that the media are helpful in providing the information, the more news they consume.[5]

OPINIONS ABOUT SOCIAL CONFLICTS IN SOCIETY AND THEIR COVERAGE IN TELEVISION NEWS

The respondents were asked to estimate the number of social conflicts that are going on simultaneously, the frequency of reporting conflicts on TV news, and the portion of the newscast devoted to stories of conflict.

Table 7.3 Mean Perceived Prominence Scores of Social Conflicts in Social Reality and Television News

	Total (1229)	U.S. (238)	UK (229)	FRG (263)	Isr. (253)	SA (246)
How many simultaneously existing real-life conflicts are there?[1]						
International conflicts	2.55	2.66	2.47	2.62	2.39	2.60
National conflicts	2.51	2.61	2.42	2.49	2.45	2.60
Local conflicts	2.45	2.46	2.41	2.47	2.39	2.50
How frequently are conflicts reported in TV news?[2]						
International conflicts	2.67	2.73	2.62	2.90	2.43	2.68
National conflicts	2.63	2.77	2.68	2.74	2.60	2.37
Local conflicts	1.88	2.08	1.71	1.82	2.19	1.60
How much of the newscast includes social conflicts?[3]	3.54	3.54	3.37	2.88	3.13	3.14

1. 1 = none; 2 = several; 3 = many.
2. 1 = hardly ever; 2 = several days per week; 3 = every day.
3. 1 = no part of the newscast; 2 = a small part of it; 3 = about half of it; 4 = most of it; 5 = the whole newscast.

The respondents in all five countries (see Table 7.3) estimated that there were fairly numerous social conflicts going on in the world. Across the five countries 56% of the respondents said that there were many conflicts going on simultaneously at the international level; 53% said that many conflicts were going on at the national level; and 48% claimed that there were many conflicts going on at the local level.

There were no differences at all among the countries concerning local conflicts. On the other hand, concerning national and international conflicts, the respondents in the United Kingdom and Israel estimated that there were fewer conflicts going on compared with the respondents in the United States, West Germany and South Africa. This finding is interesting particularly because it seemingly contradicts the findings of the content analysis, reported earlier, whereby news in Israel and the United Kingdom had the greatest relative frequency of social conflicts in their respective newscasts.

As for the perception of the prominence of social conflicts *in the news*, here, too, many conflicts were perceived to be reported. Moreover, in the case of international conflicts, in all five countries, television news was perceived as presenting more conflicts than there were in the "real" world. This was also the case for national conflicts, except for South Africa. Finally, in the case of local conflicts, television news was perceived to be presenting far *fewer* conflicts than were perceived to exist in the real world.

Comparing the perceptions of the two realms of reality, it seemed especially noteworthy to point out the extreme relative standing of the South African respondents with regard to national and local conflicts. Although South Africans maintained that there were many social conflicts in the real world, they claimed that there was relatively little reporting of social conflicts on South African television. This was particularly manifest regarding local conflicts with 13% of the respondents claiming that there were hardly any such conflicts in their country's newscasts, compared with 0% to 1% in the other countries.

As for perceived prominence of social conflicts in the newscasts, the American and British respondents claimed that their respective networks presented the greatest portions of the newscasts devoted to social conflict, and the lowest level was reported by the West German respondents, with Israel and South Africa in the middle with the same scores. Indeed, in the United States and the United Kingdom, 61% and 47% of the respondents, respectively, evaluated the full newscast or most of it as being devoted to social conflict, whereas in the three other countries the comparable figures were only from 30% to 35%.

The respondents also were asked a series of questions concerning conflict: how often certain conflicts affected other conflicts and how often conflicts were caused by past events or disputes. When examining the data of both issues, across the five countries it was evident once more that there were trends going from international to national to local conflicts (see Table 7.4). International conflicts were perceived to be most interrelated with other conflicts and to

Table 7.4 Mean Perceived Interrelatedness and Causality of Social Conflicts in Real Life[1]

	Total (1229)	U.S. (238)	UK (229)	FRG (263)	Isr. (253)	SA (246)
How often do conflicts have an impact on other conflicts?						
International conflicts	2.34	2.42	2.18	2.49	2.15	2.47
National conflicts	2.20	2.32	2.07	2.19	2.06	2.36
Local conflicts	1.64	1.68	1.51	1.57	1.74	1.69
How often are conflicts caused by past events or disputes?						
International conflicts	2.43	2.54	2.47	2.46	2.17	2.11
National conflicts	2.19	2.18	2.02	2.11	2.11	2.50
Local conflicts	1.85	1.88	1.76	1.66	1.80	2.15

1. 1 = seldom; 2 = sometimes; 3 = often.

be caused by past events and disputes, while local conflicts were perceived to be least interrelated and to be least caused by past events and disputes. The only exception to this pattern was in the South African sample, in which the respondents claimed that national conflicts more often were caused by past events and disputes than were international and local conflicts.

Regarding the perceived impact of other conflicts, it seemed that there were different patterns for the three levels of proximity. For international conflicts, the responses of the Americans, West Germans and South Africans were quite similar, while those of the British and Israelis were somewhat different. Respondents in the first group of countries (the United States, West Germany, South Africa) saw more impact of conflicts on each other compared to the latter group (United Kingdom, Israel). As for the national conflicts, the order of the countries was different, being led by South Africa and the United States, followed by West Germany, the United Kingdom and Israel. Finally, with regard to local conflicts, the scores are lower, more closely grouped, and ordered differently with Israel first followed by South Africa, the United States, West Germany, and the United Kingdom.[6]

Table 7.5 Mean Perceived Importance of Reporting on,
Utility for Society, and Reality of Presentation of
Social Conflicts in Television News

	Total (1229)	U.S. (238)	UK (229)	FRG (263)	Isr. (253)	SA (246)
Is it desirable for TV news to report on . . . ?[1]						
International conflicts	2.58	2.54	2.49	2.61	2.56	2.68
National conflicts	2.63	2.63	2.55	2.67	2.63	2.67
Local conflicts	2.42	2.50	2.29	2.51	2.36	2.42
Does TV news present . . . the way they are in real life?[2]						
International conflicts	2.23	2.21	2.17	2.32	2.38	2.06
National conflicts	2.20	2.28	2.28	2.36	2.28	1.77
Local conflicts	2.23	2.37	2.28	2.35	2.31	1.86
In real life, are conflicts good or bad for society?[3]	2.60	2.95	2.45	2.81	2.23	2.55
On TV news, are conflicts presented as good or bad for society?[4]	2.20	2.41	2.15	2.37	2.09	1.97

1. 1 = not at all desirable; 2 = desirable; 3 = very desirable.
2. 1 = not at all; 2 = to some extent; 3 = to a large extent.
3. 1 = all are bad; 2 = most are bad; 3 = about an equal amount are good and bad; 4 = most are good; 5 = all are good.
4. 1 = all presented as bad; 2 = most presented as bad; 3 = about equal; 4 = most presented as good; 5 = all presented as good.

With regard to the notion that conflicts are caused by previous events or disputes, a somewhat similar picture appeared. Concerning international conflicts, in all countries with the exception of Israel, 55% to 59% claimed this happened often (in Israel only 21%). Regarding national conflicts, "often" was selected most by the South Africans (56%), followed by the Americans (30%), the West Germans (28%), and the British (21%), while the Israelis were once again in last place with only 19%. Finally, with respect to local conflicts, in South Africa 38% of the respondents said that conflicts often are caused by previous events and disputes, compared with 15% to 18% in West Germany, the United Kingdom, and the United States and only 7% in Israel.

Regarding the perceived reality of portrayal by television news, there were very small differences among the three proximity levels (Table 7.5). In South Africa, however, the national conflicts and local conflicts were perceived to be relatively much less realistic than were the international conflicts.

There were no differences among four of the five countries, with South Africans stressing once more the disparity between the "real" world and its coverage by television. The percentages exemplify this even more dramatically: on the average, only 17% of South African respondents claimed that their television news presents social conflicts *to a large extent* like real life, whereas in the other four countries the average was 36%. Conversely, 27% of the South African sample claimed that their television news presents social conflicts *not at all* like "real" life, whereas in the other countries only 6% responded in this manner.

The data indicate that social conflicts were perceived by young adults as relatively detrimental for society, both in terms of their occurrence in real life and in terms of their presentation in television news. In the United States the respondents gave the relatively most positive evaluations of social functions of conflicts, while in Israel the evaluations of conflicts were the most negative (see Table 7.5).

As for the evaluation of social conflicts in television news, in the United States they were most positive (conflict presented as being relatively good for society), while the most negative evaluations were made in South Africa and Israel (conflict presented as relatively bad for society). There was a gap, however, in the evaluation of social conflicts in real life and their presentation on television news. Thus, for example, concerning the "real" world, an average of 50% in all the countries claimed that social conflicts were mostly or all bad for society, whereas an average of 68% claimed that most or all social conflicts are presented on the news as being bad for society.

The differences found between the countries were quite striking as well: 73% of the Israeli respondents gave negative evaluations concerning the real world compared with only 29% of the respondents in the United States; as for television news, the range was between 76% of the respondents evaluating its presentation of conflicts as negative in South Africa and 58% doing so in the United States.

Table 7.6 Mean Perceived Prominence Interrelatedness, Background Presentation, and Advocation of Positions in Social Conflicts in TV News[1]

	Total (1229)	U.S. (238)	UK (229)	FRG (263)	Isr. (253)	SA (246)
How often are ... conflicts linked together with other conflicts on TV news?						
International	1.98	2.14	1.87	2.00	2.02	1.89
National	2.03	2.20	1.99	1.98	2.02	1.97
Local	1.61	1.67	1.47	1.52	1.86	1.51
Generally, how often do news people explain the background of ... conflicts?						
International	1.87	1.75	1.77	1.97	2.19	1.67
National	1.99	1.98	2.12	2.00	2.19	1.65
Local	1.98	2.07	2.04	1.81	2.28	1.70
How often do newspeople take sides with the position of one of the opponents in ... conflicts?						
International	1.79	1.58	1.88	1.90	1.62	1.98
National	1.81	1.53	1.77	1.90	1.66	2.20
Local	1.74	1.58	1.73	1.80	1.57	2.03

1. 1 = seldom; 2 = sometimes; 3 = often.

As with the desirability ascribed to the coverage of conflicts, national conflicts were considered the most desirable type of conflict to be reported by television. This was the case in all countries except for a minuscule difference in the case of South Africa, which favored the covering of international conflicts. Local conflicts were reported as least desirable for television news coverage in all the countries.

The respondents were asked three sets of questions: how often are conflicts linked together with other conflicts on TV news; how often do newspeople explain the background of conflicts; and how often do newspeople advocate the positions of one of the opponents in the conflicts?

Regarding the linkage of conflict items across the five countries, this phenomenon clearly was more pronounced among the national and international conflicts than in local conflicts. No clear pattern emerged among the countries: the U.S. respondents scored higher than the other respondents on international and national conflicts, and the Israelis scored higher than the other four countries' respondents on local conflicts (see Table 7.6).

As for the explanations given by newspeople, across the five countries international conflicts were ranked lowest on this variable. The highest scores were given to national conflicts in the United Kingdom and West Germany and to local conflicts in the United States, Israel and South Africa. As for differences among the countries, the Israelis reported the highest degree of background explanation given in the news and the South Africans reported the least amount of background given.

Finally, as to the extent to which newspeople advocated their positions when reporting on conflict stories, it seemed that there were no meaningful differences among the three proximity levels in four of the countries; however, in South Africa there was a slight tendency to advocate positions more frequently when reporting on national conflicts compared with local or international conflicts. Moreover, when comparing the data across the five countries, the South African respondents clearly reported more advocation of positions by journalists than in any of the other countries, and the American respondents reported the least amount of such reporting. The Israelis were closest to the Americans, the West Germans were closer to the South Africans, and the British were somewhat in the middle.

Perceived Prominence of
People in the News

Two sets of questions were asked concerning the extent to which "important" (e.g., leaders and officials) and "less important" people (e.g., the man on the street) were actually presented (i.e., shown and/or interviewed) in the news when dealing with social conflicts.

Regarding the prominence of important people in the news, the highest scores in all the countries were for national conflicts (see Table 7.7). The second position was taken by international conflicts in all countries except the United States. As for the less important

Table 7.7 Mean Perceived Prominence of Important and Less Important People in TV News[1]

	Total (1229)	U.S. (238)	UK (229)	FRG (263)	Isr. (253)	SA (246)
When reporting on . . . conflicts, how often are relatively important people shown or interviewed in the newscast?						
International	2.43	2.44	2.37	2.60	2.31	2.42
National	2.55	2.52	2.59	2.61	2.43	2.58
Local	2.32	2.51	2.30	2.44	2.20	2.16
When reporting on . . . conflicts, how often are less important people shown or interviewed in the newscast?						
International	1.57	1.56	1.60	1.49	1.76	1.44
National	1.80	1.78	1.99	1.73	2.02	1.52
Local	2.09	2.15	2.28	2.13	2.24	1.63

1. 1 = seldom; 2 = sometimes; 3 = often.

people, in all the countries the highest scores were for the local conflicts, and the lowest were for the international conflicts. The cross-country examination of the data showed that for important people, the highest scores were in West Germany and the lowest in Israel, whereas for less important people the highest scores were in Israel and the lowest in South Africa.

CONCLUSIONS

This chapter examined audiences' attitudes and evaluations related to news media, social conflicts, and the way conflicts were presented in the news. Respondents in all the countries attached importance to the information on social conflicts and consumed news from various media in order to find out what was happening in the world and around the corner. Using summed rankings of the five countries for each of the three media, it was clear that the Israelis were the heaviest news consumers, followed by the respondents in the United Kingdom, South Africa, West Germany, and the United States.

And yet—beyond the absolute differences among the countries—when examining the correlation between news consumption and the various attitudes expressed by the individuals, we generally found no statistical relationship between the extent of news consumption and attitudes concerning the coverage of conflict in the media. This was similar to what we found concerning the relationship between media consumption and the perception of the dimensions of social conflicts, as we shall report in Chapter 8.

NOTES

1. In the United States, on the other hand, 49% claimed they either rarely or never watched television news. In Israel only 13% and in the United Kingdom only 14% rarely or never watched the news, and in West Germany and South Africa, respectively, 40% and 32% never watched or rarely watched the major evening newscast.

2. In addition, 57% of the South African respondents claimed that they never listen to radio news or only listen on some days, and the respective reports in the remaining four countries were 52% in the United States, 43% in the United Kingdom, 38% in West Germany, and only 9% in Israel.

3. Also, 67% of the German respondents rarely or never read the news section of a newspaper, 48% in the United States did not read the newspaper regularly, and 32% in the United Kingdom, 31% in Israel, and 29% in South Africa did not read the newspaper frequently.

4. In South Africa 32% claimed that television did not help at all, compared with a range of 5% to 19% in the other four countries.

5. For each medium, 15 zero-order correlations between the consumption and the importance of knowing about conflicts were calculated (at the three levels in the five countries). For television, only 8 correlations reached or exceeded .20, with the highest being .44 (the highest correlations were for West Germany, while none reached .20 for South Africa). For newspapers, only 10 correlations reached .22, with the highest being .37 (the United States had the highest correlations and the United Kingdom had the lowest). And for radio, of the 15 correlations, only 1 was as large as .22 (for Israel, for national conflicts). The correlations between the perceived help afforded by the media in providing information on the conflicts and consumption showed stronger and more consistent positive relationships. Of the 15 correlations with television news viewing, 8 ranged between .24 and .34. For newspaper reading, all the correlations but one (local conflicts in the United Kingdom) were higher than .20, ranging from .22 to .56. For radio, 14 correlations ranged from .24 to .44.

6. International conflicts were perceived to have an impact often by 50% in the United States, 54% in the United Kingdom, and 52% in South Africa, 27% in West Germany, and 19% in Israel. National conflicts were perceived to have an impact often by 43% in South Africa, 37% in the United States, 29% in West Germany, 21% in the United Kingdom, and only 10% in Israel. Finally, regarding local conflicts, in South Africa 14% replied using the "often" option, 13% used it in the United States, 9% in the United Kingdom, 8% in West Germany, and only 2% in Israel.

EIGHT

The Perception of Conflict Dimensions

Although the previous chapter dealt with our respondents' evaluation of several aspects of social conflicts, the present chapter is concerned with the perception of the three dimensions of social conflict in the two realms of reality—the "real" world and the world of television news. The analyses presented here are an attempt to answer four research questions.

The first question was whether in perceiving social conflicts people differentiate between the dimensions of complexity, intensity, and solvability. Based on our earlier work (Adoni, Cohen, & Mane, 1984; Cohen, Adoni, & Drori, 1983) we suggest that when people think about social conflicts they tend to distinguish among these dimensions. In the present study we were concerned with the universality of this perception process and hence wished to determine if it occurs with all social conflicts, regardless of their specific topic, location, and the nature of the parties participating and involved in them.

The second question was whether people can differentially perceive social conflicts in the realm of television news and in the realm of social reality. This question was based on the assumption that all media contents are the result of the complementary processes of selection and composition, so that presentation of social conflict on television news, by definition, cannot be identical with real social conflicts. Moreover, people's experiences with the mass media have conditioned them to notice discrepancies between the "real" world and the symbolic world, and hence they are able to draw some distinctions between the two. This argument would be in contrast with the initial-cultivation hypothesis (Gerbner & Gross, 1976) and more in line with the concepts of "mainstreaming" offered later by Gerbner and his colleagues (Gerbner, Gross, Morgan, & Signorelli, 1980).

The third research question reintroduces the notion of *proximity* as a variable that influences perceptions of social conflict. Specifically, we wished to discover if people relate differentially to conflicts that occur at close psychological and physical proximity (e.g., local conflicts) compared with conflicts that are relatively remote to the individual (e.g., international conflicts). The location of conflicts thus provides a marker variable for proximity, as local conflicts signify closeness and international conflicts indicate remoteness. National conflicts fall in between the other two categories. The assumption here was that events that occur at various distances from the person's daily experience require and provide different kinds of cues needed to understand and interpret the conflicts (Ball-Rokeach & DeFleur, 1976; Berger & Luckmann, 1967).

The fourth and final research question combines the latter two. Based on media-dependency theory, it was suggested that the more remote conflicts are from the individual's life experience (i.e., international conflicts), the more there would be congruence between the individual's perception of conflicts in social reality and the manner in which they are presented on television news. Conversely, the more proximate conflicts are to the individual's experience (i.e., local conflicts), the less similarity between the two realms of reality. Thus people's perceptions of distant conflicts would be relatively more media-defined, and hence we would expect relatively little differentiation in their perception of the two realms. In contrast, when people have more nonmedia sources of information—including the entire range of interpersonal acquaintances—they would tend to be less dependent upon media. In such cases, it would be more likely that there would be differences in people's perception of mediated portrayal in the "real" world of nearby social conflicts.[1]

The four research questions were examined in three different, yet complementary ways: first, by comparing both the mean scores of each of the variables as well as difference scores computed between the "reality" and TV news scores for each of the dimensions of social conflict at the three levels of proximity; second, by generating smallest space analysis (SSA) maps for each of the five countries in order to examine the structure of the interrelationships among the variables; and third, by analyzing the magnitudes of the relationships.

THE OVERALL PERCEPTION OF
SOCIAL CONFLICTS

The respondents in each of the five countries were asked to what extent they believed international, national, and local social conflicts were complex, intense, and difficult to solve. The nine questions resulting from all the permutations of these variables were put to the respondents separately concerning the "real" world and the world of television news (see Appendix C).

The first overall and highly consistent finding based on the mean scores was that in all the countries, for each of the dimensions and in both realms of reality, international conflicts nearly always were perceived to be the most severe—that is, more complex, more intense, and more difficult to solve (see Table 8.1).[2] The only exception to this was in the Israeli case, in which the presentations of international and national conflicts on television news were perceived to be of equal intensity. Also, local conflicts were always perceived to be the least severe (i.e., the least complex, the least intense, and the least difficult—or easiest—to solve).

The second overall finding was that, controlling for country and dimension, conflicts in the "real" world tended to be perceived as more severe than conflicts in television news. This pattern was less uniform than the effect of proximity, as there were several exceptions (13 of 45 possibilities).[3] Once again, the Israeli data

Table 8.1 Mean Scores[1] for the Three Dimensions in Both Realms
of Reality and Three Levels of Proximity

	U.S. (238)	UK (229)	FRG (263)	Isr. (253)	SA (246)
"Real" complexity					
International	2.8	2.7	2.5	2.6	2.7
National	2.4	2.3	2.4	2.5	2.4
Local	1.9	1.8	2.1	1.9	2.0
"Real" intensity					
International	2.7	2.7	2.4	2.6	2.6
National	2.3	2.4	2.3	2.4	2.2
Local	1.9	1.8	2.2	1.8	1.9
"Real" difficulty of solving					
International	2.8	2.8	2.8	2.6	2.8
National	2.2	2.2	2.2	2.4	2.5
Local	1.9	1.8	2.0	1.8	2.1
TV news complexity					
International	2.5	2.4	2.2	2.3	2.3
National	2.3	2.2	2.1	2.4	2.1
Local	1.7	1.6	1.5	1.8	1.5
TV news intensity					
International	2.7	2.5	2.5	2.5	2.6
National	2.3	2.3	2.3	2.5	2.0
Local	1.8	1.6	1.5	1.9	1.6
TV news difficulty of solving					
International	2.7	2.8	2.6	2.6	2.6
National	2.2	2.1	2.2	2.4	2.2
Local	1.8	1.7	1.9	2.0	1.8
Mean total scores by dimensions					
"Real" complexity	2.4	2.3	2.3	2.3	2.4
"Real" intensity	2.3	2.3	2.3	2.3	2.3
"Real" difficulty of solving	2.3	2.3	2.3	2.3	2.5
TV complexity	2.2	2.0	2.0	2.2	1.9
TV intensity	2.3	2.2	2.1	2.3	2.0
TV difficulty of solving	2.2	2.2	2.2	2.3	2.2
Mean total overall scores					
Reality	2.3	2.3	2.3	2.3	2.4
Television	2.2	2.1	2.1	2.3	2.1

1. Highest possible score = 3; lowest possible score = 1. Scores rounded to one digit beyond the
decimal point.

provided the greatest number of exceptions (three reversals and two ties), whereas in both the United Kingdom and South Africa there was only one tie in each country.

Based on the relative rankings, there was no systematic effect of proximity on the perception of the conflict dimensions when comparing television news and the real world. The countries did vary systematically, however, when assaying the effect of the realms on the dimensions (Table 8.2).[4] The rank order correlations within each of the two realms of reality also revealed inconsistencies.[5] In contrast, the rank order correlations of countries showed that there were indeed some noticeable regularities. For example, the South African sample consistently gave responses suggesting a high degree of difficulty in solving social conflicts at the three proximity levels. In other words, all "real" social conflicts in South Africa were perceived as highly difficult to solve. Conversely, responses from the British sample indicated the opposite (i.e., a low level of difficulty of solving "real" social conflicts).

In the realm of television news, the West German and South African respondents indicated that social conflicts at all three levels of proximity were of relatively low complexity, whereas the American sample indicated that the respondents believed that social conflicts, as presented on television news, were of high complexity at all levels of proximity.

Respondents in the United Kingdom, Israel, and the United States differentiated between international conflicts and national/local conflicts on difficulty of solvability in the realm of television news. British respondents perceived international conflicts to be the most difficult to solve while perceiving national and local conflicts as relatively easy to solve. A similar, albeit less dramatic, pattern was found for the U.S. respondents. In contrast, the Israeli respondents indicated that television news presents international conflicts as very easy to solve while presenting national and local conflicts as very difficult to solve.

Summarizing the findings of the two tables we wish to emphasize that patterns of conflict perception among all the respondents were differentiated along the three key variables of the study: the dimensions of conflict, the realms of reality, and the location.

Table 8.2 Rankings[1] of the Five Countries on the Perceptual
Dimensions in Both Realms of Reality and at the Three Proximity
Levels (based on mean scores)

	U.S. (238)	UK (229)	FRG (263)	Isr. (253)	SA (246)
"Real" complexity					
International	1	2	5	4	3
National	3	5	4	1	2
Local	4	5	1	3	2
"Real" intensity					
International	1	2	5	4	3
National	4	2	3	1	5
Local	2	5	1	4	3
"Real" difficulty of solving					
International	2	4	3	5	1
National	5	4	3	2	1
Local	3	5	2	4	1
TV complexity					
International	1	2	5	3	4
National	2	3	4	1	5
Local	2	3	4	1	5
TV intensity					
International	1	3	4	5	2
National	3	2	4	1	5
Local	2	4	5	1	3

(continued)

South African respondents perceived social conflicts as being the
most severe in the real world, while they ranked fourth in terms of
perceived severity on television news. Israelis, on the other hand,
reported social conflicts on television news as the most severe of
all the five countries, yet ranked fourth in the severity of conflicts
in the real world. And although the American sample maintained
its relative ranking in the two realms, none of the other four
countries kept the same relative position in both realms of reality.

Table 8.2 Continued

	U.S. (238)	UK (229)	FRG (263)	Isr. (253)	SA (246)
TV difficulty of solving					
International	2	1	3	5	4
National	4	5	3	1	2
Local	4	5	2	1	3
Summed Rankings for Dimensions, Proximity levels					
"Real" complexity	8	12	10	8	7
"Real" intensity	7	9	9	9	11
"Real"difficulty of solving	10	13	8	11	3
TV complexity	5	8	13	5	14
TV intensity	6	9	13	7	10
TV difficulty of solving	10	11	8	7	9
International reality	4	8	13	13	7
National reality	12	11	10	4	8
Local reality	9	15	4	11	6
International television news	4	6	12	13	10
National television news	9	10	11	3	12
Local television news	8	12	11	3	11
Overall summed rankings					
Reality	25	34	27	28	21
Television news	21	28	34	19	33

1. The rankings are based on the mean scores reported in Table 8.1. The lower the number, the higher the ranking.

THE STRUCTURE OF PERCEPTION

The structure of the perception was examined by creating SSA maps that are based on the mapping sentence in Chapter 2. Five SSA maps were produced (one per country). The conflict dimensions as well as the realms of reality were not expected to be arranged in any particular order because of their inherent non-ordinal qualitative nature, whereas the proximity variable was expected to be ordered on the scale from low proximity to high proximity.[6]

Figure 8.1 presents two schematic maps illustrating the partitioning of the space according to the three dimensions, the three values of the proximity measure, and the two realms of reality. In general, the maps for the five countries present quite similar interrelationships with regard to the three dimensions of social conflict. The division of the space among the three dimensions is evident, with two different structures emerging: one nearly identical pattern for the United Kingdom, the United States, West Germany, and South Africa, and the other for Israel. In all five countries the solvability dimension is positioned uniquely on one side of the space, and in all countries but Israel there is some fusion between the space allocated to complexity and intensity. Also, the pattern for all the countries but Israel shows the complexity data points extending in a linear fashion through the space of the intensity dimension. In the Israeli sample, the complexity dimension is situated on the other side of the space, with the intensity dimensions lying between the complexity and the solvability dimensions.

These patterns clearly answer our first research question: the respondents' perception of social conflicts was organized in terms of the three conflict dimensions. The differentiation in the patterns of perception was most evident in Israel, while in the other four countries there was some blending between the complexity and intensity dimensions. The pattern of blending these two dimensions was very similar in the maps of the four countries.

As for the second research question, in all the countries with the exception of Israel the patterns of conflict perception were organized according to the two realms of reality. For the United Kingdom, the United States, and West Germany the division was essentially into two clear halves, whereas for South Africa there was a clustering of the data points of television news in the center of the map with the data points of the "real" world forming an external concentric circle around the world of television news. In sum, the SSA maps seem to indicate that there was a clear distinction in the perception between the two realms of reality (with the exception of the Israeli sample).

The third and final component of the pattern of perception was the division according to the proximity variable. This variable

Dimensions and proximity

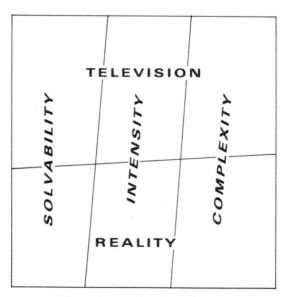

Dimensions and realms of reality

Figure 8.1. Schematic SSA Maps of the Perception of Social Conflict by Dimensions, Proximity, and Realms of Reality

organized the pattern of perception in all the countries and yielded a very clear partitioning of the space into three regions according to international, national, and local conflicts. Without exception, the international conflicts lay on one end of the space while the local conflicts lay at the other end, with national conflicts occupying the middle area.

Examining the joint partitioning of the space by realms of reality and the proximity variable, we found that the division of space by the three proximity levels appeared in the same order and in a parallel fashion for both realms of reality. This finding further reinforced the differentiation according to local, national, and international conflicts by showing that it occurred in both realms of reality.

The Media Dependency Effect
on the Perception of Conflicts

Our fourth research question, concerning the media dependency hypothesis bears upon the combined effect of realm of reality and proximity on the perception of the severity of social conflicts. Specifically, we predicted that the difference between the severity of social conflicts in the two realms would be maximal for local conflicts and minimal for international conflicts.

For each of the proximity levels we computed cross-realm correlations between the two realms, averaged across the three dimensions.[7] If our assumption was correct, the correlations should have been highest for the international social conflicts and lowest for the local social conflicts.

Our expectations were supported only partially (Table 8.3). In South Africa the pattern of correlations across the three proximity levels was as expected. In Israel and the United States the correlations were lower for the local proximity level compared with the international level, as expected, but the correlations for the national level was higher than expected. Thus we concluded that there was a weak trend, indicating that the more remote the conflicts are from people's unmediated experiences—as in the case of international conflicts—the more they are dependent upon the media for their knowledge, understanding, and interpretation of social conflicts.

Table 8.3 Mean Cross-Realm (Reality/Television)[1] Monotonicity Coefficients at each Proximity Level[2]

	U.S. (238)	UK (229)	FRG (263)	Isr. (253)	SA (246)
Proximity levels					
International	.68	.56	.29	.55	.62
National	.50	.55	.47	.58	.39
Local	.57	.56	.36	.40	.21

1. Each entry represents the mean of three coefficients: complexity of reality with complexity of television; intensity of reality with intensity of television; and solvability of reality with solvability of television.
2. The number of cases in parentheses excludes missing cases.

CONCLUSIONS

This chapter demonstrated how young adults in the five countries organized their perceptions of social conflicts in the "real" world and in the world of television news. We demonstrated that their patterns of perception tended to be ordered according to three sets of variables: the dimensions of social conflicts, their proximity, and realms of reality. What is theoretically important is that the structures of perception of all the respondents were similar. These findings suggest that this phenomenon is not culturally specific. Moreover, it is related neither to the nature of the particular social conflicts as experienced in various countries nor to the idiosyncratic manner of conflict portrayal in television news.

It is interesting to note that this differentiation was *not* related to the amount of television news viewing. This reinforces an earlier finding from an Israeli study, namely, that the amount of news viewing was not related to—and thereby could not affect—one's perception of social conflicts. What was suggested by Cohen et al. (1983) was that "if you've seen one, you've seen them all." In other words, because television news develops certain formats and rules for presenting social conflicts (which we believe is the case), once the viewer has seen a certain number of such portrayals, he or she develops a mental schema of the way the conflicts are presented. Therefore, an extremely heavy news viewer will not necessarily have a different perception of conflicts compared with a light viewer. The present data represent five independent replications of this general phenomenon, which makes it all the more significant.[8]

The findings of this study also reinforced the notion that people are able to make distinctions between the way television presents various aspects of the "real" world and what they think the world is really like. This has been found to be particularly manifest in the case of South Africa, where the gap between the way social conflicts were perceived to be in the real world and in the world of television news was the most salient.

NOTES

1. The proximity variable was operationalized in the questionnaire by using the *location* of a conflict (local, national, international). Location here partially parallels the location variable (foreign, domestic, both) in the content analysis. Specifically, *international* was used to parallel *foreign* in representing remote conflicts. In the questionnaire, however, we refined the concept of *domestic* conflicts by differentiating between national and local conflicts. By using *international*, *national*, and *local* we avoided the terms *foreign* and *domestic*, which we judged that respondents from five different countries might interpret differently.

2. In the following table we also present the percentage of "high" scores as dramatic illustrations of the differences.

	U.S. (238)	UK (229)	FRG (263)	Isr. (253)	SA (246)
"Real" complexity					
International	85	78	56	65	78
National	48	35	40	48	49
Local	15	12	27	17	27
"Real" intensity					
International	76	75	53	63	69
National	39	39	39	40	34
Local	16	16	36	14	26
"Real" difficulty of solving					
International	83	77	76	65	86
National	24	23	25	41	48
Local	8	8	13	11	27

(continued)

Continued.

	U.S. (238)	UK (229)	FRG (263)	Isr. (253)	SA (246)
TV news complexity					
International	57	48	33	37	40
National	36	23	21	44	31
Local	9	6	5	15	9
TV news intensity					
International	69	58	57	51	62
National	35	36	36	47	26
Local	15	9	7	23	12
TV news difficulty of solving					
International	74	78	65	63	65
National	21	17	22	38	32
Local	8	7	13	17	17

3. There were nine cases where the presentation of television news at any given proximity level was perceived as equal to the corresponding score for the "real" world, and four cases of reversal where the score for news was higher than for the "real world."

4. For example, comparing the ranking for "real complexity" and "news complexity" across locations revealed wide variation. The international location rankings were almost identical, yielding a Spearman rank-order coefficient of .90; the national location rankings were inconsistent, with a Spearman coefficient of only .30; and the local rankings were moderate and negatively related (–.50). A similar inconsistency appears between "real intensity" and "news intensity": for international conflicts the rank order correlation was .80; for national conflicts the correlation was .90; and for the local conflicts it was –.30. For solvability, the three rank order correlations for the international, national, and local conflicts were .10, .80, and .30, respectively. Thus there were inconsistencies for all nine dimension-location combinations when comparing realms.

5. For example, for the difficulty of solving dimension, in the realm of reality, the rank order correlation between international and national conflicts was .10; between international and local conflicts it was .80; and between national and local conflicts the rank order correlation was .50. In the realm of television news, on the other hand, the three rank order correlations were –1.00, –.90, and .90, respectively.

6. The variables in the present SSA maps were the 18 questions based on all the permutations of the dimensions (complexity, intensity, and solvability), proximity levels (international, national and local), and realms of reality (television news and social reality). The range of the individual scores for each of the variables was from 1 (which was assigned for low complexity, low intensity, and low difficulty of solving) to 3 (which was assigned for high complexity, high intensity,

and high difficulty of solving). The input for the maps was a matrix of weak monotonicity coefficients. Each run of the SSA program yielded a set of three two-dimensional maps that present the structure among all 18 variables. Initially, each SSA map was generated three times for each of the five countries: once for the respondents from the academic track; once for the respondents from the vocational track (except for the South African sample, which consisted only of academic respondents); and finally, for the entire sample in each country. Because the country maps for academic and vocational respondents were very similar and the combined sample produced a better fit between the input correlations and the SSA output (i.e., the coefficients of alienation were lower), all further country analyses are based on the maps produced by samples combining academic and vocational students.

7. Each entry in Table 8.3 is the mean of three correlations: complexity of the "real" world with complexity of TV news; intensity of the real world with intensity of TV news; and difficulty of solving in the real world with difficulty of solving on TV news.

8. In the survey questionnaire we asked the respondents two pertinent questions: "How many hours do you spend each day viewing television?" and, more specifically, "How often do you watch television news?" (in each country's questionnaire we emphasized that we were referring to the newscast that reports national and international news). As expected, we found some differences between the countries on these two variables. In general, respondents in the United States were the heaviest television viewers with an average of nearly 2 hours of viewing daily; Israeli respondents were the second highest viewers with slightly more than 1.5 hours per day; and the three other countries followed with slightly less than 1.5 hours of television viewing per day. As for the frequency of viewing television news, the most regular viewers were the British (46% claimed they watch the news several evenings per week and 40% said they watch nightly); next came the Israelis with 60% reporting viewing several times per week and 28% viewing nightly; third were the South Africans with 51% several times per week and 17% nightly; fourth came the West German respondents with 44% reporting viewing several times each week and 16% viewing nightly; and finally the United States sample indicated that 42% watched the news several times each week and 9% said they watched the news nightly. And yet—despite the variability within and among the five countries in terms of television viewing in general and the frequency of viewing television news—when we correlated these measures with the entire array of variables concerning the perception of social conflicts, the relationships obtained were mainly not significant. Whenever a coefficient was statistically significant it had, relatively, a very low absolute level. Indeed, of the 180 correlations (18 variables in each of the five countries for the two television viewing variables) only 26 (or 14%) were significant at the $p < .05$ level, and the highest absolute value for any correlation was .19. Of the 80 correlations between the television viewing variables and the overall indices only eight (or 10%) were significant at the $p < .05$ level, with the highest correlation being .14. Moreover, there was no systematic pattern in the correlations: some were positive and some were negative; and the number of significant correlations varied greatly from country to country, ranging from three significant correlations in Britain to 12 in West Germany.

PART IV

Presentation and Perception

NINE

The Correspondence Between Presentation and Perception

In the last few chapters we examined the way television news in the five countries presented social conflicts and how young adults in those countries perceived them both in the "real" world and in the symbolic world of television news. We now begin our attempt to bring together the findings concerning presentation and perception.

Two basic questions were examined in this context. First, we wanted to know to what degree people's perceptions of social conflicts on television news corresponded to the way television news actually presented the conflicts, using our content analysis. And second, we wanted to determine the degree of correspondence between the way people perceived conflicts in the "real" world and the way television presented them.

Although in the first chapters of the book we suggested that there might be some relationships between the way social conflicts are presented and the way they are perceived, we also noted the difficulty in determining these associations. The difficulty in this line of research lies in the different nature and origin of the two sets of data, one stemming from content analysis and the other from the survey research. Whereas in the present study the presentation data were obtained from newscasts produced and presented by television stations, the perception data were obtained from individual people. Thus, although both sets of information came from the same countries, the variables derived from them could not be correlated using conventional correlational techniques.[1]

The way we chose to determine if there was indeed a relationship between presentation and perception across the various countries was to compute Spearman rank order correlations between presentation variables and perception variables. Thus for several variables we ranked the five countries on both the presentation and perception scales and then computed the rankings.[2]

PRESENTATION AND PERCEPTION OF TELEVISION NEWS

The first pair of rankings we correlated was between the prominence of conflicts in the news using the observed percentage of social conflicts in the newscasts of the various countries (based on Table 4.1) and the perceived prominence of conflicts in the news (based on Table 7.3).[3] The rank order correlation was .10, indicating essentially no relationship at all between the two variables. This overall finding seemed at first glance to suggest that young adults did not grasp the full picture regarding the portrayal of conflict in the news.

The proximity factor (i.e., domestic versus foreign conflicts), however, obscured the relationship between presentation and perception. Thus we computed separate rank order correlations between the frequency of domestic and foreign conflicts (based on Table 4.3, but excluding the combined category of foreign and domestic items) and the perception of the prominence of the conflicts in the news (based once again on Table 7.3).[4] We found that for the *domestic* (or "national" and "local") conflicts the correlation was .40 and for the *foreign* (or "international") conflicts the correlation was –.40. Thus the proximity factor demonstrates that people are differentially aware of the frequency of domestic and foreign conflicts shown on television news: domestic conflicts seem to be more fully absorbed by the audience in comparison with foreign conflicts.

The next link that we examined between television presentation of conflict and the perception of news dealt with the three dimensions of conflict.[5] The rank order correlation for complexity was .33, while for the intensity and solvability indices an identical correlation of .50 was obtained. These findings indicate a moderate degree of correspondence between the presentation of the dimensions of conflicts and their perception. We suggest that the variation in the magnitude of the correlations was attributable to the nature and manifestation of the dimensions in the newscasts. Accordingly, the .50 correlations for intensity and solvability are likely a consequence of the greater frequency with which the elements of these dimensions appear on the screen (e.g., violent acts in the case of intensity, or people sitting around a table during a negotiating session in the case of solvability). On the other hand, the slightly lower .33 correlation for the complexity dimension might have resulted from the fact that at the perceptual level complexity is a much more abstract dimension, often requiring the viewer to make cognitive transformations in order to identify the opponents (who may not always be visible but only mentioned or merely implied in the verbal text of the item). In any event, there was a clear correspondence between the presentation of the dimensions and their perception.

In addition to examining conflicts as total entities, we also were interested in looking at the correspondence between the presentation and perception of the parties involved in the conflicts. To do so we examined the correspondence between the practice sometimes exhibited by journalists of advocating the position of one or more of the parties to the conflict and the extent to which this practice was perceived by viewers. Here, too, we found that there was a substantial difference in the magnitude of the rank order correlations in the case of foreign and domestic conflicts.[6] For the foreign (or international) conflicts the rank order correlation was .20, whereas for domestic (national and local) conflicts the rank order correlation was −.50.

We suggest a possible interpretation according to which this strong and perplexing shift in the direction of the relationship is an implied criticism by the viewers of the coverage of domestic conflicts. In the news items there were significantly more instances of advocation of positions by journalists in domestic items than in foreign items. With foreign conflicts, the more advocation there actually was in the news, the more the viewers tended to recognize and accept it. With regard to domestic conflicts, however, the more advocation there was in the items, the less people tended to recognize it. It is possible that the more viewers are exposed to advocation in domestic conflicts, the more they become involved in it, and therefore they evaluate it as less frequent than would be expected. These findings suggest that the coverage of foreign conflicts tended to be "accepted" as it was, whereas people were more critical of how domestic conflicts were dealt with in the news. This can be connected with an argument that despite the norms of mainstream Western journalism—according to which journalists are expected to be objective and to refrain from taking sides in reporting a conflict—news consumers do expect (or at least would like to see) the reporting of news as consonant with their personal perspective and points of view.

PRESENTATION OF TELEVISION NEWS AND THE PERCEPTION OF THE REAL WORLD

The second question dealt with the correspondence between the presentation of conflicts in the news and the perception of these conflicts as they occurred in the "real" world. Our major finding concerning this question was that there was a wide gap between the respondents' perceptions of the prominence of conflicts in the real world and the extent to which they were presented in television news. This was manifested by a rank order correlation of $-.90$ between the two variables.[7]

When controlling for the proximity variable, as we did with the previous research question, we found that for *domestic* conflicts the rank order correlation was $-.70$, while for the *foreign* conflicts the correlation was only –.20. This seems to suggest that the media-dependency hypothesis is at work here. Accordingly, when dealing with familiar conflicts (i.e., those taking place in one's local community or country) there is a distinct inverse relationship between the prominence of conflicts in the news and the frequency with which people perceive them. This suggests either viewers reject coverage or that news organizations tend to cover stories infrequently when conflict is high and frequently when conflict is low. On the other hand, when dealing with faraway conflicts, this pattern is weakened to the point where coverage and perception are nearly independent.

This finding is related to what we already reported in Table 7.5 when we discussed the extent to which people think that television presents conflicts the way they are in the real world. Once again, in accordance with the media dependency hypothesis we would expect that foreign (or international) conflicts in the real world would be perceived as more similar to their television portrayal while domestic (local and national) conflicts in the real world would be perceived as less similar to the way television presents them. This hypothesis was supported in the case of South Africa and Israel (see Table 7.5,) where domestic conflicts were perceived to have a lower correspondence with their television portrayal. In our judgment this was attributable to the particularly high conflictual level of both the Israeli and South African societies, which made people in those countries more familiar and experienced with the conflicts in an unmediated fashion.

When we examined the relationship between the way the three specific dimensions of conflict were presented in the news and the way people perceived them in the "real" world, we found that across the five countries the rank order correlation for complexity was .28, for intensity it was .30 and for solvability it was –.40. The explanation of the positive correlations with complexity and intensity are straightforward. Thus the more conflicts in the news are portrayed as being complex; and the more people tend to perceive conflicts in the real world as being more complex; and the more conflicts in the news are presented as being intense, the more people perceive conflicts in the real world as being more intense.

With regard to the negative correlation with solvability, however, it seems that it is not inexplicable if we go back to our raw data. When we looked at the actual rankings of the five countries we noted that the greatest gaps appeared for Israel and South Africa. On the one hand, although the SABC in South Africa presented its conflicts as the easiest to solve, the South African respondents perceived conflicts in their "real" world as the most difficult to solve. On the other hand, although Israel Television presented conflicts as the most difficult to solve, the Israeli respondents perceived social conflicts as the second most easy to solve (only respondents in the United Kingdom thought that conflicts were easier to solve). It is clear, then, that the Israeli and South African respondents contributed most to the negative rank order correlation of –.40, but they did so in what can be interpreted as a meaningful way.

The media-dependency hypothesis can once again help explain some of this seeming discrepancy. When we computed the rank order correlations for solvability between the perception of the real world and television's presentation separately for the domestic (national and local) and foreign (international) realms of reality, we found that for the domestic realm the correlation was –.30 whereas for the foreign realm the correlation was .68. What this clearly means is that for domestic conflicts, people were less reliant upon television and were more likely to reject its portrayal, whereas for foreign conflicts they had to rely on television presentations and hence tended to evaluate conflicts in a manner highly similar to the presentation on the air.

These findings and interpretations can be illustrated by the particular situations in Israel and South Africa during the time the surveys were conducted in 1984. In South Africa, despite some minor changes in the government's policy towards blacks, the overall domestic situation was quite difficult. World pressure was mounting against the South African position on apartheid, and various countries and business corporations were beginning to apply sanctions; the exchange rate of the South African Rand had declined drastically, as did the price of gold (one of the country's main exports and sources of revenue); and the censorship imposed on reporting outside the country about what was happening inside—including the racial riots—was causing much pressure from world public opinion. And despite all this, the SABC's presentation of social conflicts was *relatively* the most solvable, especially concerning domestic conflicts (see Table 5.6). Despite the "rosy" picture on television, however, South Africans whites seemed to be quite pessimistic (and perhaps also realistic) as to what the future held for them.

The overall domestic situation in Israel was also very difficult. The army had been deeply involved in the war in Lebanon for three years, a war that became a major confrontation between politicians on the left and on the right. There was growing consensus that the war and its escalation were not inevitable. The economic situation was deteriorating, and inflation was running at nearly 500% per year. This was what television was reporting and showing nightly. No solutions were in sight, at least as far as the presentation of television was concerned. And yet, perhaps in spite of this situation, people felt that things could not get any worse, hence they could only get better. They were anxious for solutions and were looking forward to the upcoming elections several months down the road in hope of seeing some light coming through the tunnel. Hence, despite the bleak situation presented by television, people were relatively optimistic—which might have been reflected in their perception of the "real" world.

It should be noted that support for the media-dependency hypothesis also was provided for the other two dimensions. Thus, for complexity at the domestic level, perceptions of the "real" world was correlated with television's presentation yielding a rank order correlation of −.48, whereas at the foreign level the correlation was .38. Similarly, with regard to intensity, for domestic conflicts the correlation was a negligible .10, whereas in the foreign domain the correlation was a high .70. It seems clear that the more close people were to the events being presented in the media, the less likely they were to depend on the media and to perceive the "real" world as it was presented in the news.

CONCLUSIONS

In this chapter we have attempted to bring together some of the findings on presentation and perception. We dealt here with two questions: the degree of correspondence between the presentation of conflicts in the news and the audience's perception of these presentations, and the degree of correspondence between the presentation of the conflicts and the audiences' perceptions of the real world.

We found that people perceived, made sense, and in some instances might even have been critical of the way television presented social conflicts in the news. There also seemed to be a certain degree of correspondence between the presentation and the perception of the "real" world, which was mediated to a large extent by the proximity variable that differentiates between foreign and local conflicts.

NOTES

1. Although the presentation data were based on many news items, they were presented as point estimates of the complexity, intensity, and solvability of the conflicts. The same basic notion applies to the perception data, namely, that we used the mean scores of the different variables as point estimates for the various countries. Neither with the presentation data nor with the perception data were we interested in their respective within variance. Within-variance of the presentation and perception data were of interest only when calculating relationships *within* either data set. Indeed, this was part of the methodological rationale that led us in the first place to do our cross-national research. That is, in order to correlate presentation and perception data we needed to "create" variability across the countries. This could be done by using the point estimates of the five countries and subjecting them to rank order correlations.

2. In many cases there were clear and distinct differences among the countries in terms of the percentages or mean scores, which made for meaningful rankings. In some of the cases, however, it was necessary to "force" the rankings, even when very small differences in percentages or mean scores separated any two consecutive rankings. Also, in the relatively few cases where there were ties between two countries, the halfway ranks were used (as is normally done with rank order correlations).

3. The specific rankings were based on a newly created mean score computed for a combination of all these proximity types, derived from the question "How frequently are conflicts reported in TV news?" The five countries were ranked as

follows in terms of the prominence of conflicts in the news: Israel (highest), the United Kingdom, West Germany, the United States, and South Africa (lowest). On the perception of conflicts the countries were ranked as follows: the United States (highest), West Germany, Israel, the United Kingdom, and South Africa (lowest).

4. For this correlation, combined mean scores were computed for the national and local conflicts.

5. The rankings of the dimensions of presentation utilized here were taken from Table 5.6. The rankings for the perception of presentation were based on the second half of Table 8.3.

6. For these correlations we calculated the percentage of all the parties in the conflict items where either the anchor and/or the reporter advocated that party's position. Although the overall phenomenon of the newsperson advocating a party's position was not very common, there was much variability among the countries. Thus, for the foreign conflicts, the range was from 1.9% in the United States (based on the number of items) or 0.6% (based on the total number of parties) to 8.6% or 2.6% in Israel, respectively. For domestic conflicts, the range was from only 3.2% in West Germany (based on the number of items) or 1.3% (based on the total number of parties) to 25.0% or 7.3% in the United Kingdom, respectively.

7. The data for this correlation were based on Table 4.1 and a mean of all conflicts in the "real" world in Table 7.3.

T E N

Tying the Knots

The fertile theorizing and research about the mass media during the past half century suffers somewhat from *embarassement de richesse*. This phenomenon has been typified by the generation of differing and sometimes even contradictory hypotheses concerning the social aspects of the mass communication process. Perhaps as a result of this diversity and affluence of perspectives, the intellectual history of mass communication research all too often has been compartmentalized into well defined research areas. In our context, although some researchers focused on journalistic norms and practices and the structure of media institutions, others mainly were interested in media contents while still others developed the study of media effects as a nearly autonomous domain. On the other hand, critical approaches that have long aspired to connect among various subjects and offered a more composite picture of media and mass culture all too often have rejected the avenue of empirical investigation of their ideas.

This study made it possible to examine the validity of certain claims regarding the presentation and perception of social conflicts. The questions that were investigated here stem from dilemmas and vicissitudes of scholars trained in a variety of general theoretical approaches to the study of mass communication. This

resulted in a somewhat eclectic approach in defining our conceptual framework. We permitted ourselves to extract from varying
approaches several notions that seemed to be both central and
intriguing and to converge them in our study. Our present under-
taking can be seen as one link in an increasingly growing chain of
studies that attempt to bring together some of these diverse com-
partments of communication research.

At the outset of this volume we talked about the convergence of
three kinds of reality: *symbolic* reality, which pertains to the way the
media portray and present the world; *subjective* reality, which is
how people interpret the world and what they believe about it; and
objective reality, which consists of the basic facts and ingredients
that constitute the core material of symbolic and subjective realities. In the present study we dealt with the symbolic reality by
examining the presentation of social conflicts in the news. With
regard to subjective reality we showed how people perceive social
conflicts. As for the objective reality, we were interested in two
facets: the social conflicts themselves and the media systems. We
argued that it would be difficult to describe social conflicts as they
"really" are and therefore we focused on two central factors of
objective reality that are directly pertinent: the systemic variables
of the organizational and professional structure and the modes of
media operation.

Thus, as shown in Chapter 2, we were able to place the five
countries of the study on two continua ranging from high to low
on government influence on the media and the degree of competition among the media. Accordingly, we postulated that the five
countries can be arranged in the following order: the United States,
the United Kingdom, West Germany, Israel, and South Africa. This
order simultaneously reflected both the range of political regulation over the media (with the least control in the United States and
the most control in South Africa), and the range of media competition (the most in the United States and the least in South Africa).

This made it possible, moreover, to compare and contrast various features of symbolic reality and subjective reality in the five
countries and to try to relate them to the regulation and competition factors. Such an analysis could enable us to evaluate the

relative potency of the commonly shared professional journalistic norms and values on the one hand, and the differential political and social forces on the other hand. Our assumption throughout has been that if and when we found differences among the countries, these could be attributed to variations in the nature and amount of political influence over and regulation of the media and the degree of competition among them. Conversely, we assumed that if and when we found similar trends across the countries, we could attribute them to universals of journalistic practice and common characteristics of Western democracies.

SIMILARITIES AND DIFFERENCES IN PRESENTATION

The logic of our approach, then, was first and foremost to look for ordered differences among the countries and to interpret them in the context of political regulation and media competition. When analyzing the findings showing variation among the countries in terms of the presentation of conflicts in the news and the perceptual patterns, however, we found that contrary to our initial expectations, political influence and media competition provided only a partial interpretive framework. For not a single variable did we find the five countries perfectly arranged in the hypothesized order. And for only some variables did the data place some of the countries in their expected relative positions on the continua but not others.

Having failed to find a clear-cut pattern according to the postulated continua, and having become more immersed in the data, we began to realize that several trends of similarity across the five countries of the study seemed to surface.[1]

The first similarity was the overall prevalence of social conflicts in television news. A majority of the news items in all five countries centered around social conflicts, having to do with groups of people (e.g., nations, political parties, unions, dissidents) or individuals representing such groups who opposed one another either regarding goals or the means to obtain them. If we were to add interpersonal conflicts—which were not included in our framework—we would find many more conflicts.

A second aspect of the similarity across the countries was that most of the conflict stories were concentrated in relatively few topic areas: international politics, internal politics, internal order, and labor relations. In fact, between 70% and 86% of the conflict items in the five countries fell in these topic categories. Nonconflict items, on the other hand, were much more heterogeneous and concerned a greater variety of topics.

A third feature, or group of features, relating to the similarity among the countries was that there was a greater tendency for three things to occur among conflict items as compared to nonconflict items: first, presenting conflict items in relationship to other conflict items; second, presenting conflict items connected to other events; and third, providing historical background and context. These, we believe, are poignant, because they suggest that at least one major class of news items—namely, social conflicts—is not presented as detached from one another and as lacking context, which has been a widespread criticism of television news for many years.

The above three points of similarity provide evidence that social conflict is a dominant focus of television news. News content in the five countries, despite the differences among them in the degree of political control and competition, exhibits a clear preference for the dramatic form of conflict. Moreover, although some critical theorists would argue that basic social conflicts are underplayed in the media by omitting the interconnections among them and deemphasizing their historical background and social causes, we found that by and large this was not the case. As indicated above, news items dealing with social conflict—above and beyond their dominance in the newscasts—indeed were often connected with one another and presented within a historical context. The present study indicated that social conflict in the news was not minimized and presented from afar, but rather was emphasized and presented in close-up proportions.

As we indicated in Chapter 1, many of the critical theorists and media sociologists who study journalists at work and the functioning of news organizations tend to agree that television news simplifies conflicts, presents their most intense moments, and portrays them as easily solved. These three notions are clearly relative and based on value judgments. Moreover, the bulk of the writings by these scholars, with few exceptions, presents no empirical findings nor any yardsticks that could be used to determine different levels of the conflictual dimensions.

Thus when analyzing and interpreting empirical findings, one must adopt certain criteria in order to assess whether or not such claims are empirically valid. When we examined the findings of our three dimensions of conflict, we reached the conclusion that some of the aforementioned claims were not supported by our data. For example, although some critical theorists say that conflicts are simplified by the media, using the number of parties as a criterion of complexity we found that on average all social conflict items contained between 2.8 and 3.3 parties. Keeping in mind that a conflict by definition has a minimum of two parties, we believe that a mean of nearly three parties (with some cases with as many as six or seven) is surely not oversimplifying matters. In addition, as noted earlier, the interconnectedness of conflict items with other news items and their presentation as related to previous events accentuates even further the complexity of the portrayal.

As for intensity, although many scholars suggested that television presents the news as highly intense, across the board we would tend to debate this point. What we found was that with little variation among the countries, there was *no* verbally reported physical aggression in 69% of all the conflict items, *no* visually shown physical aggression in 85% of the conflict items, *no* verbally reported verbal aggression in 85% of the conflict items, *no* visually shown verbal aggression in 94% of the conflict items, *no* verbally reported emotional display in 94% of the conflict items, and *no* visually shown emotional display in 87% of the conflict items. In short, there were relatively *low* levels of intensity in the portrayal of social conflicts in the news.[2] This does not mean, of course, that there were no very intense items (some of which we explicitly illustrated in detail), but such items were clearly a minority.

As for solvability, a similar disparity appeared between our overall findings and the claims made by some of the critical scholars. Although they would argue that conflicts are presented in the news with an emphasis on solvability, we found that the relative level of solvability was quite low. Thus, across the board, in 59% of the conflict items there was *no* call for resolution or a report of negotiations taking place between the parties, in 83% of the conflict items there was *no* expressed willingness to compromise, and in 82% of the conflict items there was *no* outcome of the conflict reported.

In sum, two dimensions of the severity of the portrayal of social conflicts were salient with relative complexity and nonsolvability being stressed, while at the same time the level of intensity was not particularly high. What this means is that social conflicts are not presented as "sensational," although they definitely are treated as serious and severe phenomena. Of course one might wonder whether the glass is half filled or half empty, but we strongly believe that in the absence of other figures, these data might be used by other scholars to refine and broaden the scope of the research further in this area.

Having said this, we still believe that our data support the critical perspective, but only when we take into account what turned out to be the major distinction between foreign and domestic social conflict items. In all five countries the relative proportion of conflicts was higher among foreign than domestic items. Foreign conflicts also were presented as being more severe than domestic conflicts. Taking each dimension separately, there were highly consistent findings. Regarding complexity, there were more parties in the foreign conflicts compared with the domestic conflicts (except for West Germany). Moreover, foreign news items consistently included more intensity components than did domestic news items. This was the case for all five countries with regard to both the physical and verbal aggression measures. Finally, across the five countries conflicts in domestic stories were more likely to be solved than were their foreign counterparts. The consistency of this finding throughout the study suggests the existence of a cross-national phenomenon that may be termed the *severity syndrome of foreign conflict news.*

The finding that the overall level of severity was higher for foreign conflicts has an important implication for the widely accepted notion that the media tend to maintain and preserve the social status quo. The picture of the world as presented in each country's news clearly suggests that "their" conflicts were more severe than "ours." In our view this can be the result of two factors. The first stems, of course, from journalistic considerations of newsworthiness. Thus foreign stories would only pass the selection threshold if they were sufficiently severe. On the other hand, domestic conflicts would be included in the news even if they were less severe, as long as they were of sufficient importance to the country of broadcast.

Another reason, which is not self-evident, could be the attempt on the part of journalists or media organizations—whether intentionally or not—to show their audiences a more tranquil domestic front in comparison with the world outside. This would be in line with "the grass is greener on our side of the fence" and hence would contribute to the maintenance of the existing social order or at least serve as a mechanism of conflict regulation. These two factors directly relate to the duality in the role of journalists that we described at the outset: on the one hand, they are members of the media profession with all that this entails; on the other hand, they are members of society who share and express the common sentiments of their fellow citizens.

The picture presented so far clearly illustrates the importance of providing empirical evidence to support or refute various intriguing theoretical assumptions proposed by the critical approach, but which by and large were not previously put to an empirical test. Although it is extremely difficult to prove or disprove them, we believe that empirical research of this nature can provide an additional perspective on these widely held beliefs. In the present instance we were able to raise serious doubts as to the validity of the generalized assumption that television news simplifies, intensifies, and underplays the difficulty of solving all social conflicts.

At the same time we offer some empirical support for the claim that the media function, at least to some extent, as the guardians of the social status quo and as social mechanisms of conflict regulation when they present foreign news.

At the outset of this study we asked ourselves to what extent journalistic norms and practices across a variety of countries create a common universe of meanings and expressions. In fact, as we reported in the various sections of this book, there is much similarity across countries in terms of the presentation of news. This, we would maintain, is indeed attributable to the highly similar processes of selection and composition of the news that is part of journalism culture and that is shared in many lands.

THE UNIQUE CHARACTERISTICS
OF THE COUNTRIES

As we have argued above, the political regulation and media competition factors did not seem to cause differences among the five countries, despite the fact that there were clear differences in the patterns of regulation and competition among them. Why, then, did the political regulation and media competition factors fall short of explaining differences among the countries?

Given the fact that our five countries can be characterized as Western parliamentary democracies,[3] we believe that Western journalistic practices are strongly dominant in all of them, leading to much commonality in journalistic output. At the same time we believe that if we were to select a different or extended sample of countries—including, for example, some from the Eastern bloc and from the Third World—we probably would find that the regulation and competition factors would have a greater impact.

We believe, moreover, that in addition to government regulation and media competition—which are relatively fixed and stable despite some changes from time to time—there is an additional set of highly pervasive factors that may be considered as transitory and relatively fluid, and that have a strong influence on political circumstances and processes in society at any given point in time.

These factors might include a variety of situations: the ascent to or descent from power of certain (usually major) political parties; particular international circumstances implicating the country, such as war or serious confrontation with outside adversaries; internal civil disturbances; and major shifts in economic conditions, including high inflation, unemployment, or recession. What happens during these situations, we would argue, can have a strong influence on the way social conflicts are presented in the news at that point in time and hence also on the way people perceive social conflicts. In order to investigate such conditions in depth it would be necessary to study such conflicts in their specific historical and social contexts, something that was not attempted in the present study. Nonetheless a brief discussion of these circumstances is warranted here, even though it is impressionistic and intuitive and does not purport to be comprehensive.

The extent to which such circumstances were operative in the present study can be illustrated by simultaneously examining two components: the idiosyncratic features of the data from each of the countries, and the countries' particular political and social conditions. By attempting to associate these two factors we can shed some light on the overall patterns of presentation and perception of social conflicts.

We begin this synthesis with West Germany (FRG)—perhaps the only country in our study where the findings correspond fairly well to its relative position on the continua of the two systemic variables of government regulation and media competition. The intermediate position on the continua, combined with the relative political and social stability in West Germany, provide the explanatory framework for the moderate presentation of conflict in that society.

West Germany in the early 1980s enjoyed a period of relative economic prosperity at home with no major external threats. Although there was concern in the Federal Republic back in 1980 regarding the situation in Poland and possible Soviet intervention, there was no direct threat to the country. Moreover, this period was characterized by the weakening of internal strife, generated in years past by several extremist groups.

In the present study we found that the prominence of social conflicts on both channels of West German television was relatively moderate, as were the various characteristics of the conflicts. The position of the conflicts on German television were by and large in the middle of all the scales, very close in most cases to the overall averages. Indeed, this position corresponded to West Germany's place in the middle of the continua of government regulation of the media and media competition.

Furthermore, West Germany's presentation of social conflicts was similar to its presentation of the entire newscast: it is a serious affair in which the anchor reads the text from paper (rather than using a TelePrompTer), and with no show-business gimmicks. The news accentuates government and public figures while deemphasizing the roles of ordinary people. Hence the only place where German news was somewhat deviant from the grand mean was the nature of the parties to the conflicts, with fewer "people" as party entities and generally low representation scores for those who were presented.

We now turn to the United States and the United Kingdom, the two countries that are positioned next to each other on one end of the regulation and competition continua. The U.S. broadcasting system, which is almost entirely commercial, is subject to the least amount of government influence and control and features the most competition. The British system, which is a balanced combination of private and public organizations, is also relatively free of regulation and has substantial competition. Accordingly, although the two countries differ, they should have exhibited fairly similar manifestations of conflict presentation, at least in terms of their relative rankings. What we found was that for some of the variables these two countries were indeed fairly similar and ranked alongside each other (as first and second place), although in many of these cases the British position was the more extreme of the two.

It should be recalled that the news in the United Kingdom contained relatively more conflicts than did news in the United States. Furthermore, we found, for example, that the complexity of the conflicts in the news was essentially the same in the two countries, while other variables related to complexity of presentation (such as giving historical background and making connections among conflict stories) was more prevalent in the United Kingdom than in the United States. These findings were in accordance with our expectations that in public service broadcasting the portrayal of conflicts is not oversimplified as much as it would be in commercial television.[4] As for intensity, however, much to our surprise, the BBC portrayal of conflicts was the most intense among the five countries. The United States, with its high degree of media competition, was ranked only in second place.

Looking at the way parties to conflict were presented indicates that in the U.S. news the parties obtained the highest representation reinforcement levels (i.e., their representatives were given highest salience in the news), while the parties in the British news were in second place. In fact, party entities in the United States were nearly twice as salient in most subject categories, compared with the overall means, while the British were quite average. This, too, would fit the standard model of U.S. commercial television.

The above examples illustrate the relatively close rankings between the United States and the United Kingdom. When looking at the foci of conflict topics in the news, however, we found that the most prevalent topics of social conflicts in the U.S. newscasts were international politics (44%) and internal politics (21%). In the United Kingdom, on the other hand, while international political conflicts also topped the list (21%), they were followed by conflicts concerning internal order and labor relations (19% for each), with only 11% and 2% for these categories in the United States, respectively.

Analogously, although government was the most prevalent party entity in all five countries, the second most frequent U.S. entity was country (23%) and in the United Kingdom the second most frequent entity was workers (14%). Also, the most salient opponent co-occurrences in the United States were country versus country and government versus government, whereas in the United Kingdom the most salient were government versus political party, government versus workers, and industry versus workers.

These findings lead us to our brief discussion of the social and political climate in these two countries at the time of the study. In the United States, the three-year period separating the two waves of content analysis (December 1980 to January 1984) occurred during President Reagan's first term. No presidential election took place during this period, and aside from normal public issues involving Congress and the Administration most of the conflicts that the United States dealt with at the time were international in nature: the Polish situation and the American hostages in Iran, both crises that had begun before the first wave of the study; the invasion of Grenada in 1983; and the heavy involvement in Lebanon in 1984. There were few dominant domestic problems, and one major labor dispute (among air traffic controllers, which ended several days after it began with the abrupt dismissal of the strikers).

In the United Kingdom, on the other hand, there were numerous problems on the home front, and a general election was held in June of 1983, following a stiff confrontation between the Labor and Conservative parties, much of which was the result of the Falklands war in 1982. Thus, for example, in 1981 the hunger strikes in the Maze prison in Belfast dominated the news, as did numerous industrial disputes involving a variety of industries. Unemployment was running very high and the problem of football (soccer) "hooligans" was in the spotlight.

By way of speculation we suggest that the events of this period in the United States were not sufficiently dominant to weaken the effects of the systemic variables. As a result the position of the United States on the continua was basically where it would be expected. In the United Kingdom, on the other hand, the conflicts that engrossed the country seemed to have an effect on the nature of news broadcasting. As a result, British news was more intensive than would be expected from a public-service system such as the BBC.

The findings concerning the last two countries in the study, Israel and South Africa, are probably the most intriguing. Both countries, whose television systems are under relatively strict government supervision and with little or virtually no competition, were positioned a priori at the other end of the continua from the

United States and the United Kingdom. And yet, time and again the findings in terms of the presentation of social conflicts in both countries did not appear to justify their proximal positions on the continua. Although the portrayal of social conflicts by South African television was often quite extreme in one direction, that of Israel was often in the opposite direction or elsewhere in the relative rankings.

Politically and socially both South Africa and Israel are engrossed in numerous conflicts, both domestic and foreign. Within South Africa the major problem, of course, has been, and still is, the administration of and attitudes toward apartheid by various social groups and political parties. Similarly, the major social and political issue facing Israel has been its confrontations with its Arab neighbors and the Palestinians.

Contrary to the situation in most countries of the world—and surely in the others of the present study—both of these major ongoing issues have been perceived over the years by their respective governments and peoples as fundamental to their very existence and survival; hence much of their politics and daily activities were anchored in these contexts. For both countries, moreover, these primary conflicts have had broad ramifications in terms of their respective relations with foreign nations, friends and foes alike.

Additional, often related, conflicts appeared in each of the countries between the two waves of our study. Thus in 1981 Israel held elections, but not before its air force bombed a nuclear reactor being built in Iraq only several days prior to the elections; in 1982 Israel completed its evacuation of the Sinai peninsula amid great internal debate; this was followed by the war in Lebanon and its extended aftermath; and at the same time, within the country, the friction between religious groups and the secular majority swelled. In South Africa during the same period, a new constitution was promulgated substituting a strong presidency for the previous parliamentary form of government; the situation in South West Africa (Namibia) was exacerbated, as were encounters with other of South Africa's neighbors; and all this was amid growing turbulence in the black townships, culminating in deadly riots and police brutality. In short, the prevalence of conflict in both countries was very high.

And yet, as the findings concerning television's presentation of conflict indicated, the Israeli level was indeed very high—more than in all the other countries—but in South Africa the portrayal was the lowest of all five countries, this despite the adjacent positions that two countries occupy on the continua. This seeming disparity can possibly be explained by drawing a distinction between the *de jure* and the *de facto* nature of the continua. On paper, both Israeli and South African broadcasting are subject to relatively strict government control; in daily practice, however, it seems that the Israeli scene is one with much less intervention than in the case of South Africa.[5]

Moreover, one should recall the difference in the gap in the percentage of domestic and foreign conflict items in these two countries. In Israel only 10% separated the level of conflict in domestic items (59%) from that of all foreign items (69%). In South Africa, however, the difference was very large: 21% of domestic items dealt with conflict, whereas 62% of foreign items contained conflict. Hence the South African case was a clear-cut example of news emphasizing conflict abroad, and thus supporting—by implication—the existing social order at home.

In terms of the dimensions, the complexity of social conflicts (as measured by number of parties to the conflicts) revealed that South African news was the most complex, and Israel stood in second. Thus these findings are a good example of public service broadcasting systems, which tend to present conflicts as relatively more complex or less simplified.

As for intensity, although Israel and South Africa overall were in third and fourth place, the distinction between foreign and domestic conflicts surfaced once more. Accordingly, although at both proximity levels the Israeli conflicts were still in third and fourth place, in South Africa the intensity of domestic conflicts was the lowest of the five countries, whereas for the foreign conflicts it was the second most intense. This once again seems to support the SABC's role in the preservation of social status quo by emphasizing foreign conflicts and minimizing domestic conflicts.

Finally, with regard to solvability, South African television presented conflicts as easiest to solve (both domestic and foreign), whereas in Israel the overall presentation indicated that conflicts were the most difficult to solve (fifth place for domestic and in a tie—with the United States—next to last for foreign conflicts). Thus we would suggest that South African television attempted to present a not-too-conflictual picture of the world and that things would turn out all right in the end. In Israel, however, this tendency was all but absent. To complement this we found that in South Africa nearly 11% of all the parties to the conflicts were mediators, arbitrators or go-betweens, whereas in Israel only 3% of the parties fulfilled roles that were oriented toward problem solving.

SIMILARITIES AND DIFFERENCES IN PERCEPTION

Turning now to the perception of social conflicts, here too we found some important similarities across the countries. The basic point was that the respondents in all five countries estimated that there were fairly numerous social conflicts going on in the world. Moreover, the respondents estimated that there were more international conflicts taking place than national conflicts, and more national conflicts than local conflicts.

Despite the different political and social contexts of the five countries of the study, we found that young adults clearly were able to make three significant distinctions in their perception of social conflicts. First, the respondents in all five countries cognitively differentiated between the "real" world and the world of television news. Second, people organized their thinking and attitudes toward conflicts, in both realms of reality, according to the three dimensions elaborated in this study: complexity, intensity, and solvability. And third, when thinking about social conflict, people tended to discern among the three levels of proximity—namely, conflicts that happened in their immediate (local) environment, those which took place at the national level, and those which occurred in other countries.

These three findings support our initial contention that the perception of social conflict is an integral part of the process of the social construction of reality. Accordingly, our respondents were able to differentiate between the "commonsense" objective reality and its symbolic representation (in this case the realm of television news). In addition, they used the dimensions of conflicts as typifications of both symbolic and "real" conflicts and organized their constructions of reality accordingly. Finally, the zones of relevance, which were operationalized in terms of three levels of conflict proximity, also were manifested in their cognitive frameworks.

In addition to the structural patterns of the dimensions and proximity levels, we also examined the absolute levels of the perception scores. Perhaps the most important finding in this context is that young adults in all countries perceived the "real" social conflicts as more severe than their portrayal in television news along all three dimensions. Almost without exception in all the countries, for each of the dimensions and in both realms of reality, we found that the international conflicts nearly always were perceived to be the most severe—that is, more complex, more intense, and more difficult to solve than local and national conflicts. In fact, the correspondence between the respondents' evaluation of differences between the presentation of domestic and foreign conflicts and our content analysis of these features was quite high. Our respondents seemed to be highly sophisticated young adults, able to understand overt messages as well as some of the subtleties of their presentation.

And yet the viewers' capability to analyze and differentiate was found to be unrelated to the amount of viewing of television news. What we suggested earlier concerning this phenomenon, namely that "if you've seen one portrayal of conflict in the news, you've seen them all," may be true. In fact, the way the different countries presented the news was highly similar, as was the perception of the conflicts, and even the amount of news viewing in the five countries was not very different.

The full significance of our findings cannot be grasped, however, without basing our interpretations on our attempt to relate the theories of the social construction of reality with the media-dependency hypothesis. This latter hypothesis enabled us to understand better not only the dynamics of the interrelationships among the three sets of variables (realms of reality, dimensions of conflict, and proximity levels), but also the patterns of correspondence between presentation of the news and the perception of both the news itself and the "real" world.

Thus in the previous chapter we were able to show that the proximity variable served as a very effective moderator in terms of bridging the gap between the findings on the presentation of conflicts in the news and the perception of the news and social reality by our young adults. In general, then, people tended to be less dependent upon the media portrayal of reality when evaluating local conflicts with which it could be assumed they were more familiar, while they were more dependent upon the media when dealing with international conflicts that were more remote from their immediate environment and zones of relevance.

To what extent, then, does television news transmit messages regarding social conflicts that might contribute to a "common-sense" understanding according to which the existing social order must prevail? Or, putting this in functional terms, does television news fulfill an integrative function for its audience and, as a consequence, a conflict-regulation function for the whole society? Our study provides several possible responses to this question, not all of which point in the same direction. First, the fact that people distinguish between reality and television seems to diminish or limit the power of television. Television, it seems, is not necessarily accepted by people as the state of the world, and hence they can be critical of its presentation of events.

Second, implied criticism toward television and the picture of the world that it presents is also expressed in the fact that viewers perceive "real" social conflicts as more severe than their portrayal in the news. This is particularly poignant in view of the fact that the portrayal of conflict on television is not simplistic, is not sensational, and does not stress only those events that might be connected with the solution of problems. Our respondents certainly realize this, inasmuch as their intuitive evaluation of the contents was quite similar to our own systematic content analysis of the conflicts. They accept the notion that there is a picture of severe social conflicts on television, but at the same time they believe that in the real world the degree of severity is even greater.

And third, the reliance of viewers on the news seems to depend on the zones of relevance that were operationalized as local, national, and international conflicts. In some instances we found that as the conflicts were more distant from the viewer, they were more dependent upon television, and their perceptions were more similar to that of television. This dependency in understanding events that are more remote does indeed support the hypothesis that television can develop perceptions that are conducive to the preservation of the status quo by shifting emphasis and attention to more remote conflicts, the evaluation of which is not direct but is based rather more on the media. This option is weakened when a particular society is in a highly and perpetually conflictual state, such as is the case in Israel and South Africa. In these countries, given the presumed more direct experience that people have with major conflicts, the media dependency for domestic conflicts is weakened and there is a growing and constant comparison between the objective reality and symbolic reality. Hence in these cases stronger criticism is likely to develop toward the presentation of domestic conflicts.

This study has demonstrated that the linkage between the presentation and perception of conflicts at the empirical level can yield findings that indicate a most elaborate relationship between social conflicts (both domestic and foreign), media organizations and their output, and media audiences, who learn about conflict from the news and can respond by means of social action. We are distinctly aware of the fact that we have provided, at best, only partial and sometimes even contradictory answers to the complicated questions we raised. In fact, we feel that we probably have opened up a wider range of new questions that should be addressed in further research. If we have been successful in initiating a discourse on some of these issues, we are content.

NOTES

1. Although we speak here of similarities, this does not mean, of course, that the findings were identical in all the countries. The question, then, is when did we consider a comparison as having yielded similar or dissimilar findings? Because, as indicated earlier, we decided not to use statistical criteria of significance as our guideline, we chose merely to use heuristic criteria. As indicated later in this chapter, there were also some situations where there were notable outstanding or idiosyncratic findings, which we will try to interpret using a different kind of rationale.

2. We wish to point out that the coding of the news items was quite liberal in the sense that coders were instructed to indicate the *presence* of any of the features of the dimensions even if they were only subtly evident.

3. Despite the a priori differences among the countries we have chosen to view all five as parliamentary democracies, based on the definition offered by Nordlinger (1972).

4. It will be recalled that in the United Kingdom only BBC newscasts were analyzed, hence the findings in that country are only based on a public-service system.

5. This point may be illustrated with several examples in which the Director General of the Israel Broadcasting Authority, a government political appointee, attempted to interfere in professional news-reporting decisions but ultimately (in most cases within days) was forced to reverse his decision because of public pressure. The most recent example was the attempt to prevent the coverage on television news of the speech by Yassir Arafat in Geneva in December 1988. The pretext for this was that the speech might incite additional riots in the occupied territories. By week's end, however, parts of the speech were broadcast within a comprehensive report on the special session of the United Nations General Assembly.

Epilogue

By way of illustration, we began our story with an incident in the village of Beita in the hills of Samaria. According to the various television reports of the event that we briefly presented in the Prologue of this volume, the incident at Beita between the Israelis and Palestinians was a very severe one. It was highly complex, it was extremely intense, and it was a sad example of how difficult it is to solve this continuing conflict.

And where does the story end? Or does it? Social conflicts will be with us always. Some are more transient and others appear to endure forever. Social scientists and media scholars have only begun to understand these intriguing social phenomena, and much is still to be done. We hope that we have offered a modest contribution.

Through several examples and numerous tables (not too many, it is hoped) as well as analysis and discussion, we have tried to illustrate how television news covers social conflicts and how people perceive them. As we asserted all along, we were interested in the phenomenon of social conflict in television news in general, and hence we did not focus on the coverage and perception of any particular conflict. At this point, however, we do feel that another complementary cross-national approach to the study of conflict in the news ought to examine in depth how specific conflicts were treated in the news (see Adoni, 1989), and what sense people made of them. This, we believe, ought to be one of the next steps in furthering our understanding of the processes by which television covers social conflicts and the image that is created in peoples' minds regarding them. This kind of research should, we believe, complement our research strategy and utilize the concepts and instruments that we developed here.[1]

Another potentially fascinating perspective for media scholars might be the expansion of the present scheme to other media, particular the printed press. Thus we would like to see this kind of research expanded and applied to print journalism. The work by Van Dijk (1988) is a promising example of research on how the press in various nations covered a particular conflict—the assassination of President-Elect Bechir Gemayel of Lebanon in 1982. That work, however, did not focus on what we consider some of the more inherently conflict-oriented variables that were of interest to us.

We believe that this kind of research ought to be expanded to other countries. The present study dealt with five Western parliamentary democracies. Surely other forms of government and media systems should be examined. In fact, by extending this kind of research to other countries greater variability would be created, which would most likely lead to stronger relationships among the systemic, presentation, and perceptual variables.

We also believe that above and beyond our specific findings, the greater significance of our work is our attempt to bring together the study of presentation and the study of perception of events. We would like to propose that the three dimensions of conflict and their respective application to the content of news, on the one hand, and to the perception by audiences, on the other hand, be used as a barometer of the level of conflictuality in society. In other words, we suggest that a sample of newscasts be drawn from time to time, and in various locations, and measures taken to determine the magnitude of the complexity, intensity, and solvability of social conflicts in the news. This information, when monitored over time, could indicate changes in the severity of conflict in the news. Also, in a similar manner, the measurement procedure could be used to gauge the way people perceive the level of conflictuality in their society. These two measures could then be used as social indicators in bringing together media analysis and public-opinion research in different countries.

Finally, in a recent paper summing up a mini-conference held in Jerusalem in 1989 on future directions in television news research

(Cohen & Bantz, 1989), we called for what we termed "start-to-finish" research—namely, research that begins with the producers and journalists of the news, continues with the product they manufacture, and terminates with the audience. The present study focused in roughly equal parts on the product and the audience, but only by way of inference did it deal with producers and journalists. They, too, should be added in a direct fashion in the next round.

NOTE

1. The study of the Falklands conflict (Glasgow University Media Group, 1985) as it was portrayed on the BBC and ITN in the United Kingdom could serve as an example of a case study approach to a major social conflict, except that it was limited to one country and hence lacked the breadth of the various intercountry factors that could broaden its academic perspective. It also did not attempt to deal with the peoples' perception of the issue, other than by discussing how some public-opinion polling done at the time in the United Kingdom was reported on television.

The Television News Systems in the Five Countries

THE UNITED STATES

In the U.S. broadcast services are provided by the combination of thousands of local television and radio stations and national networks that provide programming to most of those stations. Television and radio stations are licensed individually but within legal limits one party may own 12 radio and 12 TV stations (up to 14 if at least two are minority controlled). A multiple TV station owner is permitted to reach as much as 25% of American TV households (more if the stations are UHF).

The vast majority of television and radio stations are licensed for commercial operation. Three main commercial television networks (ABC, CBS, NBC) provide programming to affiliated stations, who in turn broadcast that programming, which is viewed by the majority of the audience. There have been several attempts to develop a fourth network, the most successful of which appears to be the current Fox network. Although there are noncommercial ("public") broadcasting stations and networks (Public Broadcasting Service, National Public Radio, American Public Radio), noncommercial broadcasting serves primarily as an alternative, emphasizing non-mass-audience music on radio (e.g., classical, jazz) and educational, informational, and non-mass audience entertainment (e.g., high drama) on television. In addition to broadcast services, cable television has become increasingly available and several cable news services are available, most notably Cable News Network (CNN), a 24-hour news service.

U.S. broadcasting policy results from the interaction of many forces. It is formally regulated by the Federal Communications Commission (FCC), a five-member body appointed by the president and confirmed by the Senate. The FCC does not operate any broadcasting operations and is constrained by law and tradition to supervising broadcasting, most directly through broadcast station licenses. Political and governmental influence on U.S. broadcasting is typically subtle and quite complex, as broadcasters have traditionally sought to avoid direct government intervention; as a result, some broadcasters are sensitive to "the raised eyebrow" that may suggest government officials are concerned about some matter. Other broadcasters, however, have overtly snubbed such influence and directly challenged the government's authority (see Krasnow, Longley, & Terry, 1982, for a discussion of these issues). The U.S. broadcasting system has been legislatively granted the protection of the First Amendment to the U.S. Constitution, which guarantees freedom of the press. However, unlike print publishing, U.S. broadcasting is legally mandated to serve the public interest. In addition, from 1949 to 1987 the FCC maintained the "Fairness Doctrine," which required broadcasters to afford a reasonable opportunity for discussion of controversial public issues and to present "both" sides in such controversies. In 1987, in the Meredith case, the FCC abolished the doctrine (see Donahue, 1989), a move that was upheld by the Supreme Court (FCC's Repeal of Fairness Doctrine, 1990).

Thus U.S. broadcasting, unlike print publishing, is mandated to present a diversity of points of view to serve the public interest. Furthermore, election coverage is constrained by the equal-time requirement that prevents broadcasters from allowing one candidate to use their airtime without providing an equal opportunity to the other candidates. Although this restriction does *not* apply to bona fide newscasts, U.S. network newscasts typically match Republican and Democratic candidates quite evenly (Epstein, 1973; Hofstetter, 1976). These mandates, combined with a professed commitment to objective journalism, encourage television news reporters to present at least two viewpoints in stories (see Epstein, 1973; Gans, 1979; Tuchman, 1978a). Given the international focus of this study, it is important to note that the Fairness Doctrine did *not* apply to foreign news topics; thus foreign stories were not under the same mandate for balance as were domestic stories.

U.S. commercial broadcasting is financed by advertising sold either by stations or networks. The commercial television networks pay their affiliated stations "compensation" for using the station's time. Noncommercial broadcasting employs a variety of means to generate revenue, including donations, memberships, and grants from governments, corporations, and foundations.

Commercial networks in the United States compete against each other, as well as against public broadcasting and cable television, for their share of audience attention. The desire to attract and maintain a large and salable (to advertisers) audience in the face of competition encourages the production of news programs that are visually attractive, technically flawless, and entertaining; such programs have been criticized as being designed more to entertain than to inform (Epstein, 1973; Gans, 1979). The competition among the commercial networks is very intense, particularly during the evening when advertising rates can be very high. During the 1980s, the relative evening viewership of the three largest television networks varied greatly, with all three networks holding the largest audience at various times. The intensity of competition and enormous revenue involved in U.S. broadcasting led Barnouw (1978), Gans (1979), Skornia (1968), and others to argue that the commercial networks are vulnerable to undue influence from their advertisers and affiliates.

The three largest national television networks transmit early evening newscasts on a daily basis (ABC's *World News Tonight*, CBS's *Evening News*, and NBC's *Nightly News*). Local stations broadcast programs at different times in the various time zones, but the most typical time is 6:30 p.m. Eastern time and 5:30 p.m. Central and Mountain time. The newscasts occupy a 30-minute time slot, but because of commercials the programs actually run approximately 22 minutes. All three newscasts stress the personality of the news presenters to the extent that he or she may become an attraction in his or her own right (Epstein, 1973; Williams, 1974). All three use a variety of techniques including videotaped and live reports from the field, extensive graphics, and complex visuals.

Although the exact news values reflected in U.S. network television news are a matter of some debate, there is a clear emphasis on national items or national themes (U.S. television stations broadcast frequent local television newscasts); on politics, with the Presidency and Congress receiving extensive coverage; and on a sense of immediacy created through on-the-scene reports, extensive video reports, and brief, compressed items. Although television news reporters frequently seek to present several sides to issues, network reporters in particular often use a closing statement to make valuative statements concerning the item and the sides to a dispute.

THE UNITED KINGDOM

The four channels of British television are divided between two broadcasting services, the British Broadcasting Corporation (BBC) and Independent Television (ITV).

The BBC is financed almost entirely by a license fee paid by television set holders at a level fixed by the government. It manages two television channels, BBC-1 and BBC-2, the latter providing a larger proportion of programs likely to appeal to minority and specialist audiences.

Independent Television, which began broadcasting in 1955, is structurally more elaborate. It includes both a regulatory agency (called the Independent Broadcasting Authority) and 15 regionally organized companies that both make programs and transmit broadcasts to a defined area of the country, plus Independent Television News (on whose board the ITV companies are represented) and TV-AM for breakfast television. Until 1982, the Independent system had only one television channel, but in that year it introduced a second channel known as Channel 4, which was authorized by an Act of Parliament. This was legislatively enjoined to provide programs that are different in kind from those scheduled by BBC and ITV-1 and to commission a significant proportion of its output from so-called independent producers, that is, producers not employed by the BBC or the ITV companies. Almost all the revenue for ITV comes from the sale of advertising. In fact, the 15 ITV companies enjoy an advertising monopoly, for they even sell the commercial time for Channel 4. The latter then receives its funds directly from the IBA, which in turn distributes contributions to the channel's budget from the companies proportionate to their financial strength.

The political status of British broadcasting is complex and subtle, notable for an arms-length relationship to government departments and the lack of a significant role for the courts. The ultimate regulatory and supervisory responsibility falls on the top broadcasting councils, the BBC governors and IBA members, appointed by the Government for five-year terms. They are expected to combine two functions (as the Annan Committee Report on the Future of Broadcasting expressed it): on the one hand "to intervene, chide or even discipline the broadcasters in the public interest"; and on the other hand, to "stand up for the broadcasters' independence and defend them if they consider that in controversy with Government, or with pressure groups of some kind or another, broadcasters are in the right" (Annan, 1977).

Thus the British broadcasting system has been designed with two somewhat opposed principles of "editorial independence" and "public accountability" in mind. The former presupposes that programming should not be under the thumb of any social or political group, particularly that of the government of the day. But the latter presumes that in return for the privileges conferred on them by royal charter and license (BBC) or statute and franchise (ITV), broadcasters should be accountable to certain broad public requirements. The main obligations are to preserve due impartiality in news and the treatment of controversial issues, not to editorialize, to provide a balanced schedule of good-quality programming, to avoid incitement to crime and offenses to decency and (for Independent Broadcasting) to control advertising for amount, misleading claims, and separation from program content.

The influence of both norms can be seen in the day-to-day role of television in British politics. Concerted attempts certainly have been made from time to time by governments, by parties in and out of power, and by bodies representing other organized interests and causes, to influence news and current affairs output—sometimes being able to elicit the desired response as well, at least up to a point. Nevertheless, the belief that such pressures should be resisted has been central to British Broadcasting philosophy. It also played a significant part in ultimately blocking the government's attempt in 1985 to prevent the broadcasting of *Real Lives*, a documentary about Northern Ireland featuring interviews with spokespersons of Protestant militants and Sinn Fein (the political wing of the Irish Republican Army).

Competition between the BBC and ITV may be described as both keen and circumscribed. Certainly, many BBC and ITV producers compete keenly with each other for professional reputation, critical approval, and audience patronage. As far as winning audiences is concerned, both BBC and ITV have aimed at, and usually succeeded in, attracting about half of the total audience over a given period of time. Although it is mainly BBC-1 that competes with ITV-1 for the mass audience, the other two channels are not entirely out of the race; both BBC-2 and Channel 4 aim for up to 10% of the total share of the audience.

Even so, competition in British television has been more circumscribed than in the United States. This is because the two branches of the broadcasting system have tapped revenues from quite different sources, ensuring that each side could afford to lose out a bit from time to time and to pursue other goals as well. It has also eased pressure on each and every program to earn its way with maximum ratings.

British television news responds to all these forces. On the one hand, attracting and holding large audiences matters especially for the news vehicles of BBC-1 and ITV, the editors, specialist correspondents, and reporters of which take keen pride in their journalistic professionalism and performance and routinely monitor each other's work closely. On the other hand, the three main evening programs, being scheduled at different times, avoid direct head-to-head competition. These include BBC-1's *9 O'Clock News* (25 minutes from 9 p.m. nightly), ITV's *News at Ten* (half an hour from 10 p.m.) and *Channel 4 News* (55 minutes from 7 p.m.).

The strict role of news values in their output also is leavened somewhat by two influences. One is sensitivity to the allegation that television news may perpetuate a "bias against understanding" if it hews too closely to the practices of conventional journalism. This may explain a heavy reliance on specialist correspondents especially in the fields of politics and economics. The other reflects the fact that British broadcasting is a creature of Parliament. This has fostered a disposition to show a degree of respect toward the country's main political institutions and a sensitivity toward expectations for broadcasting that are believed to be shared widely throughout the political establishment. Thus, election campaigns enjoy extraordinary treatment, with schedules revamped to include numerous discussion programs and news bulletins lengthened and augmented with many contributions from current affairs specialists. Between elections, coverage of the House of Commons is so extensive and regular that, "For British broadcasting, it can virtually be said that political news *is* Parliamentary news" (Blumler, 1984).

THE FEDERAL REPUBLIC OF GERMANY

The Federal Republic of Germany's broadcasting system in its present form was established by the western Allies immediately after the end of World War II (Hoffman-Riem, 1988). Because broadcasting had been used as a means of indoctrination by the Nazis, the first aim was to keep broadcasting free from any influence of the state. Therefore, instead of one centralized broadcasting system, several public corporations were set up through broadcasting acts or treaties in the federal states.

The public broadcasting stations are controlled by broadcasting councils, which consist of representatives of the public. These councils are mandated to supervise adherence to editorial principles, to advise the director-general in questions of programming policy, to deal with complaints, and to approve the budget. The other two executive bodies are the administrative council, which is basically in charge of budget administration, and the director-general, who is both the chief executive and the top administrative officer of the station as well as the person responsible for the programming output.

All public broadcasting stations are financed primarily by license fees, the amount of which has to be approved by the parliament of each federal state. Another source of income is from advertising, which can be broadcast for a maximum of 25 minutes per day during the early evening hours. Although the early evening program is operated by independent affiliates of the broadcasting stations, these are required to pass a substantial share of their profits to the public corporations.

The general legal basis, the supervisory bodies, and the financial sources apply to all public broadcasting stations in West Germany, although the two television channel systems differ in their nature and actual way of operation. In 1950, the public corporation set up by the Allies formed an association, the ARD (*Arbeitsgemeinschaft der Rundfunkanstalten Deutschlands*), in order to facilitate cooperation and share responsibilities. Each station, however, maintained editorial independence for its service area and can in fact refuse to transmit programs carried by all other stations.

Currently the ARD has 12 members, nine of which jointly operate the nationwide First TV Channel. These stations also operate the Third Channel, which can be received only in the service area of the respective station. In the beginning, the emphasis of the Third Channel was on education, training, and culture, but now more and more popular programs are shown—thus increasing competition among the public stations, in particular for prime-time audiences. To date, commercial cable or satellite TV programs are only available in certain urban areas, and thus are not yet serious competitors for public stations.

Each ARD broadcasting station contributes a precise proportion to all strands of programming on the First Channel, depending on the number of license holders in each service area. Some programs, the most important of which are the daily newscasts, are produced jointly. The main evening newscast, *Tagesschau*, is aired at 8 p.m. and runs for 15 minutes. An average of 14 items is covered each evening, some with filmed reports by correspondents, and some only read by a single newscaster.

Contrary to the federalist structure of the ARD, the Second German Television Channel—the ZDF (*Zweites Deutsches Fernsehen*)—was established in 1961 as a centralist organization. It operates on the basis of a treaty signed by all the states of the Federal Republic. From its headquarters in Mainz, the ZDF provides a nationwide full-time television service, but no radio programs like all the ARD stations. Although this public corporation is completely independent from the ARD, ZDF's director-general is required to coordinate the programming structure of the two networks by offering viewers a choice between two different kinds of programs in the same time slot rather than choosing between two similar programs at any point in time. In practice, however, this coordination agreement hardly ever has worked, at least from the viewer's perspective.

The ZDF's main evening newscast, *Heute*, is broadcast at 7 p.m. and, depending on how many commercials are to follow, runs from 20 to 25 minutes on weekdays. Contrary to the situation on the *Tagesschau*, the news items are presented by an editor who is supposed to have a better understanding of what he is reading, because he is involved in writing the messages, whereas ARD's news anchor reads texts produced by someone else. The format is more similar to the news in the United States, including a separate in-studio weather reporter. Given the greater broadcasting time slot, one *Heute* newscast usually features about 16 items, which tend to be slightly longer than on *Tagesschau* and tend to give some additional background information.

The editorial independence of German public broadcasting is guaranteed in all the states by treaties and acts of their respective parliaments. These acts also oblige them to reflect upon and discuss different and divergent ideological, political, scientific, and cultural convictions, as well as opposing views and opinions.

During the last decade, this implied plurality and overall balance of programming content has degenerated, with more entertainment and fiction programs at the expense of nonfiction. One reason for this is that the major political parties—especially the Christian Democrats and Social Democrats—gained influence on public broadcasting because they could rely not only on their official representation in the broadcasting councils, but also on delegates from other social groups who happened to be party members. They have used their influence in the beginning to appoint as many affiliated party members as possible to higher positions within the organizations, by means of negotiations with each other about the correct proportions. Currently, the need to balance political affiliation proportionately seems to carry throughout the entire organizational and editorial structure (Mahrenholz, 1983).

The consequence for television news and current affairs programs is that in addition to their obligation to present impartial and unbiased reporting, they have to make sure that none of the major parties is more present than the other, and that their portrayal is extremely fair. The political parties constantly monitor the programming output very meticulously for appropriate balance, and as a result of complaints some journalists already have been sanctioned. A news story, therefore, will with very few exceptions present the positions of both the government and the opposition.

ISRAEL

When the present study was conducted, there was only one television channel in Israel, owned by the state and operated by the Israel Broadcasting Authority (IBA). At the time of this writing, a second channel is in the advanced planning stages and "experimental" broadcasts are being conducted.

The bulk of the funding for Israel Television is channeled through the IBA, which also runs Israel's five-station radio network. Most of the revenue comes from a license fee paid by radio and television set owners. Additional revenue comes from the airing of public service announcements shown each day at several points during the broadcasting schedule (Israel Radio is permitted to broadcast commercial advertisements as well as public service announcements). The amount of time devoted to public service announcements on television has increased during the past few years, and the range of sponsors has expanded from purely "public" agencies to semi-commercial entities. Officially, however, no commercials are allowed, although this will most likely change with the formal introduction of the second channel.

The Israel Broadcasting Authority was established by an Act of the Knesseth in 1965 to regulate radio broadcasts in the country. Prior to the introduction of television in Israel in 1968, after the Six-Day War, Israel Radio was run as a department in the Prime Minister's Office. In order to introduce television, the Broadcasting Authority Law was amended. Television was given the responsibility of providing educational, entertainment, and information programs in various life areas with a view to reflecting the life, struggle, creative effort, and achievements of the state;

to foster good citizenship; to strengthen the ties with, and deepen the knowledge of, the Jewish heritage and its values; to reflect the life and cultural assets of all sections of the people from the different countries of origin; to broaden education and disseminate knowledge; to reflect the life of Diaspora Jewry; to further the aims of the State Education Law; to promote Hebrew and Israeli creative endeavors; and to provide broadcasts in Arabic for the Arab-speaking population for the promotion of understanding and peace with the neighboring states in accordance with the basic tendencies of the state.

The Broadcasting Authority is an independent body modeled to a large extent after the British Broadcasting Corporation. The IBA is administered by a plenum of 31 members and a seven-member board of governors. The plenum is appointed by the president of the state and typically consists of members of the major political parties of the country, its academic institutions, and the cultural establishment. The board of governors is selected from among the plenum members by the government. The board is usually a microcosm of the Israeli political establishment. The executive head of the IBA is the director-general, who also is appointed by the government for a five-year term.

The IBA can be considered "somewhat more closely tied to government" than is the BBC, on which it is modeled (Shinar, 1972). Roeh, Katz, Cohen, and Zelizer (1980), when discussing the IBA, point out that "the organizational structure allows for greater political influence than that of the BBC," although in their opinion "it has on the whole resisted such pressure so far" (p. 14). They observe that "in Israel, unlike England, the board of governors is appointed with a 'party key' in mind, and the director-general is appointed by the government" (p. 22).

Smith (1973) however, claims that "the entire atmosphere of Israeli television is bedeviled by politicking. . . . Israel affords an example of what can happen in any democratic system in which the broadcasting body is neither strong nor independent." Despite original intentions to exclude partisan influence, Israel is one country where the "ruling political community has gained the upper hand" and where "the actual conflict between broadcasters and politicians has . . . increased" (pp. 134-135).

In another observation, Peleg (1981) points out that actual active interference and formal control by broadcast management and the director-general over the news department is limited. This, however, creates a stronger system of self-supervision and a stricter observance by news personnel of the Broadcasting Authority Law and of professional demands.

The main television newscast, *Mabat* (meaning "view" or "outlook"), is aired nightly at 9 p.m. (except for an abridged newscast on Friday evenings when it is combined with a weekly news magazine program). It usually lasts 30 minutes, although it is extended up to an hour if the events of the day warrant it. There is also a brief news summary at the end of the evening's broadcasts, around midnight, which usually runs for about 10 minutes. In recent years, this late-night newscast has been expanded and now very often includes an in-depth interview with some person in the news or a debate between two people concerning an event of the day. The news is presented by two newscasters from a pool consisting of approximately eight women and men.

Given the single-channel environment, there is no meaningful Israeli competition. In fact, surveys conducted in Israel from time to time consistently report that about 85% of the adult viewing population watch the news on any given evening, a very high rate of viewing indeed. And yet, Israelis are able to view television programs from their neighboring Arab countries, including newscasts broadcast in Arabic, English, and even in Hebrew (from Jordan Television) that are scheduled in different time slots so as not to conflict with the Israeli *Mabat* program. Surveys have indicated that there is considerable viewing of programs from across the border (the schedule of Jordan Television even appears regularly in the daily Israeli Hebrew press).

Broadcast journalists in Israel subscribe to the basic Western standard of professional norms and news values. Over the years, there have been numerous encounters between the news department and management, or between Israel Television and the government. Recent examples of this complex relationship can be found in directives issued via the board of the IBA, with the objective of limiting coverage of events in the West Bank and Gaza, and particularly with regard to interviews conducted by Israel Television reporters with the members of the outlawed PLO.

On the domestic political front, an attempt is made to maintain a delicate balance in giving access and presenting the points of views of the numerous political parties and factions represented in the Knesseth. In particular, during election campaigns very strict laws regulate the amount of free time allocated to each party's slate of candidates to present its platform and views to the people. Moreover, it is even against the law for television to show the faces of candidates during the 30 days preceding the election, a constraint that makes it extremely difficult to cover the events of the day.

Furthermore, the format and style of news presentation falls somewhere between the British and American manner in terms of selection and composition of news items. There is no formal training of journalists in Israel at the university level. Most of the present television news staff members (particular the more senior ones) have come from radio or print journalism and have learned their roles "on the job." The IBA is strongly unionized, which has made it virtually impossible to fire tenured employees. It is also difficult to rotate jobs or change procedures without union approval. Within the relatively few years of its existence, numerous work slowdowns and strikes have plagued broadcasting in Israel (most recently in 1987 for nearly two months) both on radio and television.

THE REPUBLIC OF SOUTH AFRICA

The South African Broadcasting Corporation (SABC) was created by an Act of Parliament in 1936 to regulate radio broadcasts. It was only in 1976 that television was introduced into South Africa. There was one channel, TV1, broadcasting programs in the two "national" languages, English and Afrikaans. At the end of 1981, two more channels, TV2 and TV3, were opened with programs in African languages. A further channel, TV4, devoted in the main to entertainment has since opened, as has a private channel (called M-Net).

The SABC, therefore, held the broadcasting monopoly in South Africa with responsibility for 24 radio services in 19 languages, and four television services in seven languages. Overall responsibility for the corporation rests with a board, whose 16 members are appointed by the state president. Radio and television do not have separate administrations, and a management committee is headed by a director-general.

The SABC claims to operate in the manner of a public corporation under an independent charter. Charges, however, continue to be made that this is not so, and that it is the mouthpiece for government propaganda:

> Over the past 30 years, through judicial ministerial appointments to the Board, the government has effectively taken control of the SABC. More than half of the members of the Board are today members of the Afrikaner Broederbond, a secret and sectional organization devoted to the interests of the governing party. . . . As a result, since the accession to power of the National Party in 1948, nearly all sensitive senior positions in this semi-State monopoly have been filled with Nationalist adherents. (Dalling, 1983)

The opposition claim that these appointments result in government control of the SABC. The director-general, Riaan Eksteen, in a 1984 address to the Cape Town Press Club admitted the following:

> Because it puts the national interest first, the SABC is an unashamed ally of the state in its fight against the revolutionary onslaught. . . . I am not ashamed of what the SABC has done. Whatever it has done has been done out of sincere conviction.

The state has subsidized the SABC since its inception. Operational losses have decreased over the years, however, with, among other things, an increase in income from advertising and an increase in license fees. In 1987, about 65% of the corporations's income was derived from advertising, and about 26% from license fees (South African Broadcasting Corporation, 1987).

In 1988, at the time of the present study, SABC Television News presented three bulletins a day on the shared English/Afrikaans channel, TV1: at 6 p.m. for approximately 15 minutes, at 8 p.m., for about half an hour, and at the end of the day's transmission for approximately 10 minutes. In fact, the 8 p.m. newscast is presented in English on three alternating days each week, in Afrikaans the other three evenings, and each Sunday in one of the two languages. Each night the news bulletin was presented by a single anchor, although the 8 p.m. bulletin frequently contained in-studio commentaries by SABC journalists.

The format for the news presentations has changed somewhat since 1988. News is now presented informally during a 6 a.m. to 9 a.m. program, *Good Morning South Africa*, at 6 p.m. and at 8 p.m. The close-of-transmission broadcast has been discontinued. Moreover, the 8 p.m. news has been incorporated into an hour-long program, *Network*, consisting of the news, in-depth background information, daily economic news, sports news, and a weather forecast. A total of nearly 14% of all airtime on TV1 is devoted to news and public affairs programs (South African Broadcasting Corporation, 1987).

TV2 and TV3, the African-language programs, also broadcast the news. This could be seen as the only possible competition to the TV1 news transmission.

The 1977 annual SABC report (South African Broadcasting Corporation, 1977) published a policy code for news broadcasting. The code was set out as a series of guidelines to be adopted in order to "avoid falling into the trap—as has happened so often in other parts of the world—of being an instrument for promoting unrest and panic." The guidelines are as follows:

(a) that the dramatic potential of isolated incidents should not be exploited in a manner that would lead to a distorted presentation of the picture as a whole;

(b) that editorial judgment should be applied in any event to ensure that the material presented was representative of what actually occurred;

(c) that the opinion of the silent majority should be solicited in areas affected by disturbances and that the voice of reason should be made audible;

(d) that inciting utterances should be avoided; that cause and effect should be related to one another in any presentation of conflict situations;

(e) that rumors should be ignored and controllable facts only should be presented; and

(f) that reporting should be sober at all times to help avert the inducement of panic and emotional tensions.

Some effort has been made over the last few years, and especially before the national elections of 1987, to allow broadcasting coverage to opposition parties. In 1988, however, Eksteen, the director-general, was removed from his post after giving TV time to a member of an opposition party who had deliberately flouted a directive of the state president. By and large, the SABC has stood by its statement in the 1977 Annual Report that "controversy did not belong in news bulletins."

Critics of SABC, therefore, maintain that its news broadcasts are narrow in scope, bland in comment, antiseptic in style, and biased in content (Dalling, 1983; Hachten, 1979). With the acceleration of internal unrest in South Africa, a state of emergency was declared in 1986. This curtailed news broadcasts even further, with severe censorship being placed on details concerning conflict within the country. One official reason given for imposing the State of Emergency was to prevent sensationalistic coverage of terrorist acts.

Codebook for Content Analysis

			Column
1.	Card number		(1)
2.	Network		(2)
	1. ABC	(U.S.	
	2. ARD	(West Germany)	
	3. BBC	(United Kingdom)	
	4. CBS	(U.S.)	
	5. IBA	(Israel)	
	6. NBC	(U.S.)	
	7. SABC	(South Africa)	
	8. ZDF	(West Germany)	
3.	Wave		(3)
	1. 1980		
	2. 1984		
4.	Date (code in two columns):		(4–5)
	Code day of month using 2 column (eg, 02, 23, etc.)		
5.	Order of item in newscast (01 to xx)		(6–7)

NOTE: AT THE BEGINNING OF EACH NEW CARD
        (CARDS 2–4) COPY COLUMNS 1–7

6.	General topic of item	(8–13)
	Columns 8-10 indicate country	
	Columns 11-12 indicate generic code	
	Column 13 indicates subgroup	

Country code (8-10)

(001)	Abu Dhabi
(002)	Afghanistan
(003)	Albania
(004)	Algeria
(005)	Andorra
(006)	Angola
(007)	Argentina
(008)	Australia
(009)	Austria
(010)	Bahrain
(011)	Bangladesh
(012)	Belgium
(013)	Belize
(014)	Bhutan
(015)	Bolivia
(016)	Botswana
(017)	Brazil
(018)	Bulgaria
(019)	Burma
(020)	Burundi
(021)	Canada
(022)	Central African Republic
(023)	Chad
(024)	Chile
(025)	China—People's Republic
(026)	Colombia
(027)	Congo
(028)	Costa Rica
(029)	Cuba
(030)	Cyprus
(031)	Czechoslovakia
(032)	Denmark
(033)	Dominican Rep.
(034)	Dubai
(035)	Ecuador
(036)	Egypt
(037)	El Salvador
(038)	Equatorial Guinea

(039)	Ethiopia
(040)	Fiji
(041)	Finland
(042)	France
(043)	Gabon
(044)	Gambia
(045)	German Democratic Republic (East Germany)
(046)	Federal Republic of Germany (West Germany)
(047)	Ghana
(048)	Greece
(049)	Guatemala
(050)	Guinea
(051)	Guyana
(052)	Haiti
(053)	Honduras
(054)	Hong Kong
(055)	Hungary
(056)	Iceland
(057)	India
(058)	Indonesia
(059)	Iran
(060)	Iraq
(061)	Ireland
(062)	Israel
(063)	Judea-Samaria
(064)	Gaza Strip
(065)	Golan Heights
(066)	Israel-Occupied Territories
(067)	Italy
(068)	Ivory Coast
(069)	Jamaica
(070)	Japan
(071)	Jordan
(072)	Kampuchea
(073)	Kenya
(074)	Korea—Democratic People's Republic
(075)	Korea, Rep.
(076)	Kuwait
(077)	Laos, PR
(078)	Lebanon

(079)	Lesotho
(080)	Liberia
(081)	Libya
(082)	Liechtenstein
(083)	Luxembourg
(084)	Madagascar
(085)	Malawi
(086)	Malaysia
(087)	Maldive Islands
(088)	Mali
(089)	Mauritania
(090)	Mauritius
(091)	Mexico
(092)	Monaco
(093)	Mongolia
(094)	Morocco
(095)	Mozambique
(096)	Nepal
(097)	Netherlands
(098)	New Zealand
(099)	Nicaragua
(100)	Niger
(101)	Nigeria
(102)	Norway
(103)	Oman
(104)	Pakistan
(105)	Panama
(106)	Paraguay
(107)	Peru
(108)	Philippines
(109)	Poland
(110)	Portugal
(111)	Qatar
(112)	Rumania
(113)	Rwanda
(114)	Samoa
(115)	San Marino
(116)	Saudi Arabia
(117)	Senegal
(118)	Sierra Leone

(119)	Singapore
(120)	Somalia
(121)	South Africa
(122)	South West Africa (Namibia)
(123)	Spain
(124)	Spanish Sahara
(125)	Sri Lanka
(126)	Sudan
(127)	Swaziland
(128)	Sweden
(129)	Switzerland
(130)	Syrian Arab Rep.
(131)	Taiwan
(132)	Tanzania
(133)	Thailand
(134)	Togo
(135)	Trinidad-Tobago
(136)	Tunisia
(137)	Turkey
(138)	Uganda
(139)	USSR
(140)	U. Arab Emirates
(141)	United Kingdom
(142)	United Kingdom—Northern Ireland
(143)	UK—Wales
(144)	United States of America
(145)	Upper Volta
(146)	Uruguay
(147)	Venezuela
(148)	Vietnam
(149)	Vietnam, South
(150)	Western Sahara
(151)	Yemen Arab Rep. (North)
(152)	Yemen Peoples' Democratic (South)
(153)	Yugoslavia
(154)	Zaire
(155)	Zambia
(156)	Zimbabwe
(157)	Cameroon, U. Rep.
(158)	Vatican

(201)   British Commonwealth
(202)   European Economic Community (EEC)
(203)   Arabian Gulf States
(204).   North Atlantic Treaty Organization (NATO)
(205)   Arabian Non-Gulf States
(206)   Northern Hemisphere (Industrial)
(207)   OPEC
(208)   Southern Hemisphere (Underdeveloped)
(209)   Third World
(210)   Warsaw Pact
(211)   United Nations (UN)
(212)   Western Oil Consumers
(998)   More Than One Country
(999)   Cannot Code

Generic Code (11-12) Sub-Group Code (13)

01 *Internal politics* (power politics—power & authority related rather than policy related)

Sub-Group Code	*Examples*
1 Elections/Referendums	Ugandan elections
2 Public opinion about political personalities/ parties and developments affecting this	Public opinion poll results
3 Interparty relations	Israeli PM refusal to attend Labor Party Convention
4 Internal party relations/ single party developments	British Labor Party in-fighting; changing Chairman of Chinese Communist Party; Israeli Labor Party Convention
5 Abuse of political power, corruption of politicians	Investigation of mismanagement in Netivot; charges against Minister Abu-Hatzaira
6 Political appointments	Reagan Cabinet appointments
7 Other national administration	Begin interview; Cabinet meetings
8 Other local (nonnational) administration	
9 Other	

02 *International politics* (mainly about the lack of peace)

1	Current wars between countries	Afghanistan versus Russia (until invasion complete, then becomes internal order); Iran versus Iraq
2	International tension/conflict /sanctions implied or threatened between countries	NATO, Warsaw Pact over Poland; Syria versus Jordan; USA hostages; sanctions against S. Africa
3	International violence/ terrorism by groups against other nationals	PLO attacks in Israel (IRA terrorist attacks in England & N. Ireland—internal order)
4	International disagreements/ arguments not involving fighting or sanctions	State Dept. response to Brezhnev proposal
5	Other diplomacy; international conferences, etc. not related to above or below	
6	Single country foreign policy statements not related to above	American president's foreign policy statement
7	Diplomatic agreements, promises of aid or cooperation	Aid to Italian earthquake victims; El Salvador aid; S. Africa-Israel cooperation; U.S. & Israel settle on sinking of USS Liberty

03 *Defense* (domestic policy, not international deployment)

1	Government defense policy and actions	Missile purchases; defense appropriations
2	Protest at above	Nuclear disarmament marches

04 *Internal order*

1	Civil war/rioting within countries (groups within a country fighting government authorities/assassinating	IRA/Protestant killings, wounding, hunger strikes, nonpeaceful demonstrations; El Salvador fighting; Israeli Arab terrorist actions as opposed to non-Israeli Arab actions; all H-block protest
2	Peaceful demonstrations/ protests (no guns fired,petrol bombs thrown, or bricks & paving stones (thrown) (N. Irish would NOT normally be coded here as they are not peaceful)	

| 3 | Nonpolitical crime | Lennon murder |

3 Nonpolitical crime — Lennon murder

4 Prisons — (Not H-block protests)

5 Other disorder/petty crime — Vandalism, squatting

6 Legal measures (government action) to implement law & order

7 Other

8 Government treatment of dissidents

05 *Economic—general* (strength, state of economy, and policies for its promotion)

1 State of economy and general economic policies (the two have been merged because they often appear together in an item) — Reports on inflation, monetary matters, industrial sales production, economic indicators, interest rates, stock exchange news, employment figures plus monetary policy, fiscal policy, employment policy

06 *Labor relations and trade unions*

1 Strikes/disputes past, present & future, both employer versus employee and inter-union

2 Other labor relations

3 Other trade union matters

4 Legal measures & policy for labor relations and trade unions

07 *Business, commerce, industry*

1 Business, commercial, industrial activities — Individual firms or industries (not general trends)

2 Legal measures & policies towards business

3 International business problems

08 *Transport*

0 General — Possibility of increasing axle weight & size of lorries

09 *Agriculture and fisheries*

0   General

10 *Health, welfare and social services, and public safety measures*

0   General   *Not* disasters/ famines

11 *Population/immigration*

0   General   Large families bill

12 *Education*

0   General

13 *Communication*

1   TV, radio

2   Mail, telephones

3   Press

4   Media regulation

14 *Housing*

0   General

15 *Environment*

1   Threats   Nuclear

2   Damage   Demolition of buildings, threat
                                              to animals

3   Conservation measures   Killing stray animals

16 *Energy*

0   General   OPEC meetings

17 *Science, inventions, technology*

0   General

18 *Social relations* (social tension between groups, exploitation of groups,
             not covered in preceding codes)

1   Sexes—equality,   Women
    discrimination, etc.

2   Ethnic/Race   Busing

3   Classes

4   Age groups   Youth problems per se, the elderly

5   Religious groups

6   Internal family   Battered spouses and children

7 Other

8 Mixed problems

19 *Disasters and accidents*

1 Natural Earthquakes, floods, drought

2 Manmade, technical Fires, air crashes

3 Health Epidemics—cholera, famines

20 *Sport*

1 Reports, results

2 Anti-social behavior of Football hooligans
participants, audience

3 Government/legal/political
pressures

21 *Other cultural*

0 General

22 *Ceremonial*

0 General Royalty

23 *Other human interest*

1 Positive stories Famous people, family life,
eccentricities, awards

2 Negative stories Suicides

24 *Other*

0 General

99 *Cannot code*

0 General

7. Does this item contain social conflict? (14)
    1. yes
    2. yes, but opponent(s) unspecified or taken
       for granted (e.g., court decisions reported)
    3. no
    4. yes, journalist created
    5. yes, but conflict is inconsequential
       to main story

8. How many other social conflict items are (15)
related to this item throughout the
newscast? (0—9+)

9. How many *Non*-conflict items are related to this   (16)
    item throughout the newscast? (0—9+)

10. Does a journalist connect this item to prior events,   (17)
    i.e., is historical context or background given?
    1.   no
    2.   yes, to events of previous day
    3.   yes, to events of previous week
    4.   yes, to events of previous month
    5.   yes, to events of previous year
    6.   yes, to events prior to one year back
    7.   yes, but no reference given to precise time

11. Is the general topic of this item essentially   (18)
    1.   a domestic issue
    2.   a foreign issue
    3.   both a domestic and foreign issue

NOTE: IF RESPONSE TO VARIABLE 7 IS "1" OR "2" CONTINUE
ANALYSIS OF ITEMS.

12. Total number of OPPONENTS in item (without mediators, etc.)   (19)

13. The consequences of this conflict are likely
    to affect (USE INFORMATION FROM ITEM ONLY):   (20)
    1.   One OPPONENT only
    2.   More than one OPPONENT
    3.   Only NON-OPPONENT party or parties
    4.   An opponent and another party other than
            an opponent
    5.   Persons or groups beyond the parties in
            the conflict (including the parties)
    6.   No information about consequences available

14. Call for resolution   (21)
    (USE INFORMATION FROM ITEM ONLY):
    1.   All OPPONENTS call for resolution
    2.   At least one OPPONENT calls for resolution
    3.   No OPPONENT calls for resolution
    4.   Existence of conflict denied by at least
            one OPPONENT
    5.   Existence of conflict denied by ALL OPPONENTS
    6.   MEDIATOR/ARBITRATOR/GO-BETWEEN/IN
            TERESTED PARTY calls for resolution
    7.   6 and 1 above
    8.   6 and 2 above

9. The news media (journalist)
10. The news media and 7 or 8 above

15. State of negotiations   (22)
    (USE INFORMATION FROM ITEM ONLY):

    1. Intensive negotiations taking place
       (OPPONENTS agree not to break off
       negotiations until solution is found)
    2. Negotiations taking place
    3. Attempts to get negotiations started
    4. No negotiations taking place (or no mention
       of negotiations in item)
    5. Opposition by at least one OPPONENT to
       negotiations
    6. Negotiations took place IN THE PAST only

16. Willingness to compromise   (23)
    (USE INFORMATION FROM ITEM ONLY):
    1. All OPPONENTS willing to give up
       some demands
    2. At least one OPPONENT willing to give
       up some demands
    3. No OPPONENT willing to give up some
       demands) (or no reference is made to
       relinquishing any demands)
    4. One OPPONENT not willing to give up
       any demands
    5. One OPPONENT not willing and at least
       one OPPONENT IS willing (combining
       2 and 4 above)

17. Scope of conflict (choose BROADEST)   (24)
    1. Local
    2. Regional
    3. National
    4. International

18. Outcome of conflict (USE INFORMATION   (25)
    FROM ITEM ONLY):
    1. Withdrawal (at least one OPPONENT
       withdraws demands)
    2. Imposition (victory and defeat)
    3. Compromise (mutual concessions)
    4. Conversion (one side converts to
       other's position)
    5. No mention of solution

19. VERBALLY reported PHYSICAL aggression   (26)
    (score highest):
        0.   None
        1.   Physical aggression without damage,
                wounding or killing
        2.   Imprisonment
        3.   Damage to property (including living
                nonhumans)
        4.   Physically wounding at least one person
        5.   Damage and wounding
        6.   Killing
        7.   Damage and killing
        8.   Wounding and killing
        9.   Damage, wounding and killing

20. VISUALLY shown PHYSICAL aggression   (27)
    SAME CATEGORIES AS FOR VARIABLE 19

21. VERBALLY reported VERBAL aggression   (28)
        1.   no
        2.   yes

22. VISUALLY shown VERBAL aggression   (29)
        1.   no
        2.   yes

23. VERBALLY reported EMOTIONAL display   (30)
        1.   no
        2.   yes

24. VISUALLY shown EMOTIONAL display   (31)
        1.   no
        2.   yes

25 How many slides and photos (still pictures)   (32)
    are used? in the item (0—9+)

26. How many graphics (charts, figures, etc.)   (33)
    are used?
    in the item (0—9+)

27. How many cases of printed words (entire   (34)
    quotes counted as 1 even if broken up) other
    than photo or film IDs of people are used? (0—9+)

28. How many times is moving film used?   (35)
    (Code 1 for each geographic location if
    hops around the world are used, but not if
    just changes within building, etc.) (0—9+)

29. How many clips (film or video) or correspondents in the field are used? (Stand-ups in front of bland or nonaction background count here and not in Variable 28) (0—9+) (36)

30. Total number of seconds of ANCHOR PEOPLE in the item(in studio only) (000 to xxx) (37–39)

31. Total number of seconds of CORRESPONDENTS IN THE FIELD (not in studio) (000 to xxx) (40–42)

32. Total number of seconds of entire film, video clips or stills which contain physical aggression, of any kind (using definitions in Vars. 19 and 20) computed together for all aggressive clips in the item (000 to xxx) (43–45)

33. Total number of seconds of clips in item as defined in Variable 28 (include freeze frames which are part of clips and not separate still photos) (000 to xxx) (ALL MOVING CLIPS) (46–48)

34. Total number of voice-overs of journalists in clips used in item (each voice-over interspersed with live action counts as 1) (00 to xx) (49–50)

35. Number of cuts in whole item (including studio time) (00 to xx) (51–52)

36. Number of close-up shots (bust to extreme close-up) of Party A (each cut counts as one, zoom-ins and zoom-outs in one count as 1) (00 to xx) (53–54)

37. Close-ups of Party B (55–56)

38. Close-ups of Party C (57–58)

39. Close-ups of Party D (59–60)

40. Close-ups of Party E (61–62)

41. Close-ups of Party F (63–64)

42. How many clips (film or tape) of NON-ANCHOR news persons speaking in the studio (sit-ups) are used? (0—9+) (65)

43. Total number of seconds of NON-ANCHOR news persons in studio (sit-ups) (000 to xxx) (66–68)

44. Length of item (in seconds) (69–71)

THE FOLLOWING VARIABLES APPLY TO THE PARTIES FILE. A
MAXIMUM OF 6 PARTIES CAN BE CODED. THE PARTIES ARE
LABELED "A" THROUGH "F". THE COLUMN NUMBERS WILL
APPEAR IN A TABLE FOLLOWING THE VARIABLES.

45. Party entity (Use Appendix B)

46. Is this party
    1.   an opponent
    2.   a mediator
    3.   an arbitrator (including courts when relevant)
    4.   a go-between
    5.   an interested party (including "victims")

47. Does this party connect this conflict to prior events
     by giving it historical context or background?
    1.   no
    2.   yes, to events of previous day
    3.   yes, to events of previous week
    4.   yes, to events of previous month
    5.   yes, to events of previous year
    6.   yes, to events prior to one year back
    7.   yes, but no reference given to precise time

48. Is the entity represented
    1.   A private party
    2.   A public party—IRA
    3.   A government agency or ministry (e.g., the Pentagon,
          Treasury, CIA, Dept. of Agriculture, Social Security
          Administration)
    4.   A full government (e.g., the Israeli Govt., the govt.
          of Texas or Bavaria)
    5.   A non-organized or ad-hoc organization
    6.   Group of governments

49. How many NON-OFFICIAL persons speak for
     the party? (0—9+)

50. How many OFFICIAL persons speak for the
     party? (0—9+)

51. How many NON-OFFICIAL persons are directly or indirectly
     quoted by journalists speaking for the party ? (0—9+)

52. How many OFFICIAL persons are directly or indirectly
     quoted by journalists speaking for the party? (0—9+)
     ("informed sources" count as 1 person)

53. The position of this party is described by:
    1.   an anchor
    2.   a reporter
    3.   more than one reporter
    4.   1 and 2 above
    5.   1 and 3 above
    6.   neither reporter(s) nor anchor

54. The position of this party is advocated by:
    1.   an anchor
    2.   a reporter
    3.   more than one reporter
    4.   1 and 2 above
    5.   1 and 3 above
    6.   neither reporter(s) nor anchor

55. By how many PEOPLE is this party VISUALLY represented?
    (DO NOT count journalists, i.e., reporters or anchors).
    Include slides and still pictures.
    1.   none
    2.   one person
    3.   two or three persons
    4.   four to ten people
    5.   more than 10 to an uncountable number

56. The human representative seen or quoted who represents the
    HIGHEST position in the party entity is:
    1.   Top leader
    2.   Middle level person (including "spokesman")
    3.   Regular member

57. The human representative seen or quoted who represents the
    LOWEST position in the party entity is:
    1.   Top leader
    2.   Middle level person (including "spokesman")
    3.   Regular member

    NOTE: If only one human representative seen or quoted in item,
           score Variable 57 the same as for Variable 56.

58. How many interviewees are interviewed as representatives of this
    party? (0—9+)

59. Total number of seconds of interviewing taking place with
    representatives of this party (000—xxx)

60. During how many seconds in the item are representatives of this party present (audio and visual presence) including the interviewer (000—xxx)

61. If this party is an OPPONENT or an ARBITRATOR or a MEDIATOR, does it describe another OPPONENT'S position?
    1. yes
    2. no—irrelevant, this party is a go-between or an interested party

62. The MAXIMUM scope of this party's influence is (USE BACKGROUND KNOWLEDGE):
    1. local, community
    2. regional
    3. national
    4. international

63. From this party's point of view, who initiated the conflict (use only EXPLICIT accusations or the like made in item)
    1. This party
    2. Other party or parties
    3. This and other party/parties both responsible
    4. No information about this party's point of view
    5. The news media

64. Is this party said to have at least helped to initiate the conflict? (use only EXPLICIT statements or accusations or the like made in item)
    1. Yes, by an anchor
    2. Yes, by a reporter
    3. Yes, by both a reported and an anchor
    4. No

THE FOLLOWING TABLE INDICATES THE LOCATION OF VARIABLES 45-64 FOR EACH OF THE 6 PARTIES (A THROUGH F). THE FORMAT OF THE TABLE SPECIFIES THAT THE NUMBER TO THE LEFT OF THE SLASH (/) IS THE CARD NUMBER AND THE NUMBER(S) TO THE RIGHT OF THE SLASH (/) IS/ARE THE COLUMN NUMBER(S).
NOTE: COLUMNS 1-7 OF CARD 1 MUST BE COPIED IN CARDS 2-4.

VARIABLE PARTY	PARTY A	PARTY B	PARTY C	PARTY D	PARTY E	PARTY F
45	2/8-12	2/37-41	3/8-12	3/37-41	4/8-12	4/37-41
46	2/13	2/42	3/13	3/42	4/13	4/42
47	2/14	2/43	3/14	3/43	4/14	4/43
48	2/15	2/44	3/15	3/44	4/15	4/44
49	2/16	2/45	3/16	3/45	4/16	4/45
50	2/17	2/46	3/17	3/46	4/17	4/46
51	2/18	2/47	3/18	3/47	4/18	4/47
52	2/19	2/48	3/19	3/48	4/19	4/48
53	2/20	2/49	3/20	3/49	4/20	4/49
54	2/21	2/50	3/21	3/50	4/21	4/50
55	2/22	2/51	3/22	3/51	4/22	4/51
56	2/23	2/52	3/23	3/52	4/23	4/52
57	2/24	2/53	3/24	3/53	4/24	4/53
58	2/25	2/54	3/25	3/54	4/25	4/54
59	2/26-28	2/55-57	3/26-28	3/55-57	4/26-28	4/55-57
60	2/29-31	2/58-60	3/29-31	3/58-60	4/29-31	4/58-60
61	2/32	2/61	3/32	3/61	4/32	4/61
62	2/33	2/62	3/33	3/62	4/33	4/62
63	2/34	2/63	3/34	3/63	4/34	4/63
64	2/35	2/64	3/35	3/64	4/35	4/64

The last two variables are the length of the newscast, in two versions. They should only be computed once and inserted for each line.

65. Running time of newscast (without commercials and weather but including headlines (in minutes and seconds)　　(2/66–68)

66. Total length of all *items* in newscast (in seconds)　　(2/69–72)

NOTE: Column 36 is left blank in cards 2–4 to enable a visual check on punching.

Coders' Guide

A basic reminder: *A social conflict is a dispute between two or more social groups or their representatives concerning at least one issue, goal, topic or idea.*

Variable 6: Topic Code

First three columns are country of the TOPIC, not necessarily the country where the story takes place. Thus U.S. foreign policy story is 144 (United States), Meeting of NATO foreign ministers is 204 (NATO) rather than Belgium where the meeting takes place. 998 (more than one country) applies if the TOPIC includes more than once country—e.g., East-West confrontation.

Variable 10: Historical Context

Note this does NOT include historical references that are the substance of the story—i.e., a government report on the housing industry in 1983. Historical context is presented when you find out the background for the story, i.e., the report was ordered when the housing industry collapsed in 1981. Typical examples of historical context are discussions of prior related events—in first wave, story of potential Soviet invasion of Poland was background often by discussions of previous Soviet invasions of Hungary and Czechoslovakia.

Variable 11: Domestic-Foreign

Domestic must be purely domestic (e.g., Israeli report of a transit strike in Tel Aviv); Foreign must be purely foreign (e.g., South African report of Canadian strike); Domestic and foreign combined, often by tying domestic concerns into foreign stories (e.g., American report of U.S. Navy shelling Beirut; British report of U.S. drought, including its effect on price of pasta in Britain).

Variable 13: Consequences

Code 5 may include parties and others, i.e., persons or groups beyond the parties in the conflict OR persons beyond the parties AND the parties.

Variable 15: State of Negotiations

If more than one code applies, e.g., opposition by one opponent and attempts to get negotiations started,then code most negative/recalcitrant (e.g., opposition by one opponent).

Variables 19 and 20: Physical Aggression

Code 1 (physical aggression without damage, wounding or killing) includes the verbal or visual report of troops marching, tanks, planes, etc., on display. For example, the May Day parade in Moscow would be coded as 1.

Variables 21 and 22: Verbal Aggression

Examples of verbal aggression include: use of profane language, heated formal debate, general yelling, general threats, threats made to property of a party, threats made to a party's well-being or life.

Variables 23 and 24: Emotional Display

Examples of emotional display include: nonverbal emotion such as grief, fear, or joy vocal (nonlinguistic) behavior such as laughing, crying, shouting sounds, applauding; and hysteria, euphoria, wailing, continuous screaming, extreme quiet or stoicism, ecstasy.

Variable 25: Number of Still Photos

Count each photo as 1.

Variable 26: Number of Graphics

Computer-generated graphics count here. As long as it is the same graphic, even though it may have movement in the graphic, count it as 1. Thus a chart of economic growth counts as only 1 even though they superimpose two different curves on it.

Variable 27: Number of Printed Words

DO NOT count IDs of people ("Peter Jennings, Parking Lot in Poland") or of locations ("Moscow"). Count extended quotations as only 1 case of printed words.

Variable 28: Number of Moving Film/Tapes

Beware of changes of film within a building, they do not count separately. ONLY count changes when there is a location change.

Variable 32: Seconds of Film/Tape with Aggression

Time the film/tape. Do not include still photos in timing. Do include freeze frames.

Variable 34: Number of Voice-Overs

These are voice overs by JOURNALISTS only. Note they count as 1 until interrupted by live action sound.

Variable 35: Number of Cuts

Begin counting cuts with the opening cut (i.e., from previous program). Count each full screen change as a cut (zooms do NOT count as cuts, nor do inserts count as cuts).

Variables 36-41: Number of Close-Ups

Count only bust shots to extreme close-ups. Use coat pocket as a good measure of bust shot. If shot opens wide and zooms to a close-up count as a close-up. If shot opens as a close-up and zooms wide count as a close-up.

Variable 42: Number of Sit-Ups

Count number of nonanchor JOURNALISTS appearing during the item.

Variable 44: Total Length of Items in Newscast

Sum the item times and enter here. The same number is recorded for all items on that day.

Variable 46: Party Type

Opponents are directly involved in producing the conflict; Mediators are involved in trying to solve the conflicts; Arbitrators have the power to solve the conflict (e.g., courts); Go-betweens simply carry messages between the opponents; Interested parties are concerned/affected by the conflict and its outcome (victims are a good example).

Variable 47: Historical Context

Same as for Variable 10.

Variable 48: Entity

A private party is defined as individuals, profit-making corporations, privately funded organizations. A public party includes nonprofit-making corporations or institutions funded by the general public, nationalized industries, political parties, etc.

Variables 49 and 51: Nonofficial Persons

A nonofficial person is a person NOT holding an official position in any capacity in the group, organization, etc. Note this would mean a local union president is official.

Variables 51 and 52: Quotations Seen or Heard

Note that indirect quotations (paraphrases) count for both variables. Thus statements like: "President Reagan told reporters today that he was losing his mind" is a quotation for the purpose of these variables.

Variables 50 and 52: Official Person

Official person holds some official position in the group or the organization.

Variable 55: Number of Visual Representatives

You must see people, not just tanks, cars, etc.

Variables 56 and 57: Level of Human Representative

Top level means policy-making authority (e.g., foreign minister); Middle level equals person not in charge of policy-making, but who is in charge of implementing policy (e.g., ambassadors); Regular member equals a person with no policy-making authority nor policy implementing responsibilities. 0=nobody represented.

Variable 58: Number of Interviews

Count the appearance of a party as an interview UNLESS it is clear that they are making a statement or giving a speech. This sometimes requires judgement as you may feel PM Thatcher is first shown making a statement, then later shown answering questions. You might code the second appearance as an interview, NOT the first.

Variable 59: Interviewing Time

Count all time when it appears an interview is taking place (using the definition of an interview mentioned in Variable 58). Include time when live questions are asked and live answers are presented.

Variable 60: Seconds of Visual and Audio Presence

Count time when representatives are seen on still photos as well as moving film/tape and when representatives are HEARD.

Variables 63 and 64: Explicit Accusations of Initiating Conflict

This must be accusations about INITIATION of conflict, not about behavior during conflict.

APPENDIX C

Survey Questionnaire

COVER LETTER (U.S. VERSION)

UNIVERSITY OF MINNESOTA

March, 1984

Dear Student,

In the following pages you will find a few sets of questions about social conflicts. We will also ask you some questions about your TV viewing habits and use of other mass media.

This questionnaire is being used simultaneously in several countries as part of a large international project which compares the opinions of Americans with those of people your age and education in the other countries. This is *not* a test, so that there are no correct or incorrect answers. We are *not* asking you to provide your name nor any other information which would identify you personally, thus your responses will be anonymous and confidential. We ask that you, therefore, give your own opinions as truthfully as possible so that the information we get will be meaningful. Your participation in completing this questionnaire is, of course, voluntary.

Before you begin with the questions, here are some brief explanations.

Every time we mention the term "social conflict" we mean a dispute between groups, organizations, governments, etc., concerning some issue(s) or topic(s). By "social conflict" we do *not* mean a dispute between individual people concerning personal matters.

When we mention *international* social conflicts we mean a dispute between countries like between Vietnam and Cambodia or between the U.S. and Iran; when we mention *national* social conflicts, we refer to disputes between different *national*-level groups *within* the country like between political parties or between government and / or public agencies; and when we say *local* social conflicts, we mean disputes between *local*-level groups within the city, country or state, such as here in Minneapolis or Minnesota.

Since we *cannot* possibly ask you about *all* social conflicts, we will ask you about conflicts "*in general*" or about "*typical*" conflicts. We know that it is sometimes difficult to tell if something is typical or not; in any event, try as best you can to relate to the general situation and not to deal with any specific example.

For each question, just circle the number of the answer which seems most appropriate for you. Sometimes you will be asked to add a few words as part of your answer. If you cannot answer a question, simply leave it blank. If you have any questions, please raise your hand and someone will come over and assist you. If you have any questions at a future date please contact either of us at the address above.

Thank you very much for your cooperation.

> Dr. Charles Bantz and Dr. Akiba Cohen
> Project Directors

Office Use Only:

1 = Country
2 = Track
3-5 = ID number
6 = Card number

HERE ARE SOME GENERAL QUESTIONS ON DIFFERENT KINDS OF CONFLICTS.

7. How important is it for you to know about *international* counflicts (disputes between countries)?

   1. very important
   2. quite important
   3. not so important
   4. not important at all

8. How important is it for you to know about *national* conflicts (disputes between national-level groups)?
   1.   very important
   2.   quite important
   3.   not so important
   4.   not important at all

9. How important is it for you to know about *local* conflicts (disputes between local-level groups)?
   1.   very important
   2.   quite important
   3.   not so important
   4.   not important at all

10. How much does *TV news* help you get information on *international* conflicts?
    1.   helps me very much
    2.   helps me quite a lot
    3.   helps me a little
    4.   doesn't help me at all

11. How much does *TV news* help you get information on *national* conflicts?
    1.   helps me very much
    2.   helps me quite a lot
    3.   helps me a little
    4.   doesn't help me at all

12. How much does *TV news* help you get information on *local* conflicts?
    1.   helps me very much
    2.   helps me quite a lot
    3.   helps me a little
    4.   doesn't help me at all

13. How much does *radio news* help you get information on *international* conflicts
    1.   helps me very much
    2.   helps me quite a lot
    3.   helps me a little
    4.   doesn't help me at all

14. How much does *radio news* help you get information on *national* conflicts?
    1.   helps me very much
    2.   helps me quite a lot
    3.   helps me a little
    4.   doesn't help me at all

15. How much does *radio news* help you get information on *local* conflicts?
    1. helps me very much
    2. helps me quite a lot
    3. helps me a little
    4. doesn't help me at all

16. How much do *newspapers* help you get information on *international* conflicts?
    1. help me very much
    2. help me quite a lot
    3. help me a little
    4. don't help me at all

17. How much do *newspapers* help you get information on *national* conflicts?
    1. help me very much
    2. help me quite a lot
    3. help me a little
    4. don't help me at all

18. How much do *newspapers* help you get information on *local* conflicts?
    1. help me very much
    2. help me quite a lot
    3. help me a little
    4. don't help me at all

THE FOLLOWING QUESTIONS ARE TO FIND OUT WHAT YOU THINK CONFLICTS ARE ACTUALLY LIKE IN *REAL LIFE*.

19. At any given time, in *real life*, how many *international* conflicts are going on simultaneously?
    1. many
    2. several
    3. none

20. At any given time, in *real life*, how many *national* conflicts are going on simultaneously?
    1. many
    2. several
    3. none

21. At any given time, in *real life*, how many *local* conflicts are going on simultaneously?
    1. many
    2. several
    3. none

We would now like to ask you about the *complexity* of conflicts in *real life*. How complex are the majority of these conflicts?

22. In *real life, international* conflicts are usually . . .
    1. high complexity
    2. medium complexity
    3. low complexity

23. In *real life, national* conflicts are usually of . . .
    1. high complexity
    2. medium complexity
    3. low complexity

24. In *real life, local* conflicts are usually of . . .
    1. high complexity
    2. medium complexity
    3. low complexity

Now we will ask you about the *intensity* of conflicts in *real life*. How intense are the majority of these conflicts?

25. In *real life, international* conflicts usually are . . .
    1. high intensity
    2. medium intensity
    3. low intensity

26. In *real life, national* conflicts usually are of . . .
    1. high intensity
    2. medium intensity
    3. low intensity

27. In *real life, local* conflicts usually are of . . .
    1. high intensity
    2. medium intensity
    3. low intensity

Now here are some questions on the *solvability* of conflicts, that is, on how *easy* or *difficult* it is to solve social conflicts. How easy or difficult is it to solve the majority of these conflicts?

28. In *real life, international* conflicts usually are . . .
    1. solved quite easily
    2. solved with some difficulty
    3. solved with much difficulty or not at all

29. In *real life, national* conflicts usually are . . .
    1. solved quite easily
    2. solved with some difficulty
    3. solved with much difficulty or not at all

30. In *real life*, *local* conflicts usually are . . .
    1. solved quite easily
    2. solved with some difficulty
    3. solved with much difficulty or not at all

31. In *real life*, how often do *international* conflicts have an impact on other conflicts (either international, national or local)?
    1. often
    2. sometimes
    3. seldom

32. In *real life*, how often do *national* conflicts have an impact on other conflicts (either international, national or local)?
    1. often
    2. sometimes
    3. seldom

33. In *real life*, how often do *local* conflicts have an impact on other conflicts (either international, national or local)?
    1. often
    2. sometimes
    3. seldom

34. In *real life*, how often are *international* conflicts caused by past events or other historical disputes?
    1. often
    2. sometimes
    3. seldom

35. In *real life*, how often are *national* conflicts caused by past events or other historical disputes?
    1. often
    2. sometimes
    3. seldom

36. In *real life*, how often are *local* conflicts caused by past events or other historical disputes?
    1. often
    2. sometimes
    3. seldom

THE FOLLOWING QUESTIONS ARE ABOUT CONFLICTS AS THEY ARE REPORTED IN TV NEWS. ANSWER THESE QUESTIONS BASED ON YOUR VIEWING OF NATIONAL NETWORK NEWS (either ABC's *WORLD NEWS TONIGHT* or the *CBS EVENING NEWS* or *NBC NIGHTLY NEWS*)

37. Generally, how much of the news is taken up by stories of conflict?
    1. the whole newscast
    2. most it
    3. about half of it
    4. a small part of it
    5. no part of the newscast

38. Are most of the conflicts on TV news concerned with *international, national* or *local* issues?
    1. most are international
    2. most are national
    3. most are local
    4. most are international and national
    5. most are international and local
    6. most are national and local
    7. about the same of all three kinds

39. How frequently are *international* conflicts reported on TV news?
    1. every day
    2. several days a week
    3. hardly ever

40. How frequently are *national* conflicts reported on TV news?
    1. every day
    2. several days a week
    3. hardly ever

41. How frequently are *local* conflicts reported on TV news?
    1. every day
    2. several days a week
    3. hardly ever

We would now like to ask you about the *complexity* of conflicts as they are reported *in TV news*. How complex are the majority of these conflicts?

42. In *TV news, international* conflicts are usually of . . .
    1. high complexity
    2. medium complexity
    3. low complexity

43. In *TV news, national* conflicts are usually of . . .
    1. high complexity
    2. medium complexity
    3. low complexity

44. In *TV news, local* conflicts are usually of . . .
    1. high complexity

2.   medium complexity
3.   low complexity

Now we will ask you about the *intensity* of conflicts as they are reported *in TV news*. How intense are the majority of these conflicts?

45. In *TV news, international* conflicts usually are of . . .
1.   high intensity
2.   medium intensity
3.   low intensity

46. In *TV news, national* conflicts usually are of . . .
1.   high intensity
2.   medium intensity
3.   low intensity

47. In *TV news, local* conflicts usually are of . . .
1.   high intensity
2.   medium intensity
3.   low intensity

And now are some questions on the *solvability* of conflicts, that is, on how *easy* or *difficult* it is to solve conflicts. How easy or difficult is it to solve the majority of these conflicts?

48. In *TV news, international* conflicts usually are . . .
1.   solved quite easily
2.   solved with some difficulty
3.   solved with much difficulty or not at all

49. In *TV news, national* conflicts usually are . . .
1.   solved quite easily
2.   solved with some difficulty
3.   solved with much difficulty or not at all

50. In *TV news, local* conflicts usually are . . .
1.   solved quite easily
2.   solved with some difficulty
3.   solved with much difficulty or not at all

51. How often are *international* conflicts linked together with other conflicts (either international, national or local) *on TV news*?
1.   often
2.   sometimes
3.   seldom

52. How often are *national* conflicts linked together with other conflicts (either international, national or local) *on TV news*?
1.   often

2.   sometimes
3.   seldom

53. How often are *local* conflicts linked together with other conflicts (either international, national or local) *on TV news*?
   1.   often
   2.   sometimes
   3.   seldom

54. Generally, how often do news people explain the background of *international* conflicts?
   1.   often
   2.   sometimes
   3.   seldom

55. Generally, how often do news people explain the background of *national* conflicts?
   1.   often
   2.   sometimes
   3.   seldom

56. Generally, how often do news people explain the background of *local* conflicts?
   1.   often
   2.   sometimes
   3.   seldom

57. How often do news people take sides with the position of one of the opponents in *international* conflicts?
   1.   often
   2.   sometimes
   3.   seldom

58. How often do news people take sides with the position of one of the opponents in *national* conflicts?
   1.   often
   2.   sometimes
   3.   seldom

59. How often do news people take sides with the position of one of the opponents in *local* conflicts?
   1.   often
   2.   sometimes
   3.   seldom

60. When reporting on an *international* conflict, how often are relatively *important* people such as top leaders of government or elected

officials, top military people or experts quoted, shown or interviewed in the newscast?
   1.   often
   2.   sometimes
   3.   seldom

61. When reporting on an *international* conflict, how often are relatively *less important* people such as the "man in the street" or regular people quoted, shown or interviewed in the newscast?
   1.   often
   2.   sometimes
   3.   seldom

62. When reporting on a *national* conflict, how often are relatively *important* people such as top leaders of government or elected officials and heads of national organizations quoted, shown or interviewed in the newscast?
   1.   often
   2.   sometimes
   3.   seldom

63. When reporting on a *national* conflict, how often are relatively *less important* people such as the "man in the street" and rank-and-file members of national organizations quoted shown or interviewed in the newscast?
   1.   often
   2.   sometimes
   3.   seldom

64. When reporting on a *local* conflict, how often are relatively *important* people such as mayors, city council members or leaders of local groups quoted, shown or interviewed in the newscast?
   1.   often
   2.   sometimes
   3.   seldom

65. When reporting on a *local* conflict, how often are relatively *less important* people such as the "man in the street", residents of the community or members of local groups quoted shown or interviewed in the newscast?
   1.   often
   2.   sometimes
   3.   seldom

66. How often are photographs of people in the news shown on the TV screen when reporting on conflicts?
   1.   whenever such a conflict is reported

    2.   when some of these conflicts are reported
    3.   they are never shown on the screen

67. How often are "printed words" (such as quotations or translation) shown on the TV screen when reporting on conflicts?
    1.   whenever such a conflict is reported
    2.   when some of these conflicts are reported
    3.   they are never shown on the screen

68. Do you think that TV news presents *international* conflicts the way they are in real life?
    1.   to a large extent
    2.   to some extent
    3.   not at all

69. Do you think that TV news presents *national* conflicts the way they are in real life?
    1.   to a large extent
    2.   to some extent
    3.   not at all

70. Do you think that TV news presents *local* conflicts the way they are in real life?
    1.   to a large extent
    2.   to some extent
    3.   not at all

71. Do you think that in *real life* conflicts are good or bad for society?
    1.   all conflicts are good for society
    2.   most are good and some are bad for society
    3.   about an equal amount are good for society
    4.   most are bad and some are good for society
    5.   all conflicts are bad for society

72. On *TV news*, are conflicts presented as good or bad for society?
    1.   all conflicts are presented as good for society
    2.   most are presented as good and some as bad for society
    3.   about an equal amount are presented as good and as bad
    4.   most are presented as bad and some as good for society
    5.   all conflicts are presented as bad for society

73. Have you had *first-hand* experience with *international* conflicts?
    1.   a lot of experience, such as _____
    2.   some experience, such as _____
    3.   no, but a relative or friend of mine did, such as _____
    4.   no experience at all

74. Have you had *first-hand* experience with *national* conflicts?
    1. a lot of experience, such as _____
    2. some experience, such as _____
    3. no, but a relative or friend of mine did, such as _____
    4. no experience at all

75. Have you had *first-hand* experience with *local* conflicts?
    1. a lot of experience, such as _____
    2. some experience, such as _____
    3. no, but a relative or friend of mine did, such as _____
    4. no experience at all

76. In your opinion, is it desirable for TV news to report on *international* conflicts?
    1. very desirable
    2. desirable
    3. not desirable at all

77. In your opinion, it is desirable for TV news to report on *national* conflicts?
    1. very desirable
    2. desirable
    3. not desirable at all

78. In your opinion, it is desirable for TV news to report on *local* conflicts?
    1. very desirable
    2. desirable
    3. not desirable at all

[Second Computer Record]

7. Do you think that your view of life is similar or different to that of your *parents*?
   1. very similar
   2. somewhat similar
   3. somewhat different
   4. very different

8. Do you think that your view of life is similar or different to that of your *friends*?
   1. very similar
   2. somewhat similar
   3. somewhat different
   4. very different

9. Do you think that your view of life is similar or different to that of *people your age in other Western countries*?

1. very similar
2. somewhat similar
3. somewhat different
4. very different

HERE ARE SOME QUESTIONS ABOUT YOUR USE OF THE MASS MEDIA.

10. How many *hours* do you *generally* watch TV each day, Monday through Friday?

    _____ hours

11. Do you watch the *national* evening news on TV?
    1. regularly, every evening
    2. several times a week
    3. only on rare occasions
    4. never

12. Do you spend any time reading the *news section* of a newspaper (*not* including the sports and the comics)?
    1. every day
    2. almost every day
    3. only on rare occasions
    4. never

13. Do you listen to the news on the radio?
    1. several times each day
    2. once or twice each day
    3. only once each day
    4. only on some days
    5. never

FINALLY, HERE ARE SOME QUESTIONS ABOUT YOURSELF. YOUR ANSWERS TO THE QUESTIONS WILL *NOT* IDENTIFY YOU PERSONALLY, BUT WILL HELP US WITH OUR ANALYSES OF THE RESULTS OF THE STUDY.

14. Are you . . .
    1. male
    2. female

15. Country of birth _____

16. Your father's country of birth _____

17. Your mother's country of birth _____

18. Your father's occupation _____

19. Your mother's occupation _____

20. Your religious affiliation _____

21. How many people live in your household (including yourself)?
   _____

THANK YOU VERY MUCH FOR YOUR COOPERATION.

References

Abel, E. (1984). Television in international conflict. In A. Arno & W. Dissanayake (Eds.), *The news media in national and international conflict* (pp. 63-70). Boulder, CO: Westview.

Adoni, H. (1989). Supplementary strategies in comparative news research. *American Behavioral Scientist, 33,* 234-237.

Adoni, H., & Cohen, A. A. (1978). Television economic news and the social construction of economic reality. *Journal of Communication, 28,* 61-70.

Adoni, H., Cohen, A. A., & Mane, S. (1984). Adolescents' perception of social conflicts in social reality and television news. *Journal of Broadcasting, 28,* 33-49.

Adoni, H., & Mane, S. (1984). Media and the social construction of reality: Towards an integration of theory and research. *Communication Research, 11,* 323-340.

Adorno, T. W., & Horkheimer, M. (1972). *The dialectics of enlightenment.* New York: Seabury.

Alexander, J. C. (1981). The mass media in systemic, historical, and comparative perspective. In E. Katz & T. Szecsko (Eds.), *Mass media and social change* (pp. 17-51). London: Sage.

Altheide, D. L. (1976). *Creating reality: How TV news distorts events.* Beverly Hills, CA: Sage.

Althusser, L. (1971). Ideology and ideological state apparatuses. In *Lenin and philosophy and other essays.* London: New Left Books.

Annan. (1977). *Report of the committee on the future of broadcasting.* London: HMSO.

Arno, A., & Dissanayake, W. (1984). *The news media in national and international conflict.* Boulder: Westview.

Ball-Rokeach, S. J. (1985). The origins of individual media-system dependency. *Communication Research, 12,* 485-510.

Ball-Rokeach, S., & DeFleur, M. (1976). A dependency model of mass media effects. *Communication Research, 3,* 3-21.

Bantz, C. R., McCorkle, S., & Baade, R. C. (1980). The news factory. *Communication Research, 7,* 45-68.

Barnes, B. (1988). *The nature of power.* Oxford: Polity Press.

Barnouw, E. (1978). *The sponsor: Notes on a modern potentate.* New York: Oxford University Press.

Benjamin, W. (1970). *Illuminations.* London: Cape.

Berger, P. L., & Luckmann, T. (1967). *The social construction of reality.* New York: Anchor.

246

Blumer, H. (1933). *Movies and conduct*. New York: Macmillan.

Blumler, J. G. (1980). Mass communication research in Europe: Some origins and prospects. *Media, Culture and Society, 2,* 367-376.

Blumler, J. (1984). The sound of Parliament. *Parliamentary Affairs, 37,* 250-266.

Blumler, J., & Gurevitch, M. (1975). Towards a comparative framework for political communication research. In S. Chaffee (Ed.), *Political communication* (pp. 165-193). Beverly Hills, CA: Sage.

Blumler, J., & Gurevitch, M. (1981). Politicians and the press: An essay on role relationships. In D. Nimmo & K. Sanders (Eds.), *Handbook of political communication* (pp. 467-493). Beverly Hills, CA: Sage.

Blumler, J., & Gurevitch, M. (1986). Journalists orientations to social institutions: The case of parliamentary broadcasting. In P. Golding et al. (Eds.), *Communication politics* (pp. 67-92). Leicester: Leicester University Press.

Boorstin, D. J. (1961). *The image*. New York: Harper & Row.

Boulding, K. (1962). *Conflict and defense*. New York: Harper.

Braestrup, P. (1977). *Big story: How the American press and television reported and interpreted the crisis of Tet 1968 in Vietnam and Washington*. Boulder, CO: Westview.

Carey, J. (1977). Mass communication research and cultural studies: An American view. In J. Curran, M. Gurevitch, & J. Woollacott (Eds.), *Mass communication and society* (pp. 409-425). London: Open University Press.

Cohen, A. A., Adoni, H., & Drori, G. (1983). Differential perceptions of social conflicts in social reality and television news. *Human Communication Research, 10,* 203-225.

Cohen, A. A., & Bantz, C. R. (1989). Where did we come from and where are we going? Some future directions in television news research. *American Behavioral Scientist, 33,* 135-143.

Coleman, J. (1957). *Community conflict*. New York: Free Press.

Connel, I., Curti, L., & Hall, S. (1976). The "unity" of current affairs TV. *WPCS9.* Birmingham: Centre for Contemporary Cultural Studies.

Coser, L. A. (1956). *The functions of social conflict*. Glencoe, IL: Free Press.

Dahlgren, P. (1981). TV news and the suppression of reflexivity. In E. Katz & T. Szecsko (Eds.), *Mass media and social change* (pp. 101-113). London: Sage.

Dahrendorf, R. (1959). Conflict groups, group conflicts and social change. In R. Dahrendorf (Ed.), *Class and class conflict in industrial society* (pp. 206-240). London: Routledge & Kegan Paul.

Dalling, D. (1983, November). *State of the media and press freedom in South Africa.* Unpublished manuscript.

Davison, P. (1974). *Mass communication and conflict resolution*. New York: Praeger.

DeFleur, M. L., & Ball-Rokeach, S. J. (1989). *Theories of mass communication* (5th ed.). New York: Longman.

Donahue, H. C. (1989). *The battle to control broadcast news: Who owns the First Amendment?* Cambridge: MIT Press.

Epstein, E. J. (1973). *News from nowhere*. New York: Vintage.

FCC's Repeal of Fairness Doctrine survives Supreme Court. (1990). *Broadcasting,* January 15, pp. 56-57.

Foucault, M. (1977). *The archaeology of knowledge*. London: Tavistock.

Galtung, J. (1964). A structural theory of aggression. *Journal of Peace Research, 1*, 95-119.

Galtung, J., & Ruge, M. (1965). The structure of foreign news. *Journal of Peace Research, 1*, 64-90.

Gamson, W. A. (1975). *The strategy of social protest.* Homewood, IL: Dorsey.

Gans, H. J. (1979). *Deciding what's news.* New York: Vintage.

Gerbner, G., & Gross, L. (1976). Living with television: The violence profile. *Journal of Communication, 26*, 172-199.

Gerbner, G., Gross, L., Signorielli, N., & Morgan, M., (1980). Aging with television: Images on television drama and conceptions of social reality. *Journal of Communication, 30*, 37-47.

Gerbner, G., Morgan, M., & Signorielli, N. (1980). The mainstreaming of America: Violence profile No. 11. *Journal of Communication, 30*, 10-29.

Giddens, A. (1982). Class structuration and class consciousness. In A. Giddens & D. Held (Eds.), *Classes, power and conflict* (pp. 157-175). London: Macmillan.

Gitlin, T. (1978). Media sociology: The decline of the dominant paradigm. *Theory and Society, 6*, 205-245.

Gitlin, T. (1980). *The whole world is watching.* Berkeley: University of California Press.

Glasgow University Media Group (1976). *Bad news.* London: Routledge & Kegan Paul.

Glasgow University Media Group (1985). *War and peace news.* Milton Keynes, UK: Open University Press.

Golding, P. (1981). The missing dimensions: News media and the management of social change. In E. Katz & T. Szecsko (Eds.), *Mass media and social change* (pp. 63-81). London: Sage.

Golding, P., & Elliott, P. (1979). *Making the news.* London: Longman.

Graber, D. A. (1988). *Processing the news: How people tame the information tide* (2nd ed.). New York: Longman.

Gramsci, A. (1971). *Selections from the prison notebooks.* London: Lawrence & Wishart.

Gratch, H. (1973). *25 years of social research in Israel.* Jerusalem: Jerusalem Academic Press.

Greenberg, B. S. (1980). *Life on television: Content analysis of U.S. TV drama.* Norwood: Ablex.

Gurr, T. R. (1980). Introduction. In T. R. Gurr (Ed.), *Handbook of political conflict.* New York: Free Press.

Guttman, L. (1977). What is not what in statistics. *The Statistician, 26*, 81-107.

Guttman, L. (1968). A general nonmetric technique for finding the smallest coordinate space for a configuration of points. *Psychometrika, 33*, 469-506.

Hachten, W. (1979). Policies and performance in South African television. *Journal of Communication, 29*, 62-72.

Hall, S. (1977). Culture, the media, and the ideological effect. In J. Curran, M. Gurevitch, & J. Woollacott (Eds.), *Mass communication and society* (pp. 315-348). London: Open University Press.

Hall, S. (1981). A world at one with itself. In S. Cohen & J. Young (Eds.), *The manufacture of news: Social problems, deviance and the mass media* (pp. 147-156). Beverly Hills, CA: Sage.

Hartley, J. (1982). *Understanding news.* London: Methuen.

Hartmann, P., & Husband, C. (1972). The mass media and racial conflict. In D. McQuail (Ed.), *Sociology of mass communications* (pp. 435-456). Harmondsworth, UK: Penguin.

Hawkins, R., & Pingree, S. (1982). Television's influence on social reality. In D. Pearl, L. Bouthilet, & J. Lazar (Eds.), *Television and behavior: Ten years of scientific progress and implications for the eighties* (pp. 224-247). Washington, DC: National Institute of Mental Health.

Hoffman-Riem, W. (1988). Federal Republic of Germany. In P. T. Rosen (Ed.), *International handbook of broadcasting systems* (pp. 91-103). New York: Greenwood.

Hofstetter, C. R. (1976). *Bias in the news: Network television coverage of the 1972 election campaign*. Columbus: Ohio University Press.

Hovland, C. I., Lumsdaine, A. A., & Sheffield, F. D. (1949). *Experiments in mass communication*. Princeton, NJ: Princeton University Press.

Johnstone, J. W. L., Slawski, E. J., & Bowman, W. W. (1976). *The news people*. Urbana: University of Illinois Press.

Katz, E. (1977). *Social research on broadcasting: Proposals for further development*. London: British Broadcasting Corporation.

Katz, E. (1989). Journalists as scientists: Notes towards an occupational classification. *American Behavioral Scientist, 33*, 238-246.

Kellner, D. (1981). Network television and American society. *Theory and society, 10*, 31-62.

Kepplinger, H. M., & Hachenberg, M. (1986). Media and conscientious objection in the Federal Republic of Germany. In D. Paletz (Ed.), *Political communication research: Approaches, studies, assessments* (pp. 109-129). Norwood: Ablex.

Krasnow, E. G., Longley, L. D., & Terry, H. A. (1982). *The politics of broadcast regulation* (3rd ed.). New York: St. Martin's.

Kriesberg, L. (1973). *The sociology of social conflicts*. Englewood Cliffs, NJ: Prentice-Hall.

Lang, K. (1979). The critical functions of empirical communication research: Observations on German-American influences. *Media, Culture and Society, 1*, 83-96.

Lasswell, H. (1948). The structure and function of communications in society. In L. Bryson (Ed.), *The communication of ideas* (pp. 37-51). New York: Harper.

Lazarsfeld, P. F., Berelson, B., & Gaudet, H. (1944). *The people's choice*. New York: Duell, Sloan and Pearce.

Lazarsfeld, P. F., & Merton, R. (1948). Mass communication, popular taste and organized social action. In L. Bryson (Ed.), *The communication of ideas* (pp. 95-118). New York: Harper.

Lewin, K. (1948). *Resolving social conflicts*. New York: Harper.

Lippman, W. (1922). *Public opinion*. New York: Harcourt Brace.

Lull, J. (1982). A rules approach to the study of TV and society. *Human Communication Research, 9*, 3-16.

Mahrenholz, E. G. (1983). Meinungsfreiheit—Rundfunkfreiheit. In L. Franke (Ed.), *Die Dedienzukunft, GEP Mediendokumentation, 11*. Frankfurt/Main.

Marcuse, H. (1964). *One dimensional man*. London: Routledge & Kegan Paul.

Martin, L. J., & Chaudhary, A. G. (1983). *Comparative mass media systems*. New York: Longman.

McCombs, M. E., & Shaw, D. L. (1972). The agenda setting function of the press. *Public Opinion Quarterly, 36,* 176-187.

McGuire, W. J. (1981). Theoretical foundations of campaigns. In R. E. Rice & W. J. Paisley (Eds.), *Public communication campaigns* (pp. 41-70). Beverly Hills, CA: Sage.

McQuail, D. (1972). *Sociology of mass communications.* Harmondsworth, UK: Penguin.

Merton, R. (1968). *Social theory and social structure.* New York: Free Press.

Murdock, G. (1973). Political deviance: The press presentation of a militant mass demonstration. In S. Cohen & J. Young (Eds.), *The manufacture of news: Social problems, deviance, and the mass media* (pp. 156-175). London: Constable.

Noelle-Neumann, E. (1974). The spiral of silence: A theory of public opinion. *Journal of Communication, 24,* 43-51.

Noelle-Neumann, E. (1984). *The spiral of silence—Our social skin.* Chicago: University of Chicago Press.

Nordlinger, E. A. (1972). *Conflict regulation in divided societies.* Cambridge, MA: Center for International Affairs, Harvard University.

Oberschall, A. (1973). *Social conflict and social movements.* Englewood Cliffs, NJ: Prentice-Hall.

Park, R. (1940). News as a form of knowledge. In R. H. Turner (Ed.), *On social control and collective behavior* (pp. 32-52). Chicago: University of Chicago Press.

Peleg, I. (1981). *Objectivity in television news.* Unpublished doctoral dissertation, Hebrew University of Jerusalem.

Pirages, D. C. (1980). Political stability and conflict management. In T. R. Gurr (Ed.), *Handbook of political conflict* (pp. 425-460). New York: Free Press.

Rapoport, A. (1965). Game theory and human conflict. In E. McNeil (Ed.), *The nature of human conflict.* Englewood Cliffs, NJ: Prentice-Hall.

Raveh, A. (1978). Finding periodic patterns in time series with monotone trend: A new technique. In S. Shye (Ed.), *Theory construction and data analysis in the behavioral sciences* (pp. 371-390). San Francisco, CA: Jossey-Bass.

Rex, J. (1981). *Social conflict: A conceptual and theoretical analysis.* London: Longman.

Robinson, J., & Levy, M. R. (1986). *The main source.* Beverly Hills, CA: Sage.

Roeh, I., Katz, E., Cohen, A. A., & Zelizer, B. (1980). *Almost midnight: Reforming the late night news.* Beverly Hills, CA: Sage.

Roper Organization (1985). *Trends in attitudes towards television and other media: A twenty-six year review.* New York: Television Information Office.

Rosengren, K. E. (1981). Mass media and social change: Some current approaches. In E. Katz & T. Szecsko (Eds.), *Mass media and social change* (pp. 247-263). London: Sage.

Roshco, B. (1975). *Newsmaking.* Chicago: University of Chicago Press.

Schellenberg, J. A. (1982). *The science of conflict.* Oxford: Oxford University Press.

Schiller, H. (1973). *The mind managers.* Boston: Beacon Press.

Schlesinger, P. (1978). *Putting reality together.* London: Constable.

Schramm, W. (1959). *One day in the world's press.* Stanford: Stanford University Press.

Schudson, M. (1978). *Discovering the news.* New York: Basic Books.

Schutz, A. (1967). *The phenomenology of the social world.* Evanston, IL: Northwestern University Press.

Shye, S. (1978). On the search for laws in the behavioral sciences. In S. Shye (Ed.), *Theory construction and data analysis in the behavioral sciences* (pp. 2-24). San Francisco, CA: Jossey Bass.

Shinar, D. (1972). The structure and content in television broadcasting in Israel. In G. A. Comstock & E. R. Rubinstein (Eds.), *Television and social behavior, Vol. 1* (pp. 493-532). Rockville, MD: National Institute of Mental Health.

Siune, K. (1983). The campaigns on television: What was said and who said it. In J. Blumler (Ed.), *Communicating to voters: Television in the first European parliamentary elections* (pp. 223-240). London: Sage.

Simmel, G. (1955). *Conflict.* Glencoe, IL: Free Press.

Skornia, H. J. (1968). *Television and the news: A critical appraisal.* Palo Alto, CA: Pacific.

Smith, A. (1973). *The shadow in the cave.* London: Allen & Unwin.

South African Broadcasting Corporation. (1977). *Annual Report.*

South African Broadcasting Corporation. (1987). *Annual Report.*

Stagner, R. (1967). The analysis of conflict. In R. Stagner (Ed.), *The dimensions of human conflict* (pp. 131-167). Detroit: Wayne State University Press.

Stohl, M. (1980). Theory and research on international conflict. In T. R. Gurr (Ed.), *Handbook of political conflict* (pp. 297-330). New York: Free Press.

Tichenor, P. J., Donohue, G. A. & Olien, C. N. (1970). Mass media and the differential growth in knowledge. *Public Opinion Quarterly, 34,* 158-170.

Tichenor, P. J., Donohue, G. A., & Olien, C. N. (1980). *Community conflict and the press.* Beverly Hills, CA: Sage.

Tuchman, G. (1973). Making news by doing work: Routinizing the unexpected. *American Journal of Sociology, 79,* 110-131.

Tuchman, G. (1978a). *Making news: A study in the construction of reality* (pp. 3-38). New York: Free Press.

Tuchman, G. (1978b). The symbolic annihilation of women by the mass media. In G. Tuchman, A. Kaplan-Daniels, & J. Benet (Eds.), *Hearth and home: Images of women in the mass media.* New York: Oxford University Press.

Tunstall, J. (1971). *Journalists at work.* London: Constable.

Turow, J. (1984). *Media industries: The production of news and entertainment.* New York: Longman.

Van Dijk, T. A. (1988). *News analysis: Case studies of international and national news in the press.* Hillsdale, NJ: Lawrence Erlbaum.

Van Poecke, L. (1988). The myth and rites of newsmaking: Hard news versus soft news. *Communications: The European Journal of Communication, 14,* 23-54.

Wehr, P. (1979). *Conflict regulation.* Boulder, CO: Westview.

Williams, R. (1974). *Television: Technology and cultural form.* London: Fontana.

Zimmerman, E. (1980). Macro-comparative research on political protest. In T. R. Gurr (Ed.), *Handbook of political conflict* (pp. 167-237). New York: Free Press.

Index

About the Authors

Hanna Adoni (Ph.D., Hebrew University of Jerusalem) is Senior Lecturer at the Department of Communication and the Graduate School of Library Science of the Hebrew University. Her main research interests concern the functions of mass media, mainly the role of news in the political socialization process. She also is interested in the sociology of mass culture, with special emphasis on books, reading, and popular music. Her publications on these subjects appear in numerous scholarly journals and book chapters.

Charles R. Bantz (Ph.D., Ohio State University) has been a member of the faculties of the University of Colorado at Boulder and the University of Minnesota before joining Arizona State University in Tempe in 1986. He is currently Associate Professor and Chair of the Department of Communication. His scholarly work focuses on both mass and organizational communication with publications in *Communication Monographs*, *Quarterly Journal of Speech*, *Journal of Broadcasting and Electronic Media*, *Communication Research*, *Communication Studies*, *American Behavioral Scientist*, and other journals. He coedited *Foundations of Organizational Communication* and is finishing *Understanding Organizations: Interpreting Organizational Communication Cultures*.

Jay G. Blumler is Emeritus Professor at the University of Leeds in England, where he directed its Centre for Television Research from 1963-1989, and a Professor of Journalism at the University of Maryland (since 1983). He is president of the International Communication Association, co-editor of the *European Journal of Communication*, specialist adviser to the British parliamentary Select Committee on Television (Proceedings of the House of Commons), and research adviser to the Broadcasting Standards Council (London). He has written extensively on communication roles in politics, audience uses and gratifications, the comparative analysis of mass media systems, and (since 1985) the policy implications of recent transformations in the television industries of both England and the United States.

Gabriele Bock (Ph.D., Technische Universität Berlin) teaches mass communication, empirical methodology, and technical communication at TU Berlin; has conducted research on cross-cultural mass communication dealing with television news and drama programs, as well as television systems in other countries and the future of broadcasting in a global context; and, in cooperation with Friedrich Knilli, has conducted a study on the images of Jews in German mass media.

Akiba A. Cohen (Ph.D., Michigan State University) is Associate Professor and Chair at the Department of Communication, Hebrew University of Jerusalem. Previous published works include: *Almost Midnight: Reforming the Late Night News* (with Roeh, Katz, & Zelizer, 1980); *The Television News Interview* (1987); and "Future Directions in Television News Research" (special issue of *American Behavioral Scientist*). He is on the editorial boards of the *Journal of Broadcasting and Electronic Media*, *Communications: The European Journal of Communication*, and the *International and Intercultural Communication Annual*.

Alison Ewbank was a researcher at the Centre for Television Research, Leeds University, England, at the time when the ideas for this book were formulated and investigated. The emphasis of her previous work at the Centre had been on political communications. Currently, she works freelance and is editing a case-study book about the interactions between indigenous and imported music in other countries.

Michael Gurevitch is Professor at the College of Journalism, the University of Maryland. He is coauthor of *The Secularization of Leisure* (with Elihu Katz), and coeditor of *Mass Communication and Society*, editor of *Culture, Society, and the Media*, and *Mass Communication Review Yearbook, volumes 5 and 6*. He is author of numerous articles and book chapters, primarily in the area of political communication, and currently is conducting a comparative analysis of meanings in television news.

Karen Honikman (M.A., University of Cape Town) is currently a private consultant and trainer in organizational communication. She held the position of lecturer in the Professional Communication Unit at the University of Cape Town for 10 years, where she devised and taught programs in communication skills relevant to professional and business careers. She has also been engaged in a number of research projects investigating the special problems associated with communication in South Africa.

Friedrich Knilli, an Austrian, is Professor of German Literature at Technische Universität Berlin, where he has focused on mass media since 1972; he has published books on radio plays, film semiotics, Harlan's movie *Jew Suess*, and the television series *Holocaust*. In collaboration with Gabriele Bock, he has studied the images of Jews in German mass media; and has research interests in cross-cultural communication, especially international media relations and television news.

Deanna C. Robinson (Ph.D., University of Oregon) has taught at the Ohio State University and the University of Oregon. Currently, she is an Associate Professor at the University of Oregon and directs the International Youth Culture Consortium and PacCom, both international research teams. She has published numerous articles, is the first author of *Music at the Margins: World Popular Music Production and Cultural Diversity* (forthcoming from Sage) and is working on a book about the South Korean informatization process. She is interested in interaction among communication systems and policies and other social forces.